CHILDREN OF THE WHALES

Story and Art by Abi Umeda

Volume

16

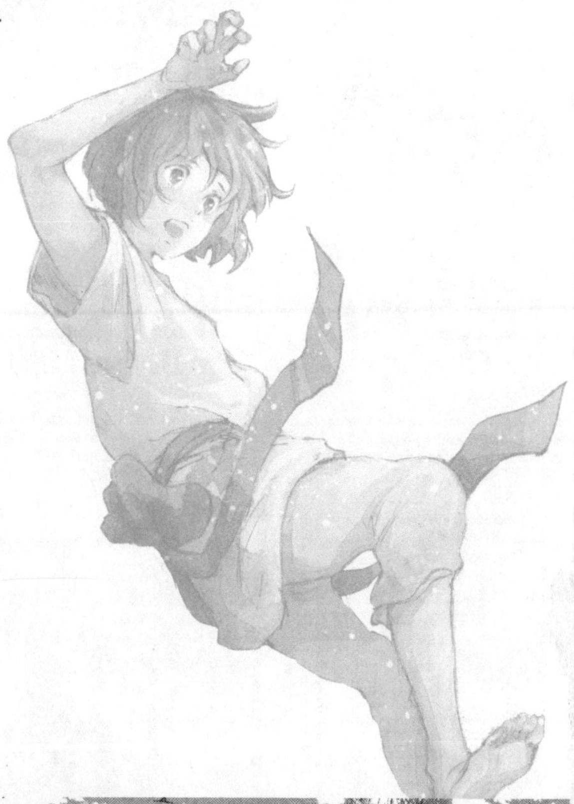

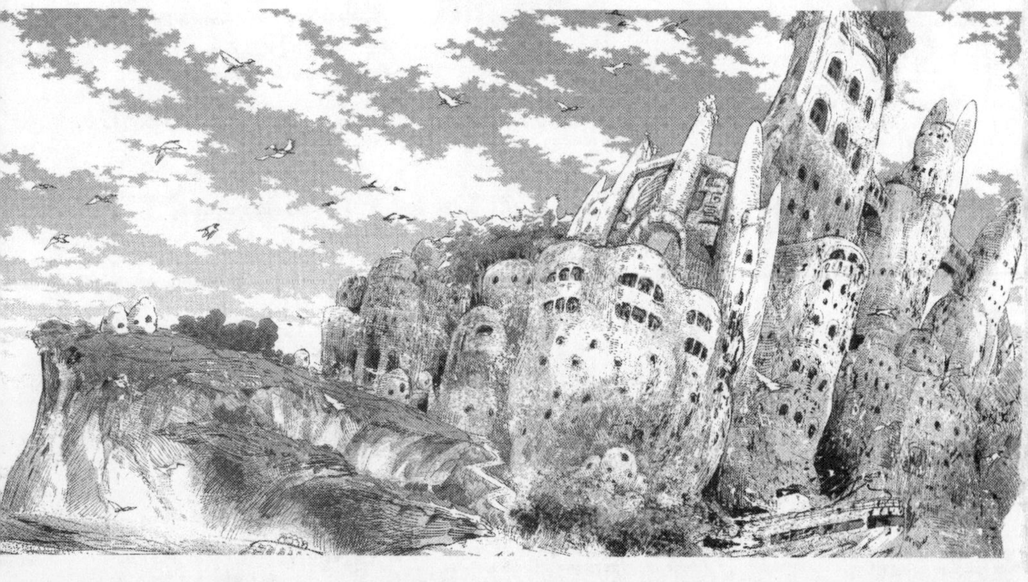

On the Mud Whale

Ouni
(Marked, 16 years old)

A very powerful thymia user who possesses the strength of a daimona. He is being held on Karcharías after being defeated by Orca.

Lykos
(Marked, 14 years old)

A girl from the Allied Empire who comes aboard the Mud Whale. She is captured by Orca but is saved by Chakuro and others.

Chakuro
(Marked, 14 years old)

The young archivist of the Mud Whale. He sneaks onto Karcharías to save Lykos and Ouni and in so doing gets a look into Orca's heart.

Former Allied Empire

Orca
(Marked)

A powerful thymia user and Lykos's brother. He has seized the battleship Karcharías and declared his independence from the empire.

Shuan
(Marked, 26 years old)

Former commander of the Vigilante Corps. He accompanies Suou to Karcharías as his bodyguard after Suou asks him for help.

Suou
(Unmarked, 17 years old)

Mayor of the Mud Whale. He secretly goes to Karcharías to rescue his friends and attempts to negotiate with Orca.

Allied Empire

The Emperor

The most powerful man in the empire bears an uncanny resemblance to Chakuro. He seeks Faláina and plans to crush Orca's insurrection.

Former Allied Empire

Itía

The archivist on the battleship Skyros before it sank. Although she is Orca's fiancée, she sympathizes with Chakuro and agrees to help him.

Former Allied Empire

Liontari
(Marked)

Joined the invasion of Amonlogia as Orca's jester and stays on Karcharías after the revolt.

Glossary of the Sea of Sand

The Mud Whale	A huge, drifting island-ship. Those in the empire who resisted giving up their emotions were exiled here, along with all their descendants.
Thymia	Telekinetic power derived from emotions.
The Marked	The 90 percent of the Mud Whale population who are thymia users. They are all short-lived.
The Unmarked	The members of the Mud Whale population who cannot use thymia. Unlike the Marked, they are long-lived.
Nous	A unique organism that obtains energy from peoples' emotions and gives people the power of thymia in return.
Nous Fáláina	A Nous that dwells deep within the Belly of the Mud Whale. Unlike other Nouses, it consumes the life force of humans rather than their emotions.
The Allied Empire	A large nation on the Sea of Sand that controls its citizenry through the Nouses and their absorption of emotions.
Daímonas	A legend from the empire. A being said to be able to destroy a Nous.

A Record of the Mud Whale and the Sea of Sand

Year 93 of the Sand Exile.

The Mud Whale drifts endlessly through the Sea of Sand, home to about 500 people who know nothing of the outside world.

With the help of Itía, Chakuro and the others successfully rescue Lykos. But before they can leave, Orca leads them deep into Karcharías, where he tells them his plan to cleanse the world of the Nous. When Itía is hurt, Orca's hidden personality emerges. Using his sasa as a medium, the god of death weaves a vision that exposes Chakuro and the others to the true record of his heart.

Orca wants to take Lykos to the new Kitrino so that she can smile again. But Lykos tells him "On Faláina, on the Mud Whale, I am smiling." In despair, he turns his sword on himself and...

"The Mud Whale was our entire world."

Table of Contents

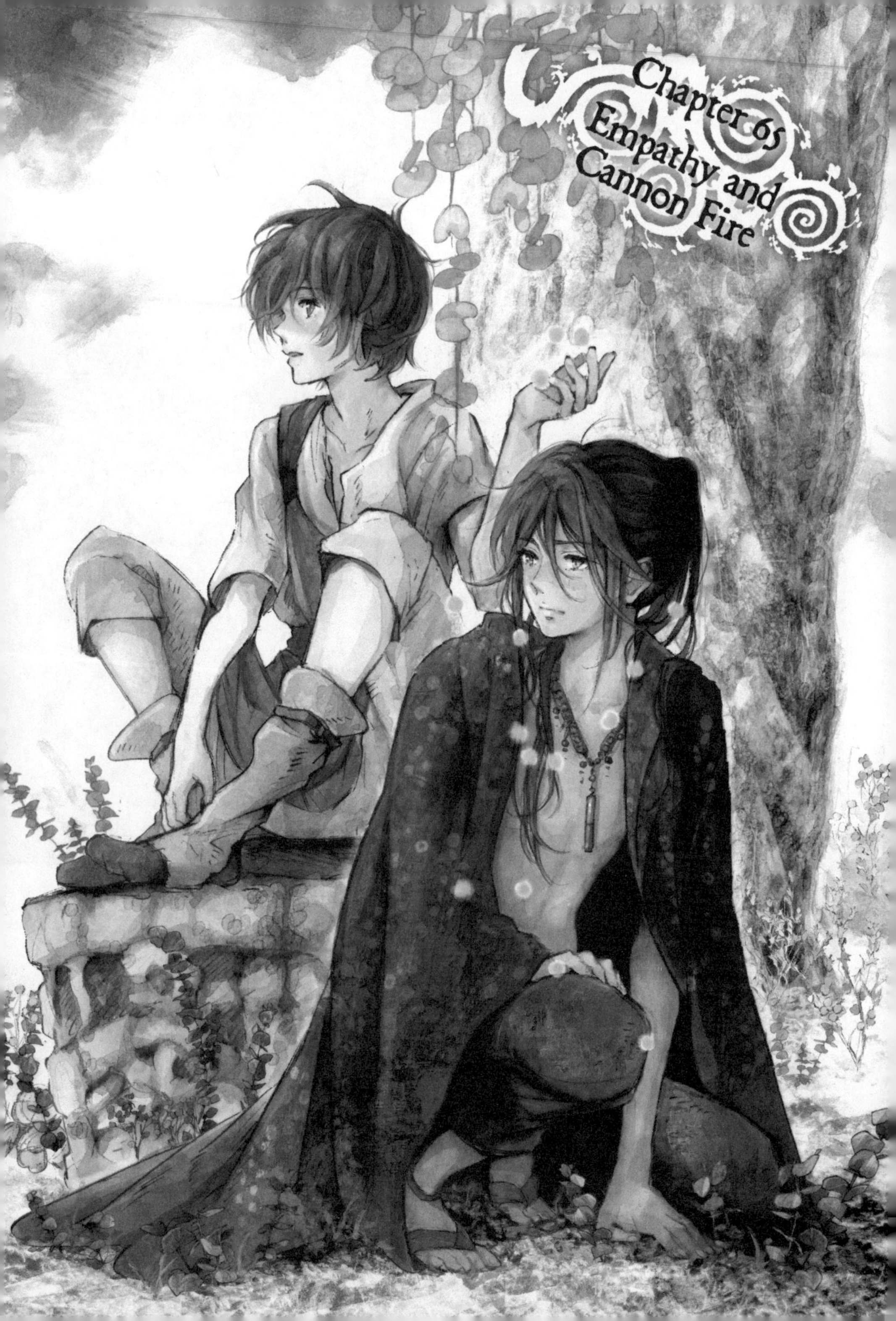
Chapter 65
Empathy and Cannon Fire

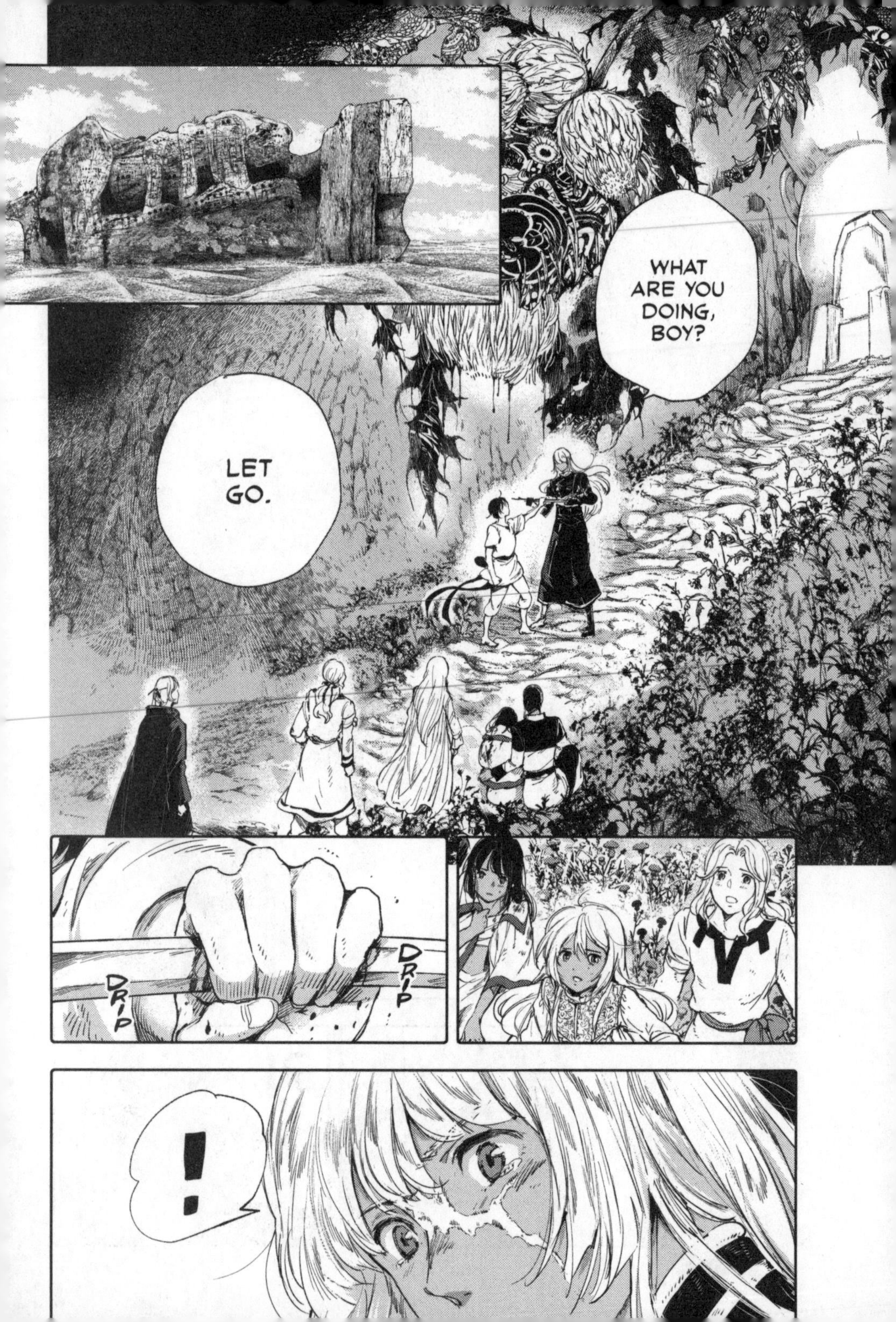

WHAT ARE YOU DOING, BOY?
LET GO.
DRIP
DRIP
!

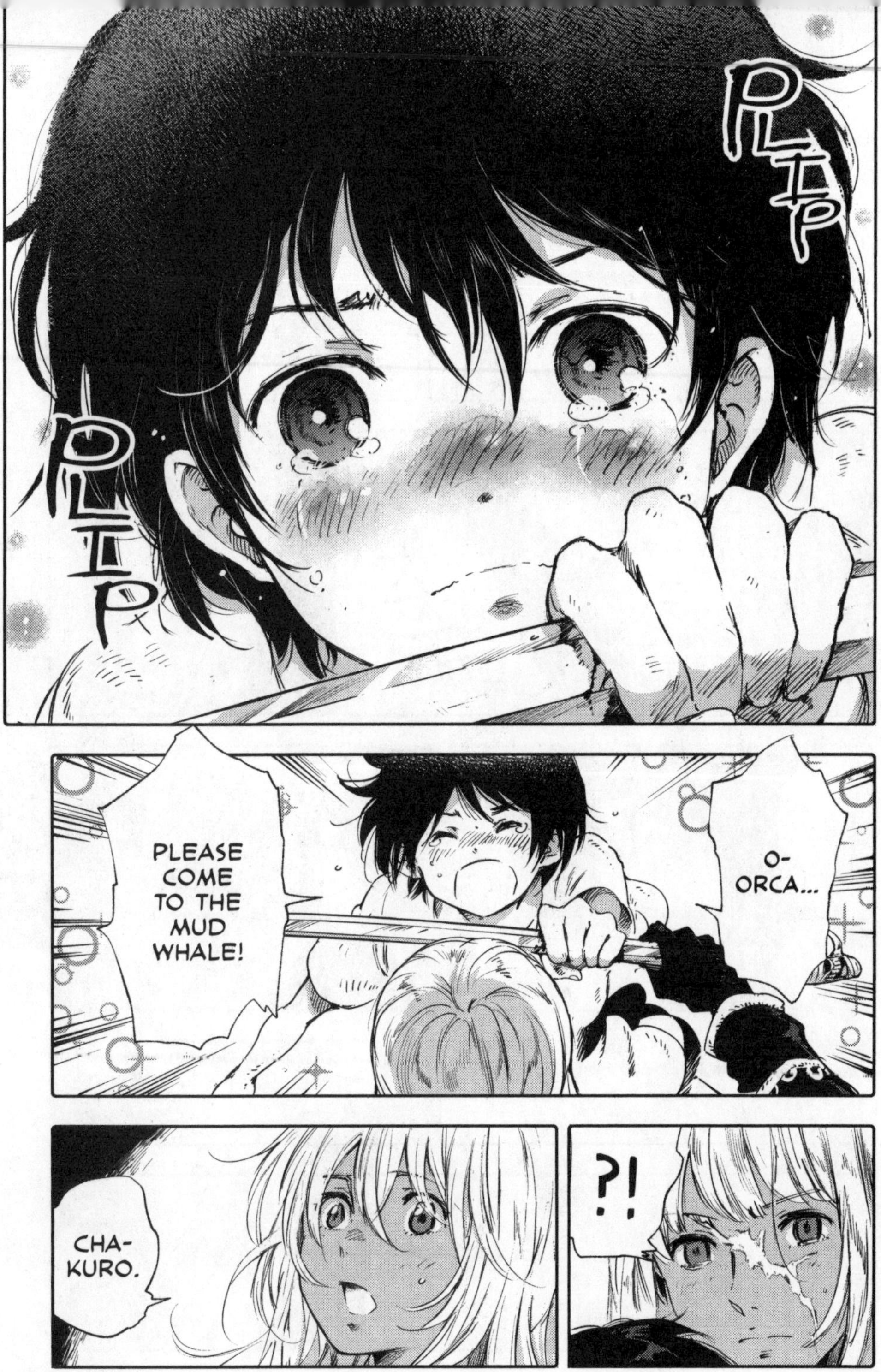
PLIP
PLIP
O-ORCA...
PLEASE COME TO THE MUD WHALE!
?!
CHA-KURO.

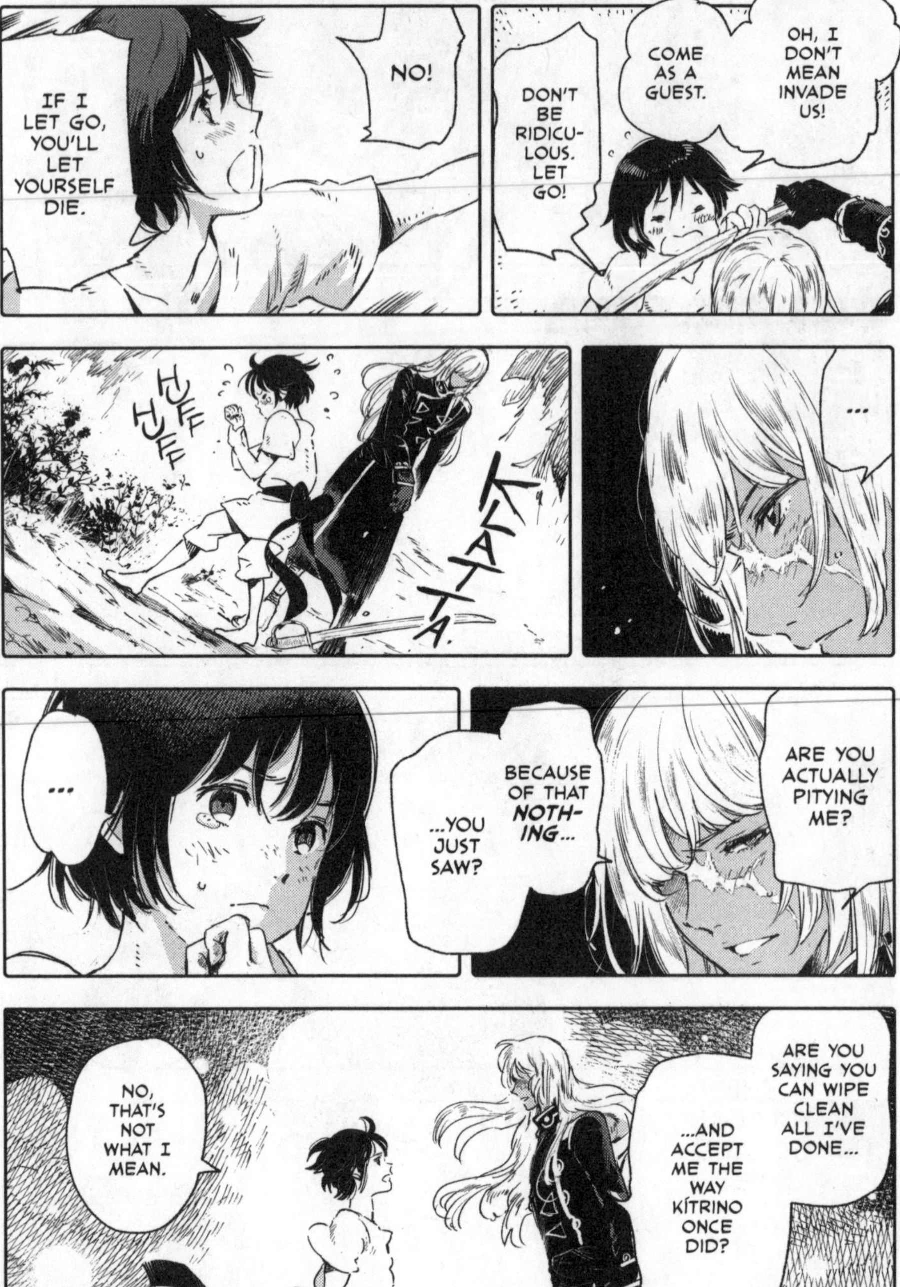
OH, I DON'T MEAN INVADE US!
COME AS A GUEST.
DON'T BE RIDICULOUS. LET GO!
NO!
IF I LET GO, YOU'LL LET YOURSELF DIE.
...
HUFF HUFF
KLATTA
ARE YOU ACTUALLY PITYING ME?
BECAUSE OF THAT NOTHING...
...YOU JUST SAW?
...
ARE YOU SAYING YOU CAN WIPE CLEAN ALL I'VE DONE...
...AND ACCEPT ME THE WAY KÍTRINO ONCE DID?
NO, THAT'S NOT WHAT I MEAN.

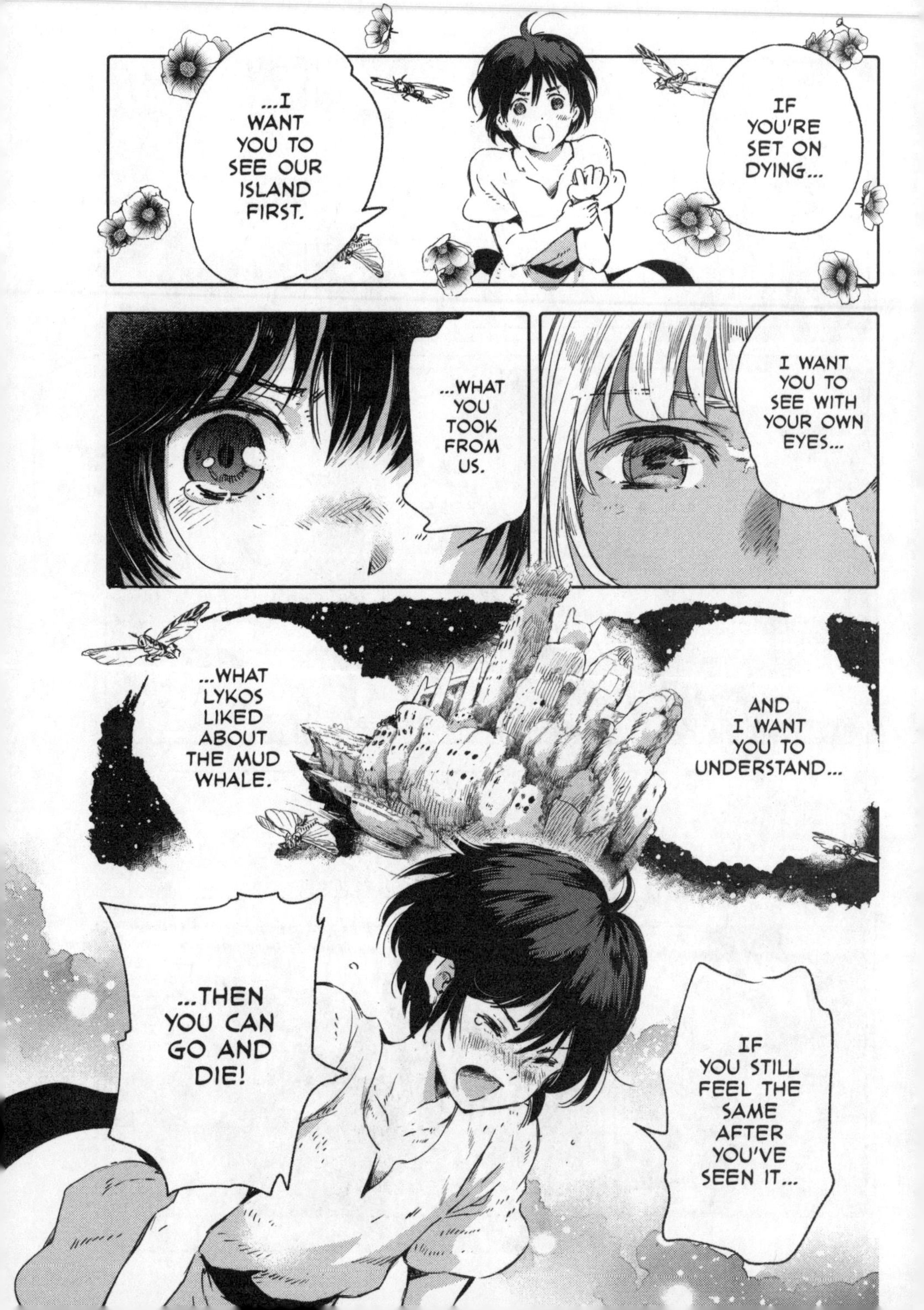
IF YOU'RE SET ON DYING...
...I WANT YOU TO SEE OUR ISLAND FIRST.
I WANT YOU TO SEE WITH YOUR OWN EYES...
...WHAT YOU TOOK FROM US.
AND I WANT YOU TO UNDERSTAND...
...WHAT LYKOS LIKED ABOUT THE MUD WHALE.
IF YOU STILL FEEL THE SAME AFTER YOU'VE SEEN IT...
...THEN YOU CAN GO AND DIE!

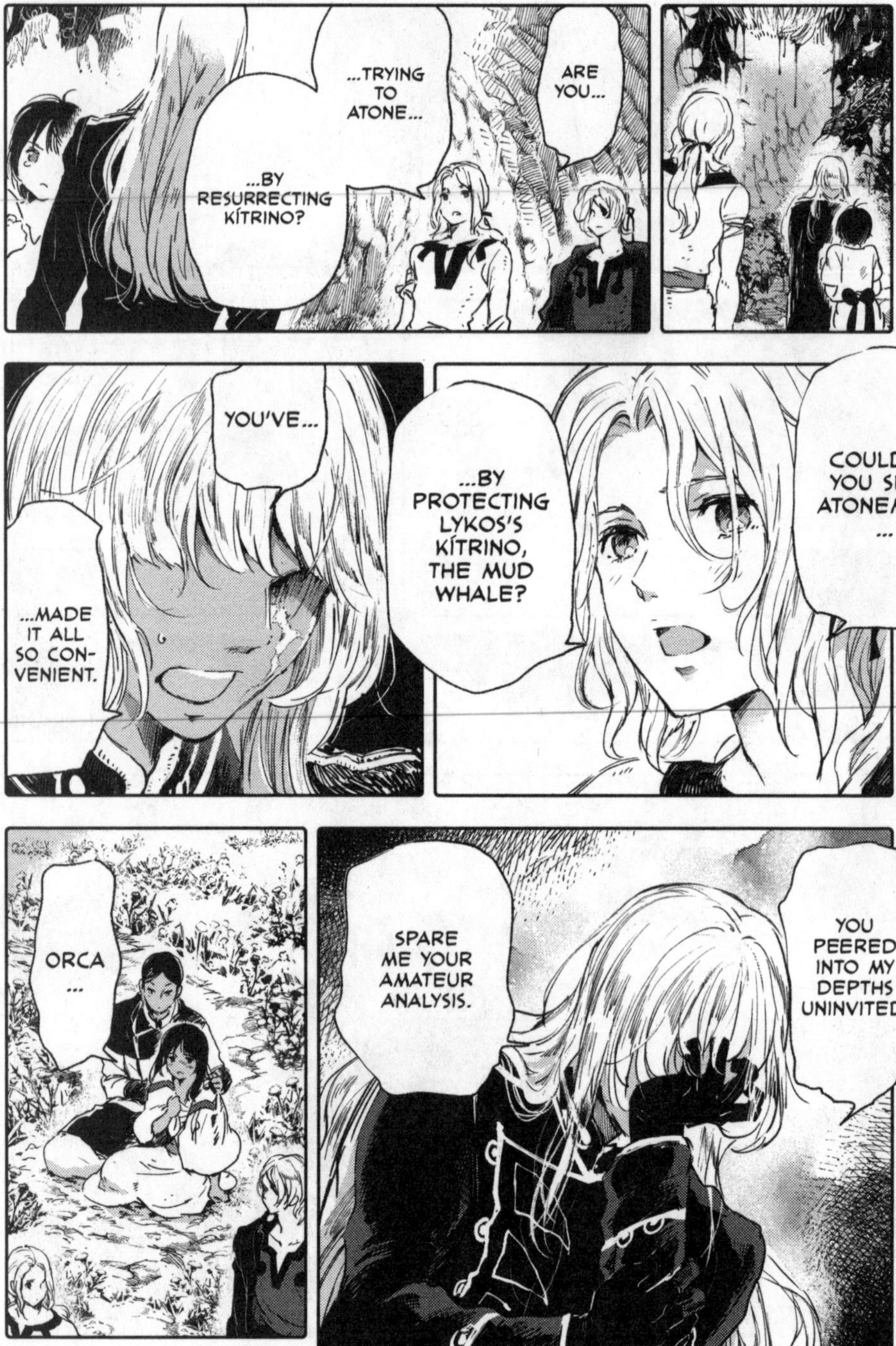
ARE YOU...
...TRYING TO ATONE...
...BY RESURRECTING KÍTRINO?
COULDN'T YOU SEEK ATONEMENT ...
...BY PROTECTING LYKOS'S KÍTRINO, THE MUD WHALE?
YOU'VE...
...MADE IT ALL SO CON-VENIENT.
YOU PEERED INTO MY DEPTHS UNINVITED.
SPARE ME YOUR AMATEUR ANALYSIS.
ORCA ...

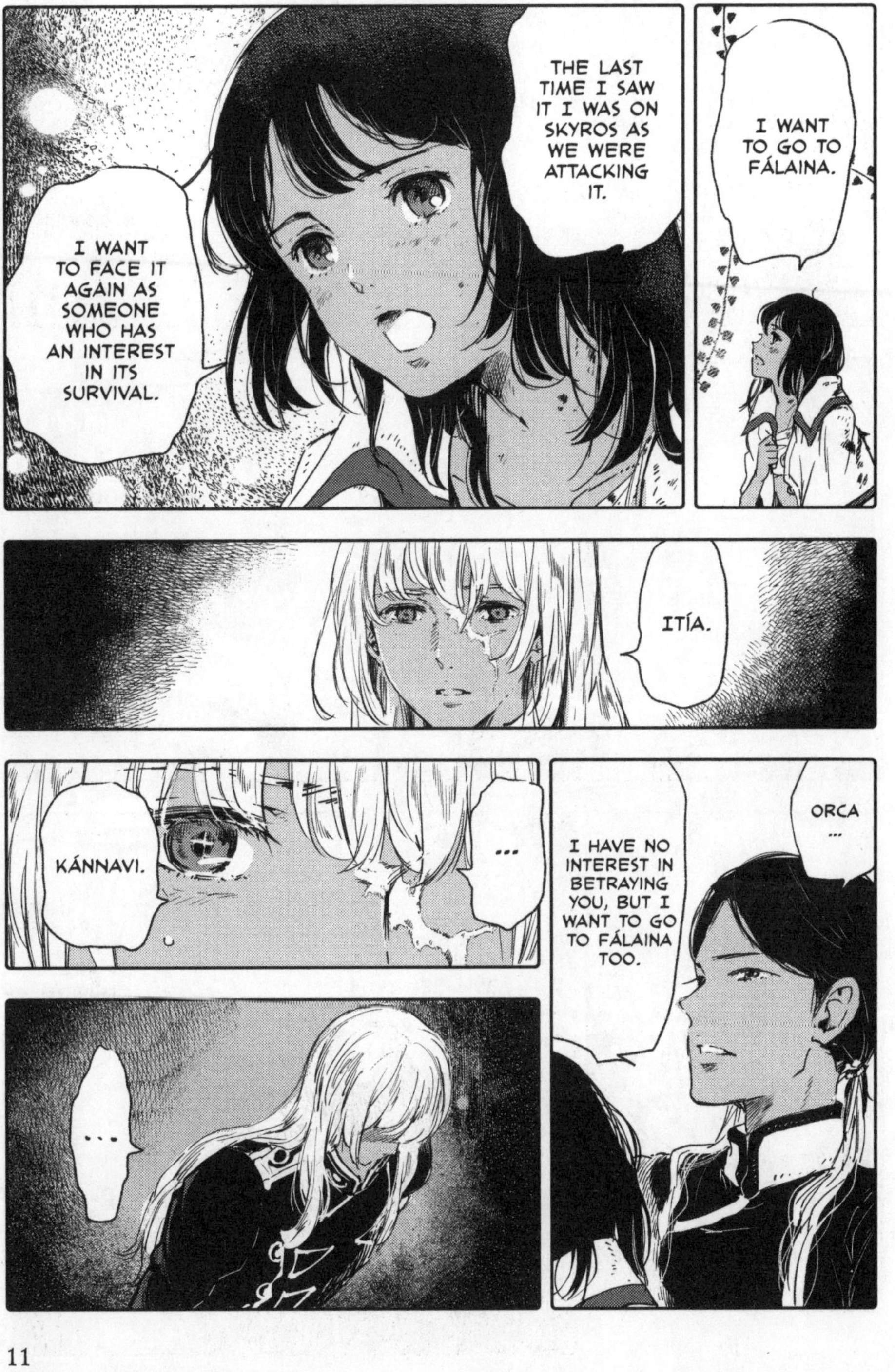
I WANT TO GO TO FÁLAINA.
THE LAST TIME I SAW IT I WAS ON SKYROS AS WE WERE ATTACKING IT.
I WANT TO FACE IT AGAIN AS SOMEONE WHO HAS AN INTEREST IN ITS SURVIVAL.
ITÍA.
ORCA ...
I HAVE NO INTEREST IN BETRAYING YOU, BUT I WANT TO GO TO FÁLAINA TOO.
...
KÁNNAVI.
...

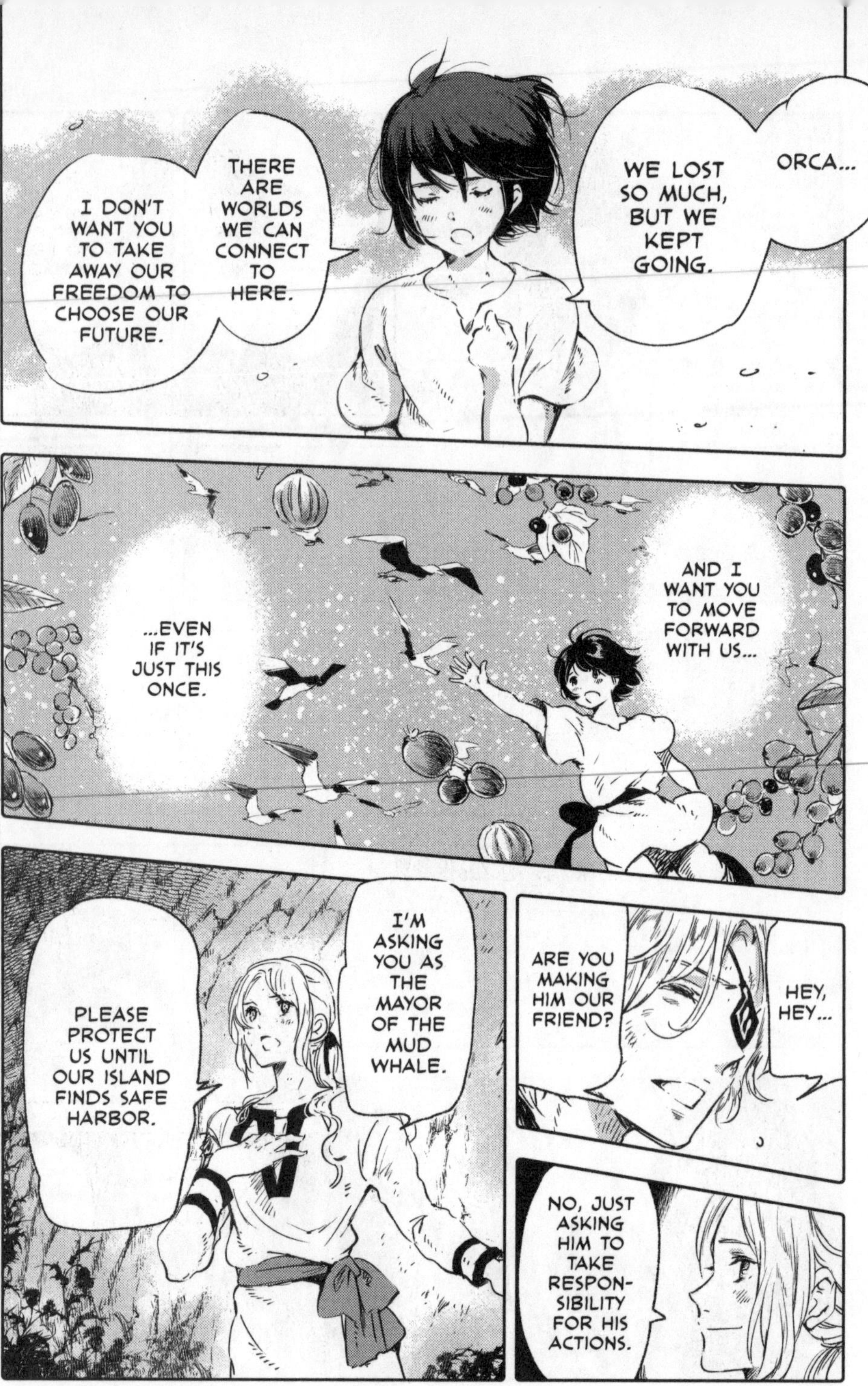
ORCA...
WE LOST SO MUCH, BUT WE KEPT GOING.
THERE ARE WORLDS WE CAN CONNECT TO HERE.
I DON'T WANT YOU TO TAKE AWAY OUR FREEDOM TO CHOOSE OUR FUTURE.
AND I WANT YOU TO MOVE FORWARD WITH US...
...EVEN IF IT'S JUST THIS ONCE.
HEY, HEY...
ARE YOU MAKING HIM OUR FRIEND?
NO, JUST ASKING HIM TO TAKE RESPON-SIBILITY FOR HIS ACTIONS.
I'M ASKING YOU AS THE MAYOR OF THE MUD WHALE.
PLEASE PROTECT US UNTIL OUR ISLAND FINDS SAFE HARBOR.

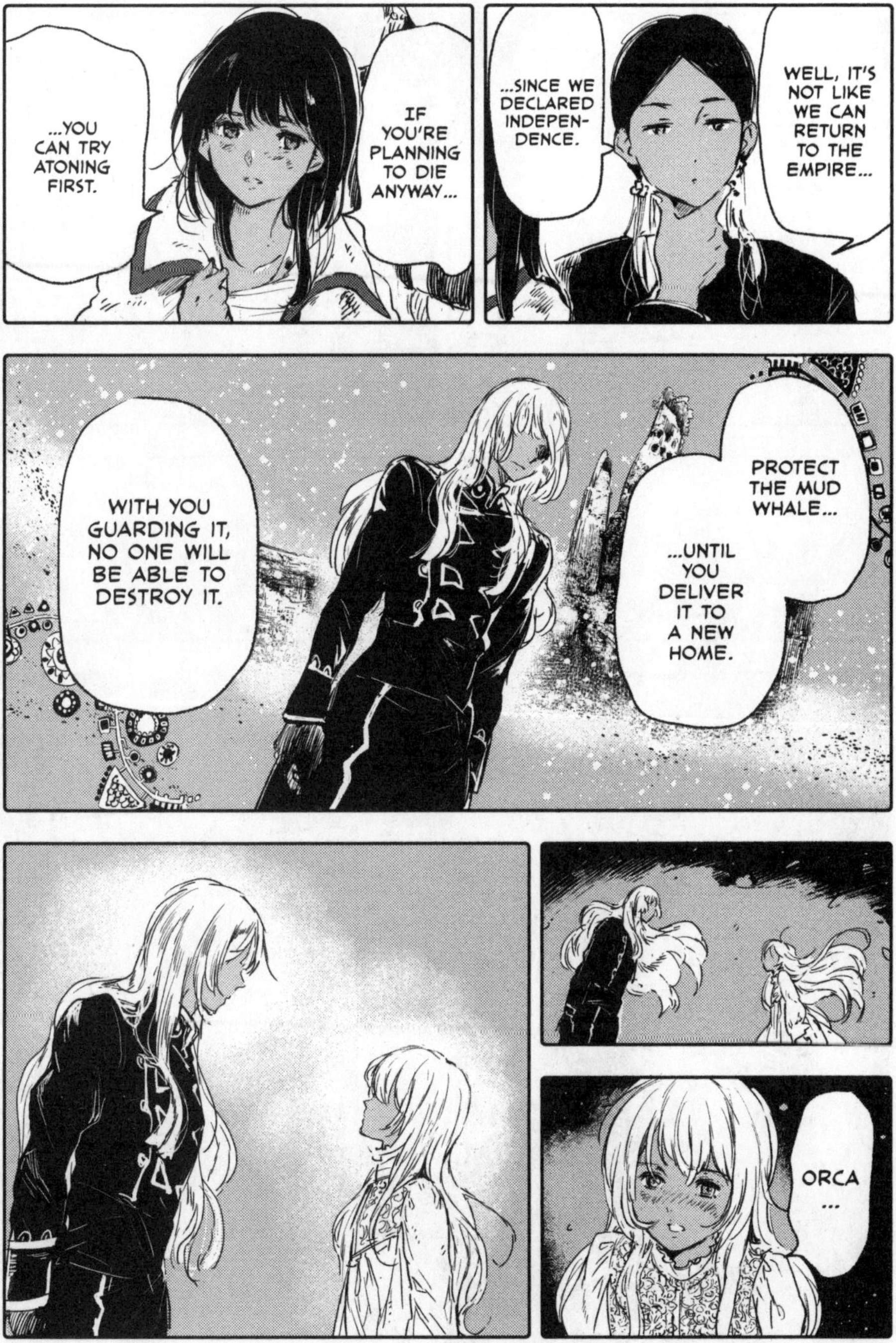
WELL, IT'S NOT LIKE WE CAN RETURN TO THE EMPIRE...
...SINCE WE DECLARED INDEPEN-DENCE.
IF YOU'RE PLANNING TO DIE ANYWAY...
...YOU CAN TRY ATONING FIRST.
PROTECT THE MUD WHALE...
...UNTIL YOU DELIVER IT TO A NEW HOME.
WITH YOU GUARDING IT, NO ONE WILL BE ABLE TO DESTROY IT.
ORCA ...

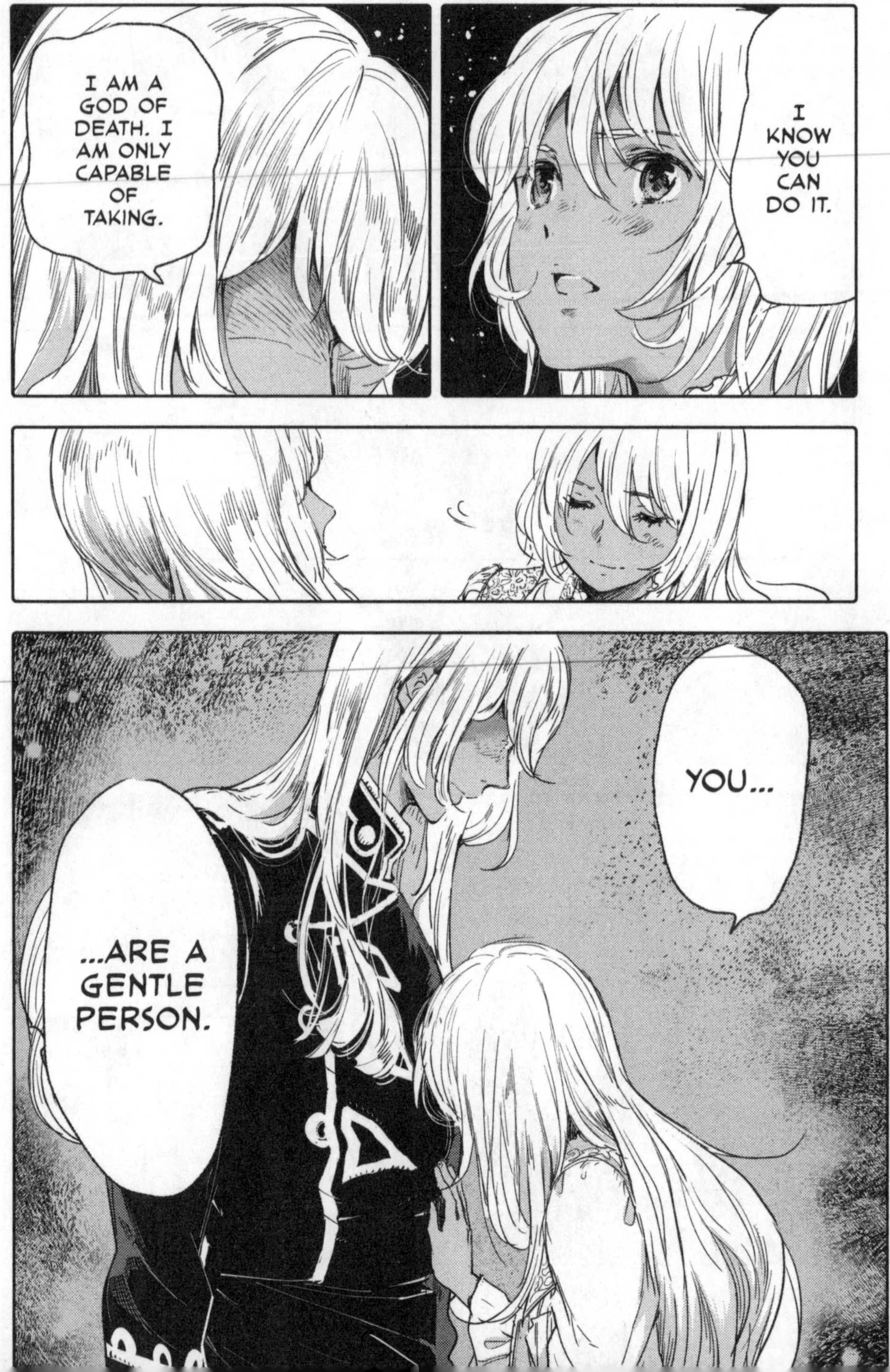
I KNOW YOU CAN DO IT.
I AM A GOD OF DEATH. I AM ONLY CAPABLE OF TAKING.
YOU...
...ARE A GENTLE PERSON.

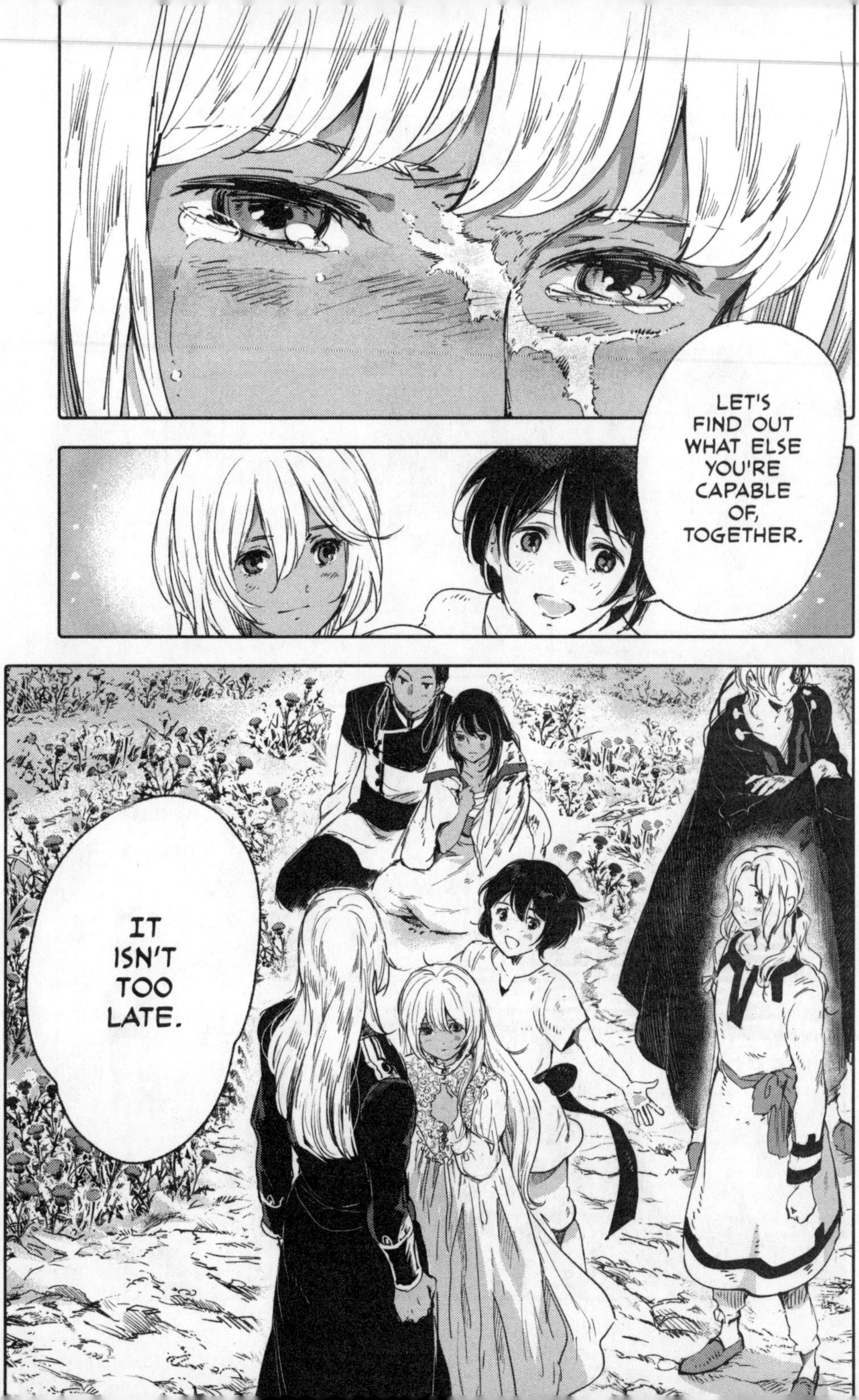
LET'S FIND OUT WHAT ELSE YOU'RE CAPABLE OF, TOGETHER.
IT ISN'T TOO LATE.

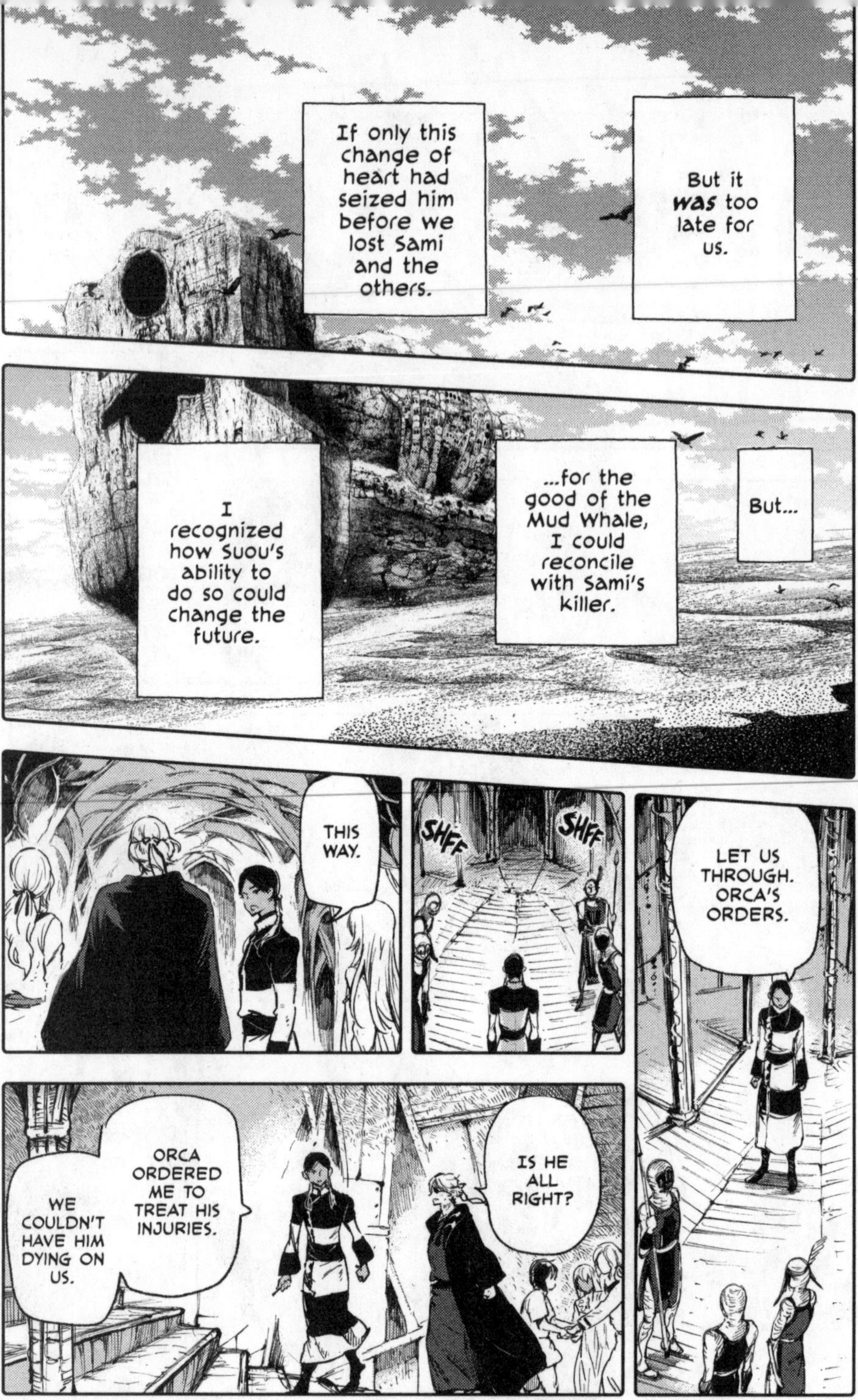
But it was too late for us.
If only this change of heart had seized him before we lost Sami and the others.
But...
...for the good of the Mud Whale, I could reconcile with Sami's killer.
I recognized how Suou's ability to do so could change the future.
LET US THROUGH. ORCA'S ORDERS.
SHFF
SHFF
THIS WAY.
IS HE ALL RIGHT?
ORCA ORDERED ME TO TREAT HIS INJURIES.
WE COULDN'T HAVE HIM DYING ON US.

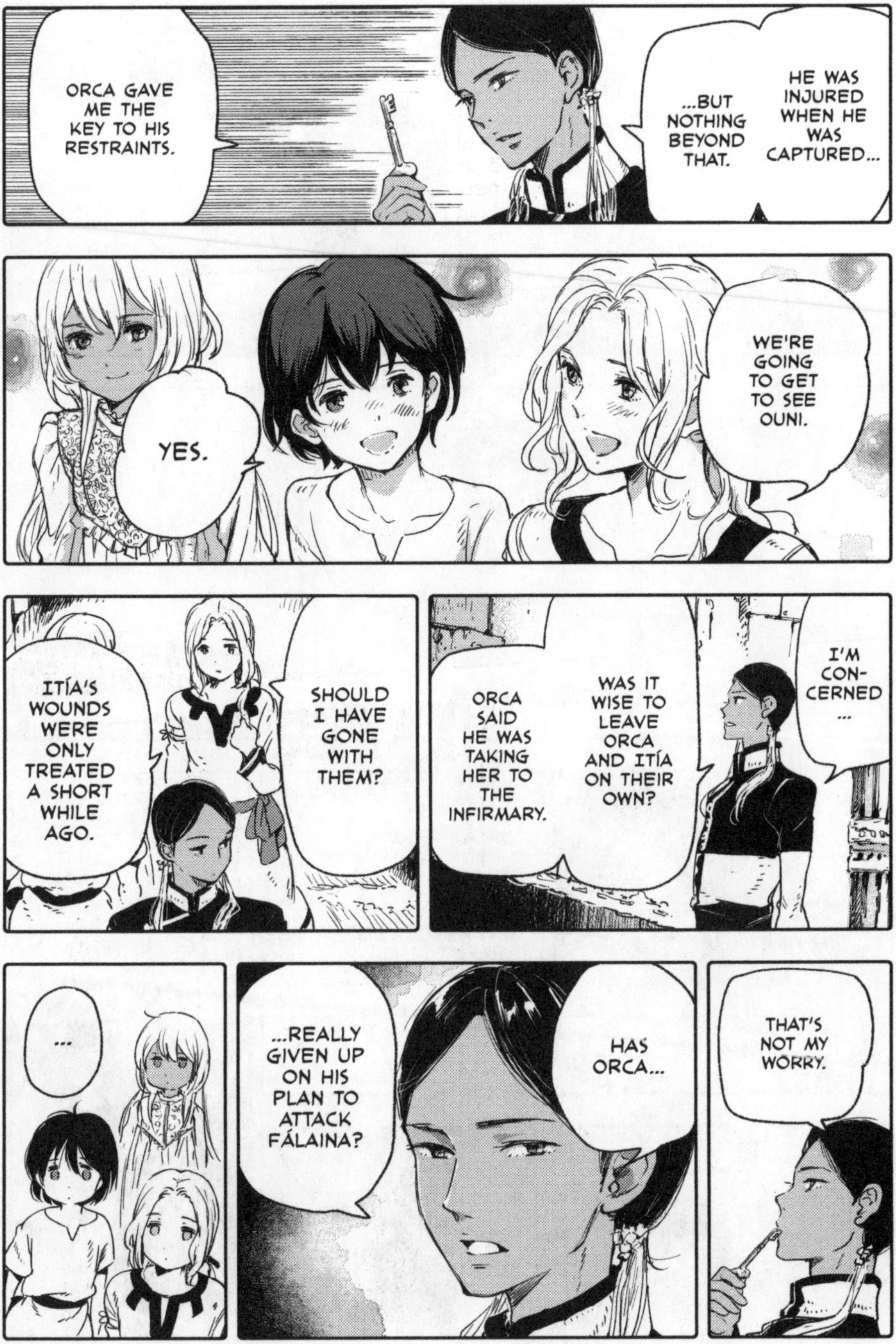
HE WAS INJURED WHEN HE WAS CAPTURED...
...BUT NOTHING BEYOND THAT.
ORCA GAVE ME THE KEY TO HIS RESTRAINTS.
WE'RE GOING TO GET TO SEE OUNI.
YES.
I'M CON-CERNED ...
WAS IT WISE TO LEAVE ORCA AND ITÍA ON THEIR OWN?
ORCA SAID HE WAS TAKING HER TO THE INFIRMARY.
SHOULD I HAVE GONE WITH THEM?
ITÍA'S WOUNDS WERE ONLY TREATED A SHORT WHILE AGO.
THAT'S NOT MY WORRY.
HAS ORCA...
...REALLY GIVEN UP ON HIS PLAN TO ATTACK FÁLAINA?
...

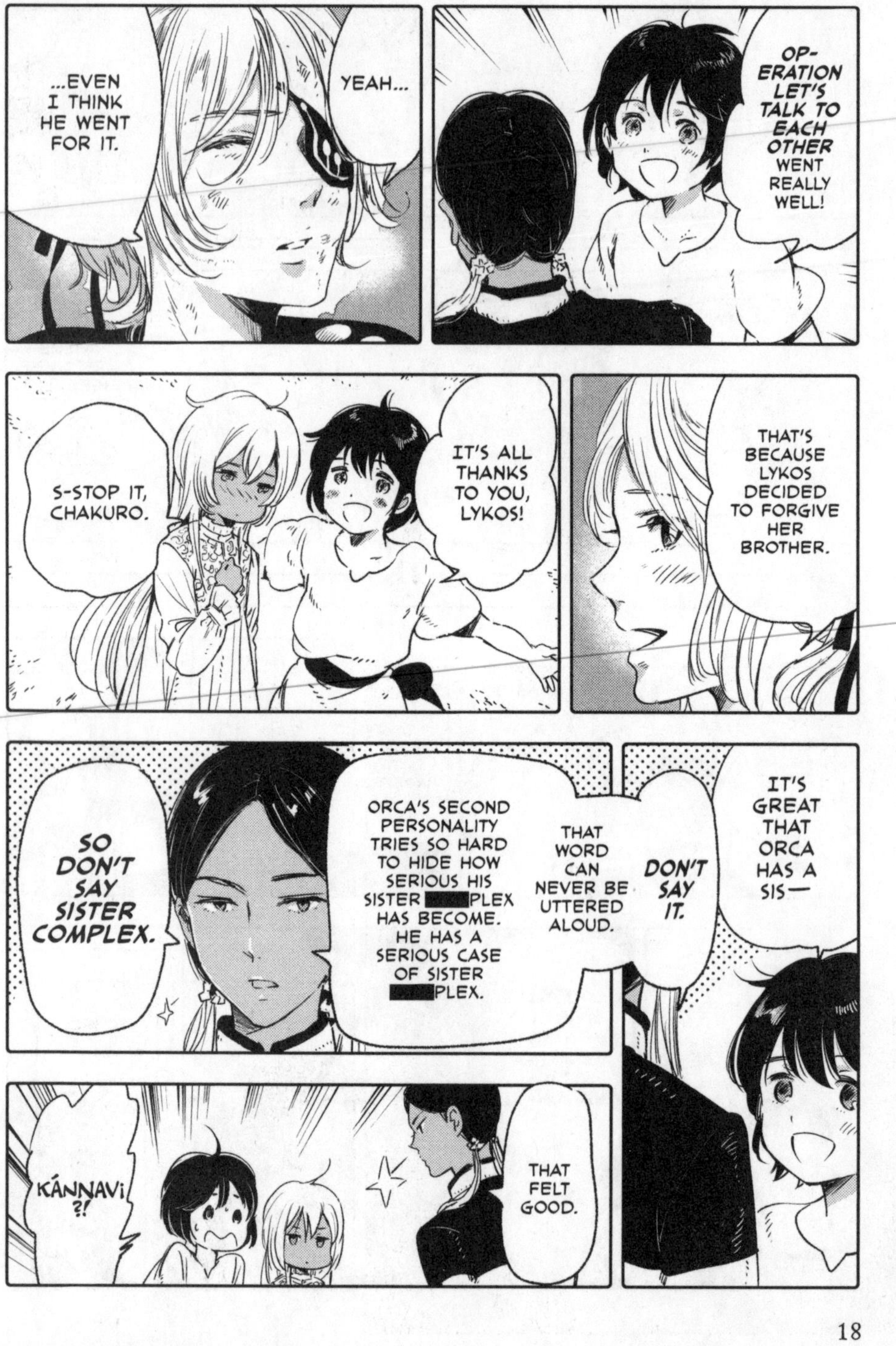
OPERATION LET'S TALK TO EACH OTHER WENT REALLY WELL!
YEAH...
...EVEN I THINK HE WENT FOR IT.
THAT'S BECAUSE LYKOS DECIDED TO FORGIVE HER BROTHER.
IT'S ALL THANKS TO YOU, LYKOS!
S-STOP IT, CHAKURO.
IT'S GREAT THAT ORCA HAS A SIS—
DON'T SAY IT.
THAT WORD CAN NEVER BE UTTERED ALOUD.
ORCA'S SECOND PERSONALITY TRIES SO HARD TO HIDE HOW SERIOUS HIS SISTER [redacted]PLEX HAS BECOME. HE HAS A SERIOUS CASE OF SISTER [redacted]PLEX.
SO DON'T SAY SISTER COMPLEX.
THAT FELT GOOD.
KÁNNAVI ?!

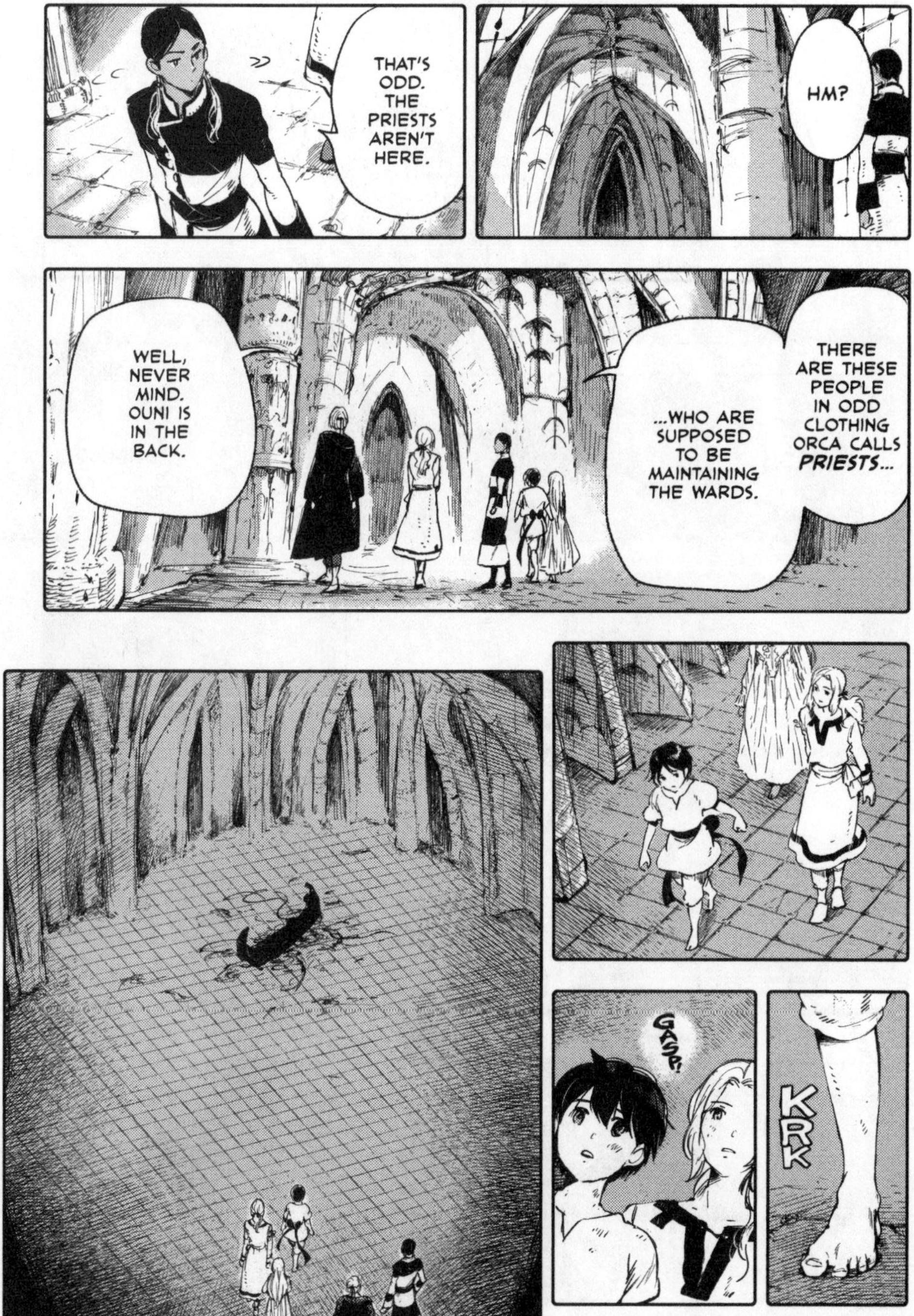
HM?
THAT'S ODD. THE PRIESTS AREN'T HERE.
THERE ARE THESE PEOPLE IN ODD CLOTHING ORCA CALLS *PRIESTS*...
...WHO ARE SUPPOSED TO BE MAINTAINING THE WARDS.
WELL, NEVER MIND. OUNI IS IN THE BACK.
KRK
GASP!

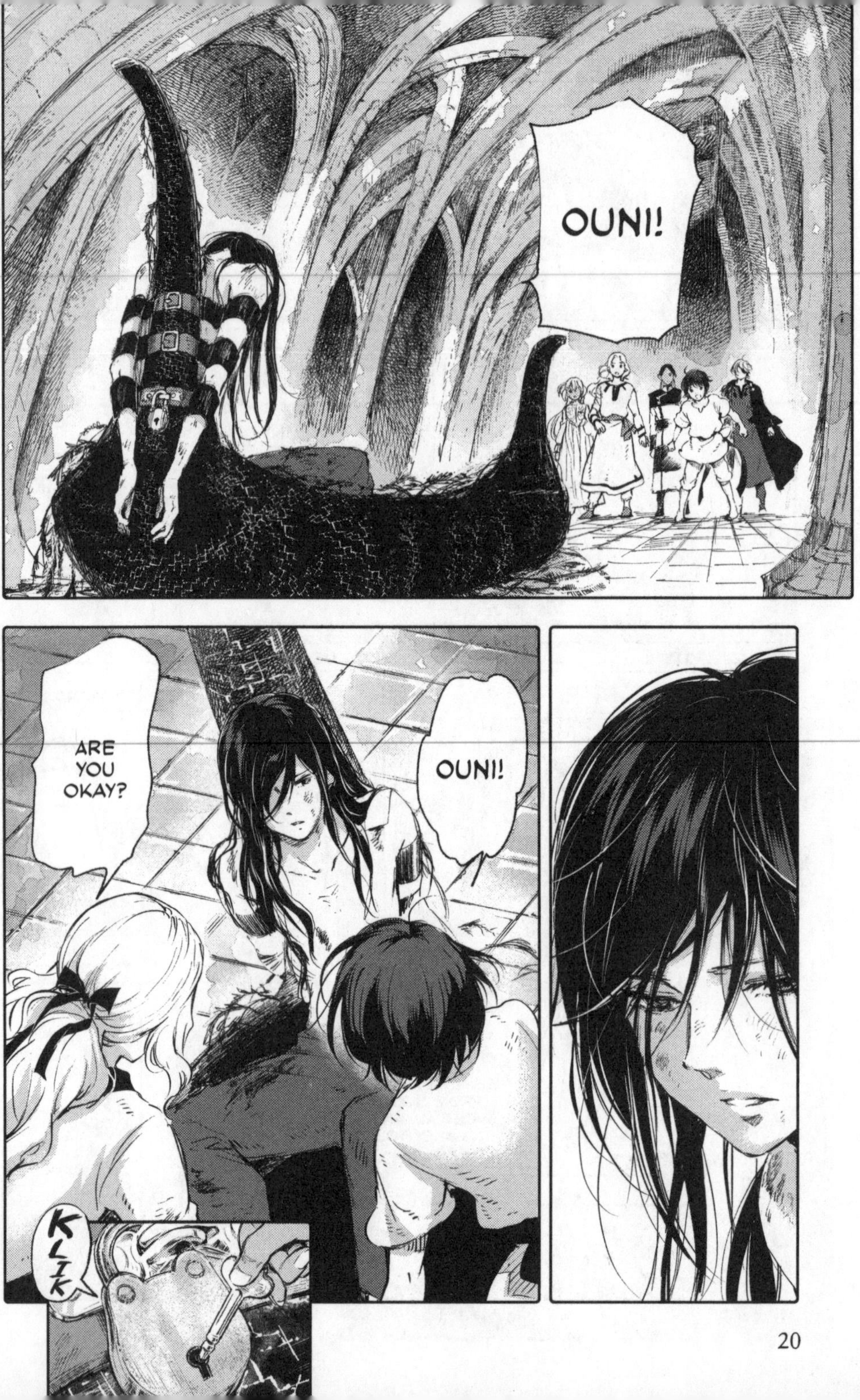
OUNI!
OUNI!
ARE YOU OKAY?
KLIK

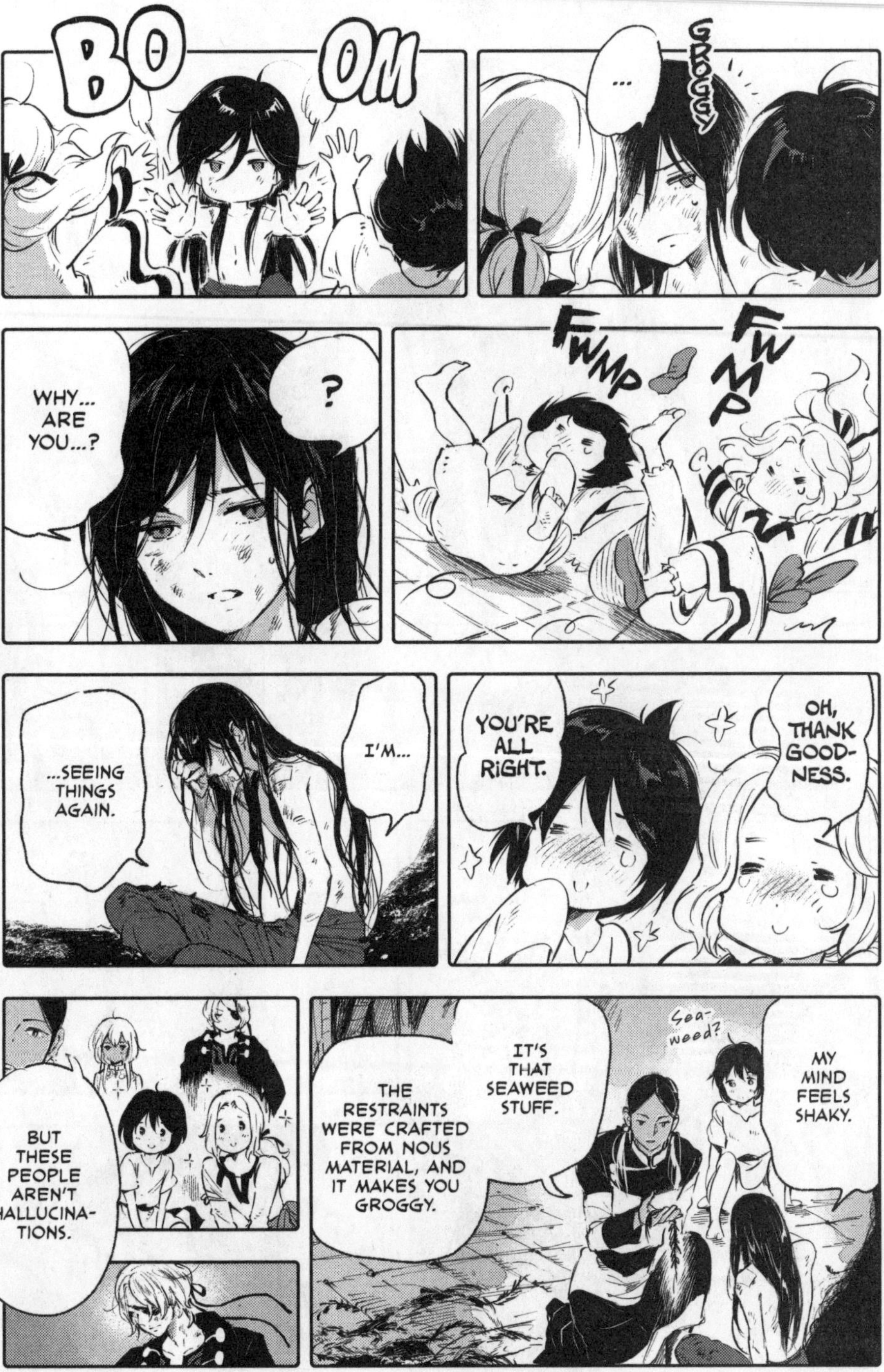
...
GROGGY
BOOM
FWMP
FWMP
?
WHY... ARE YOU...?
OH, THANK GOODNESS.
YOU'RE ALL RIGHT.
I'M...
...SEEING THINGS AGAIN.
MY MIND FEELS SHAKY.
Sea-weed?
IT'S THAT SEAWEED STUFF.
THE RESTRAINTS WERE CRAFTED FROM NOUS MATERIAL, AND IT MAKES YOU GROGGY.
BUT THESE PEOPLE AREN'T HALLUCINATIONS.

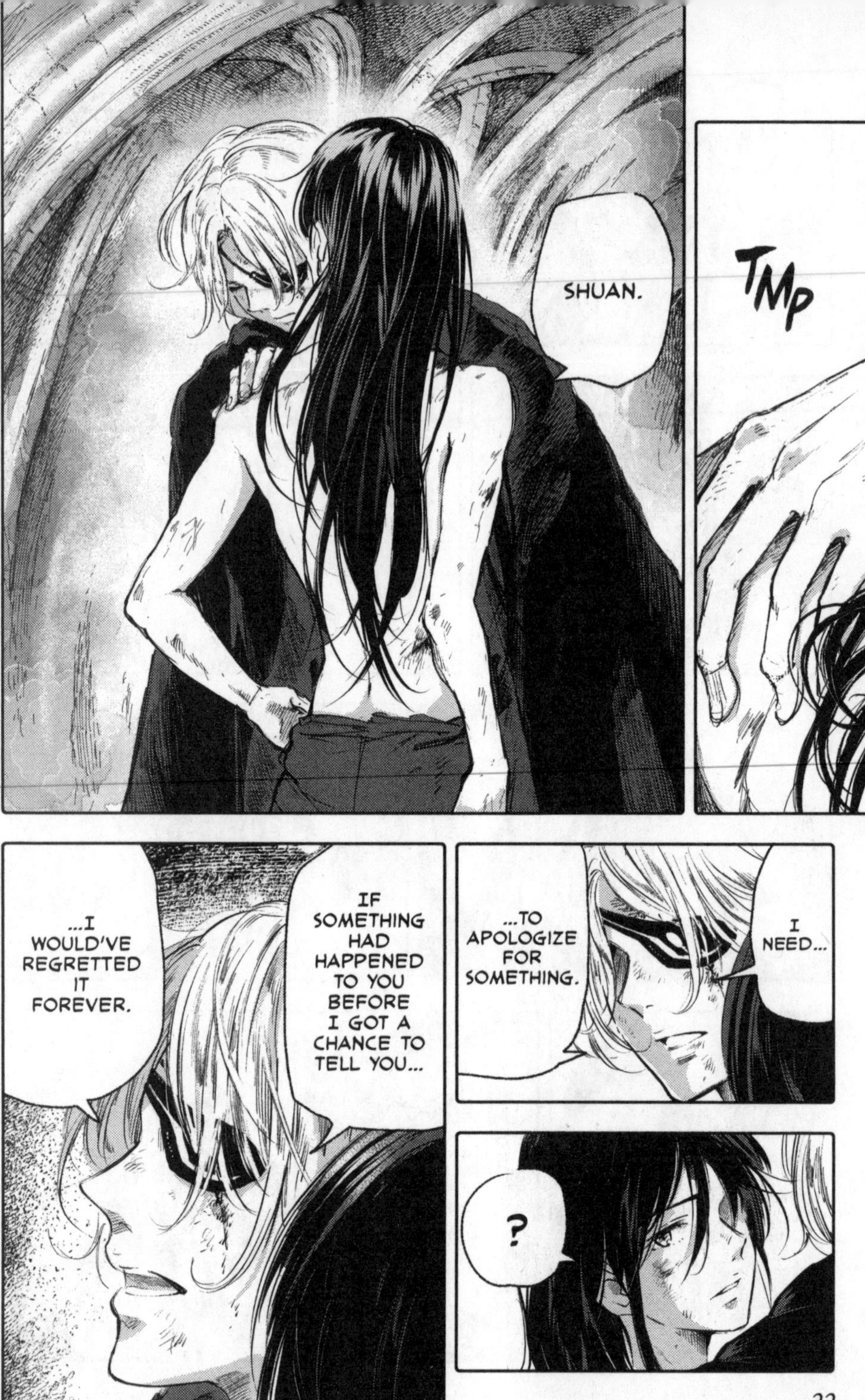
TMP
SHUAN.
I NEED...
...TO APOLOGIZE FOR SOMETHING.
?
IF SOMETHING HAD HAPPENED TO YOU BEFORE I GOT A CHANCE TO TELL YOU...
...I WOULD'VE REGRETTED IT FOREVER.

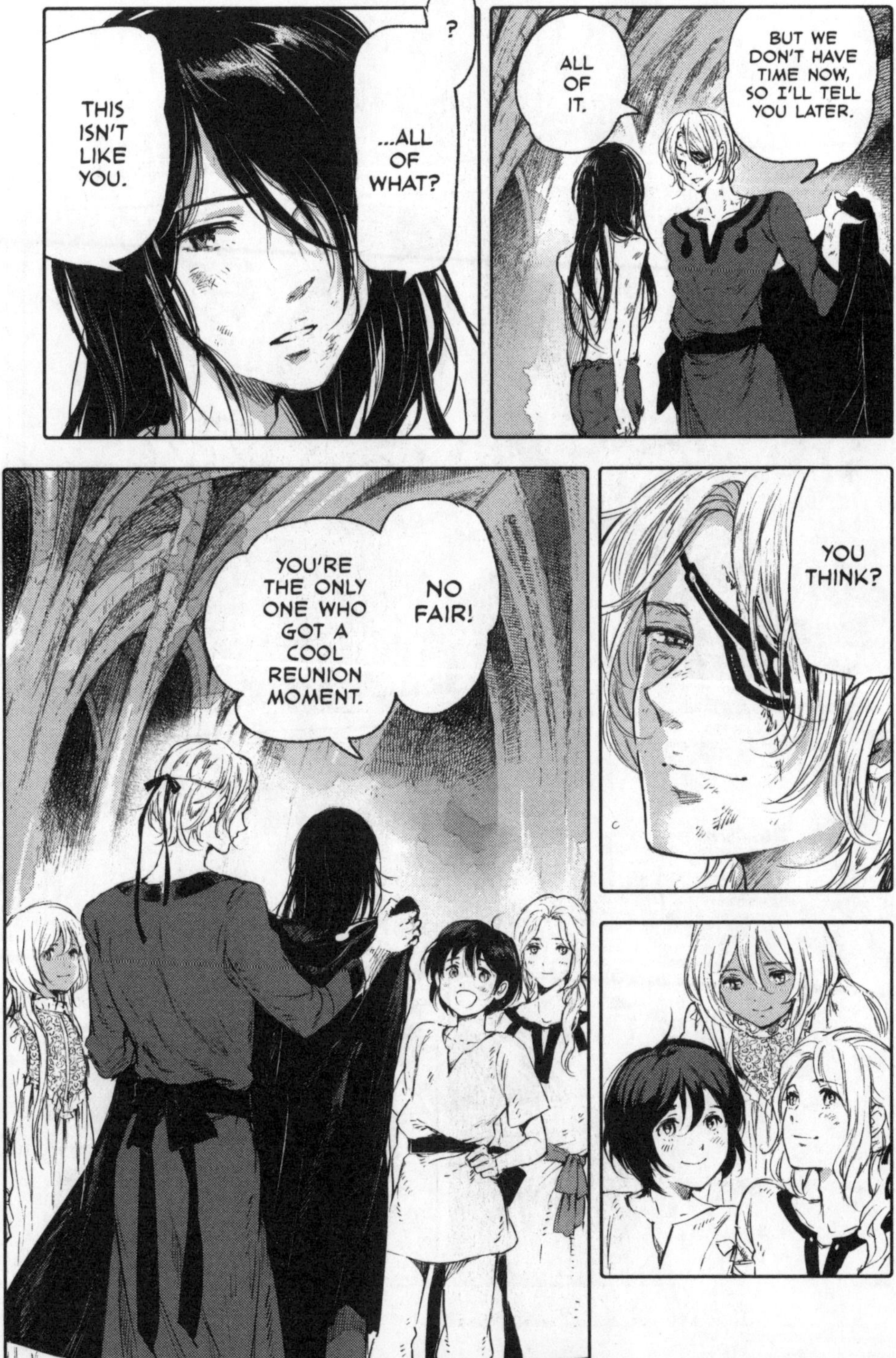
BUT WE DON'T HAVE TIME NOW, SO I'LL TELL YOU LATER.
ALL OF IT.
?
...ALL OF WHAT?
THIS ISN'T LIKE YOU.
YOU THINK?
NO FAIR!
YOU'RE THE ONLY ONE WHO GOT A COOL REUNION MOMENT.

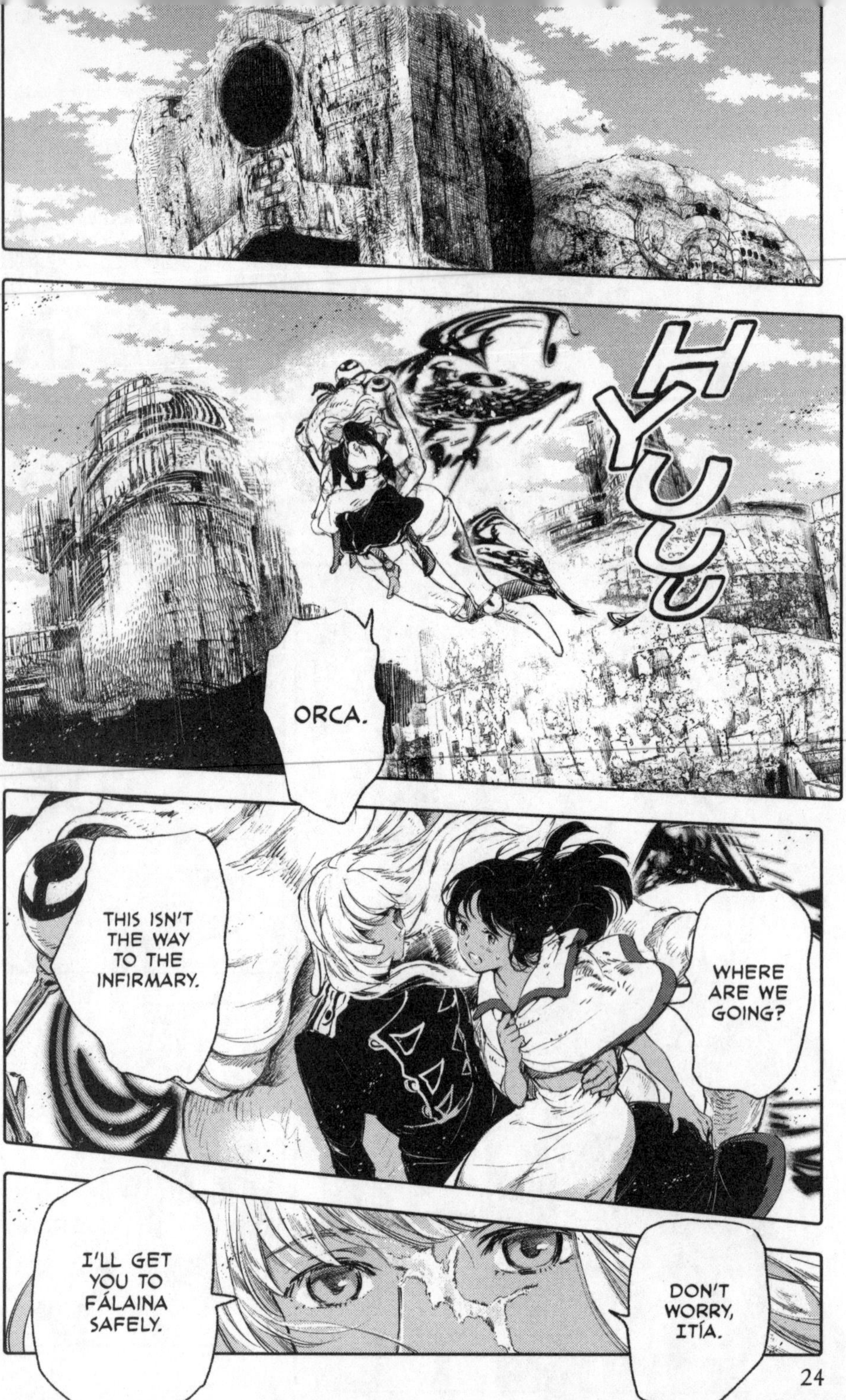
HYUUU
ORCA.
WHERE ARE WE GOING?
THIS ISN'T THE WAY TO THE INFIRMARY.
DON'T WORRY, ITÍA.
I'LL GET YOU TO FÁLAINA SAFELY.

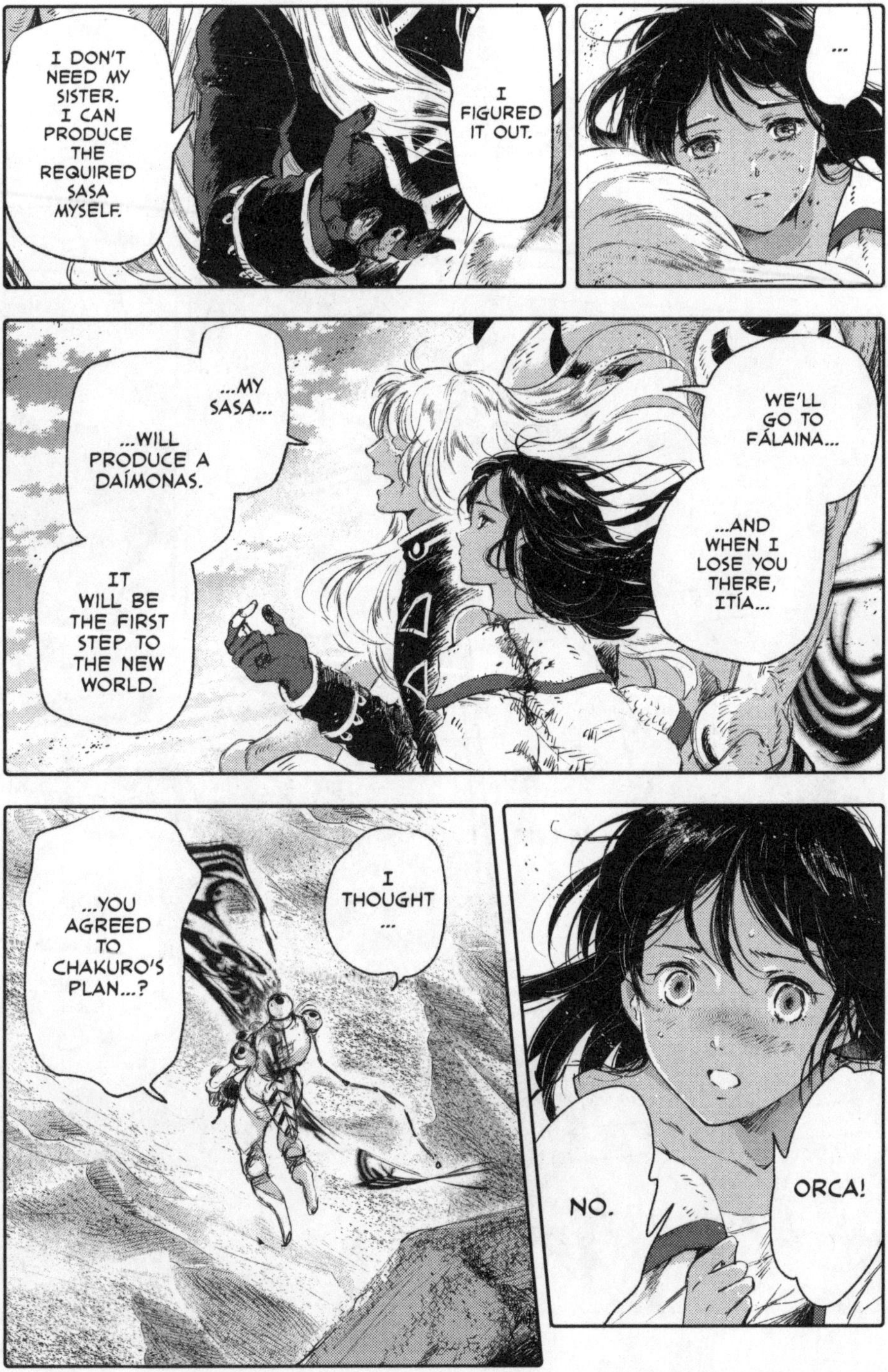
...
I FIGURED IT OUT.
I DON'T NEED MY SISTER. I CAN PRODUCE THE REQUIRED SASA MYSELF.
WE'LL GO TO FÁLAINA...
...AND WHEN I LOSE YOU THERE, ITÍA...
...MY SASA...
...WILL PRODUCE A DAÍMONAS.
IT WILL BE THE FIRST STEP TO THE NEW WORLD.
ORCA!
NO.
I THOUGHT ...
...YOU AGREED TO CHAKURO'S PLAN...?

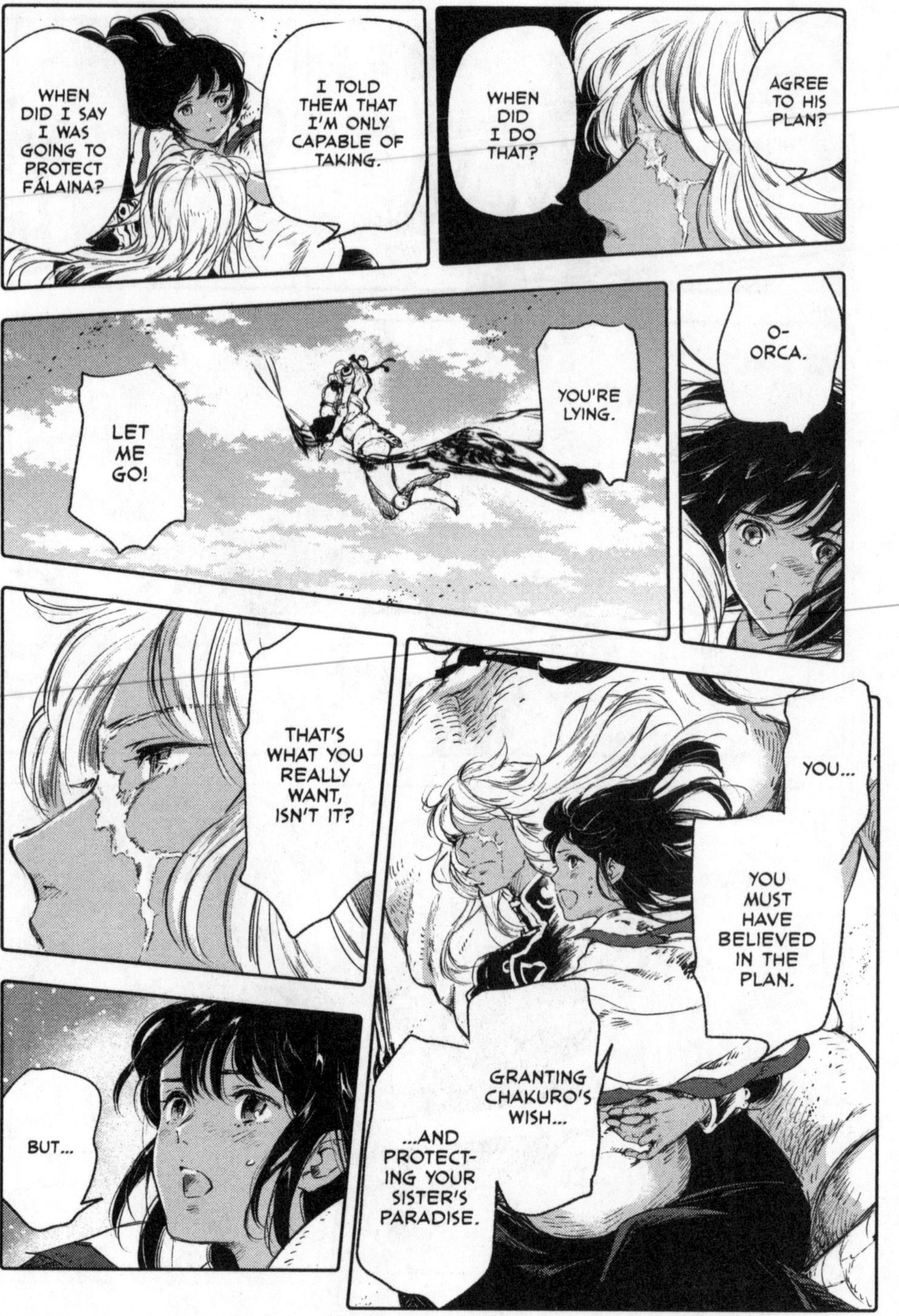
WHEN DID I DO THAT?
AGREE TO HIS PLAN?
I TOLD THEM THAT I'M ONLY CAPABLE OF TAKING.
WHEN DID I SAY I WAS GOING TO PROTECT FÁLAINA?
O-ORCA.
YOU'RE LYING.
LET ME GO!
YOU...
YOU MUST HAVE BELIEVED IN THE PLAN.
GRANTING CHAKURO'S WISH...
...AND PROTECTING YOUR SISTER'S PARADISE.
THAT'S WHAT YOU REALLY WANT, ISN'T IT?
BUT...

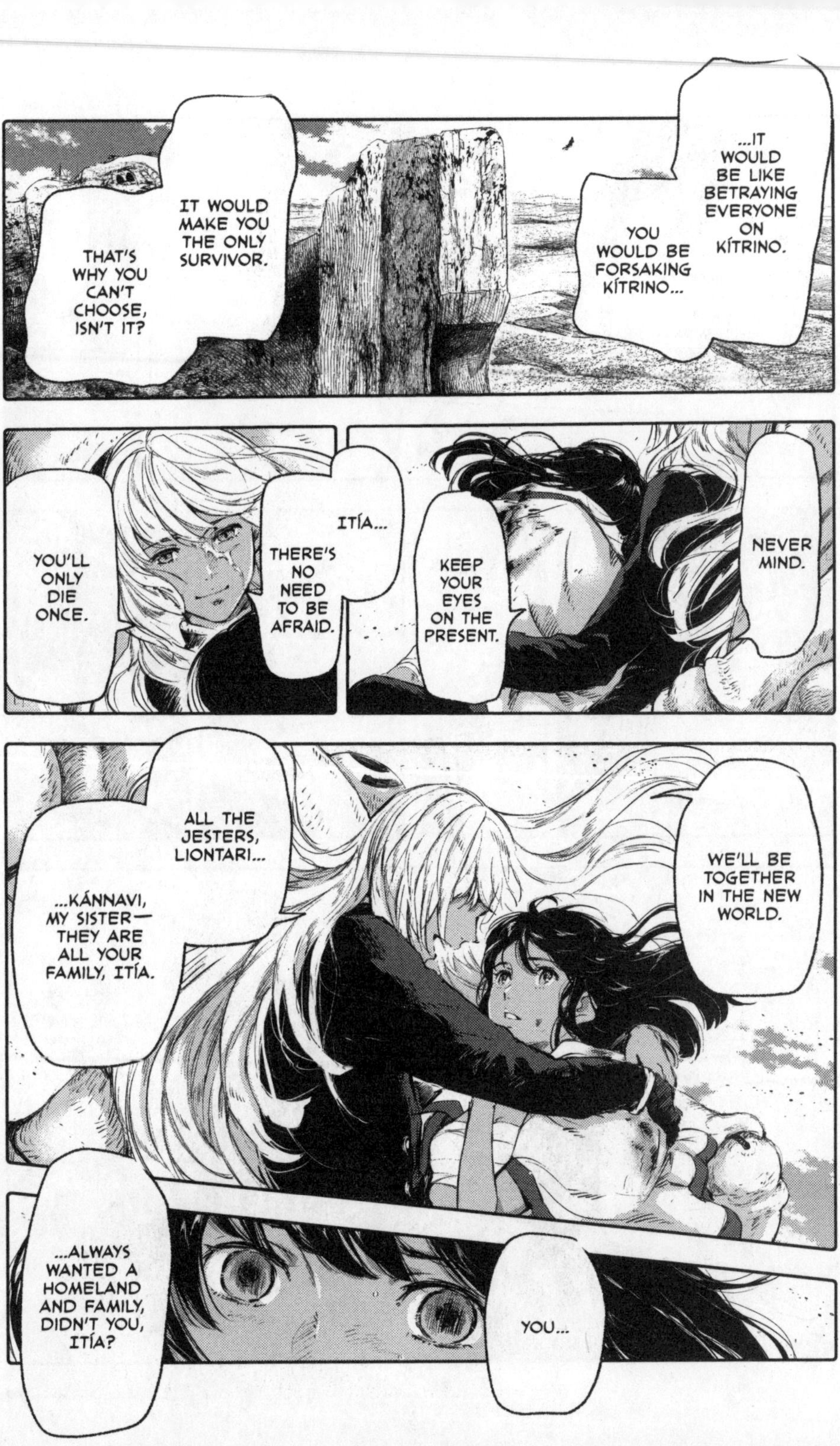
...IT WOULD BE LIKE BETRAYING EVERYONE ON KÍTRINO.
YOU WOULD BE FORSAKING KÍTRINO...
IT WOULD MAKE YOU THE ONLY SURVIVOR.
THAT'S WHY YOU CAN'T CHOOSE, ISN'T IT?
NEVER MIND.
KEEP YOUR EYES ON THE PRESENT.
ITÍA... THERE'S NO NEED TO BE AFRAID.
YOU'LL ONLY DIE ONCE.
WE'LL BE TOGETHER IN THE NEW WORLD.
ALL THE JESTERS, LIONTARI... ...KÁNNAVI, MY SISTER— THEY ARE ALL YOUR FAMILY, ITÍA.
YOU...
...ALWAYS WANTED A HOMELAND AND FAMILY, DIDN'T YOU, ITÍA?

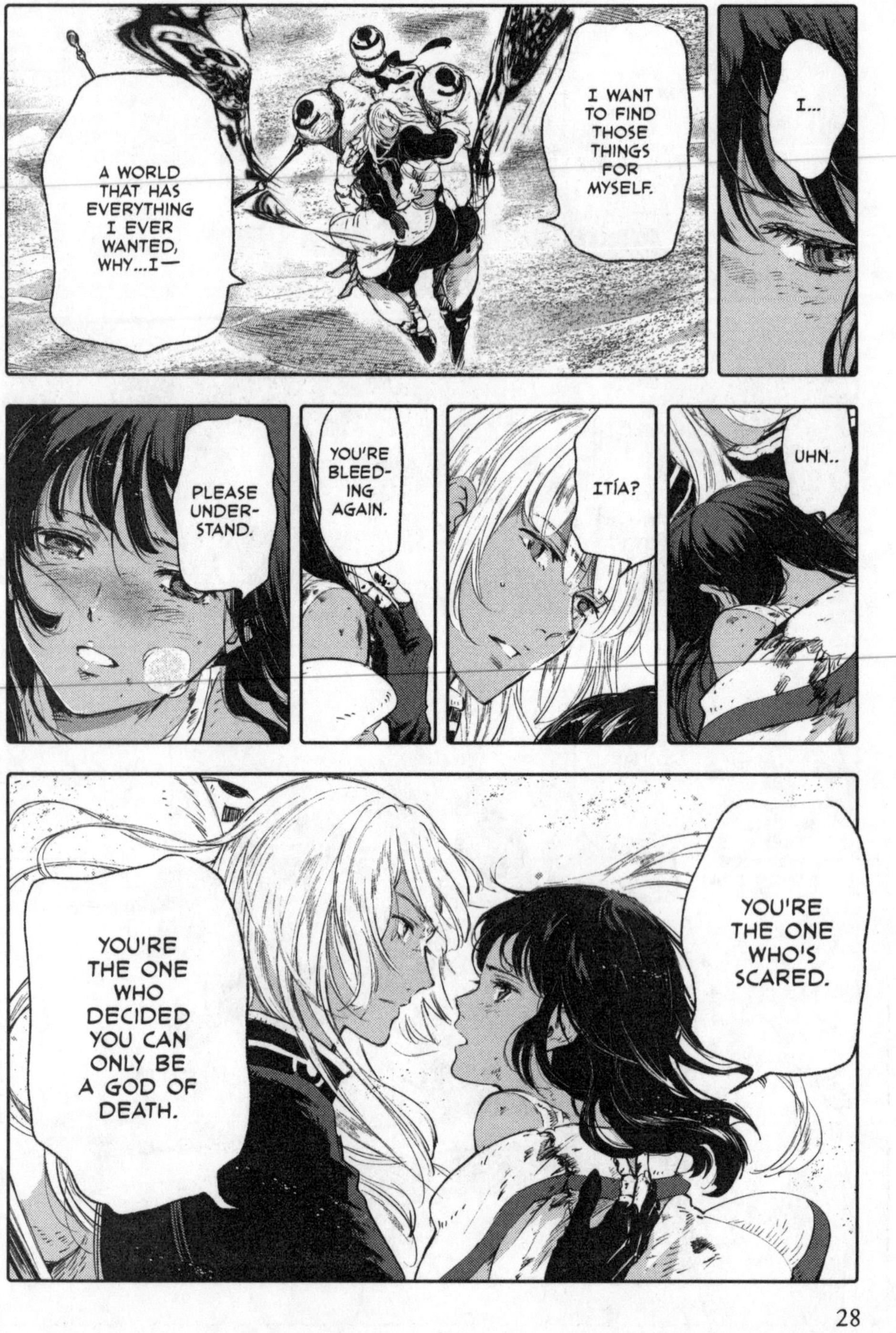
I...
I WANT TO FIND THOSE THINGS FOR MYSELF.
A WORLD THAT HAS EVERYTHING I EVER WANTED, WHY...I—
UHN..
ITÍA?
YOU'RE BLEED-ING AGAIN.
PLEASE UNDER-STAND.
YOU'RE THE ONE WHO'S SCARED.
YOU'RE THE ONE WHO DECIDED YOU CAN ONLY BE A GOD OF DEATH.

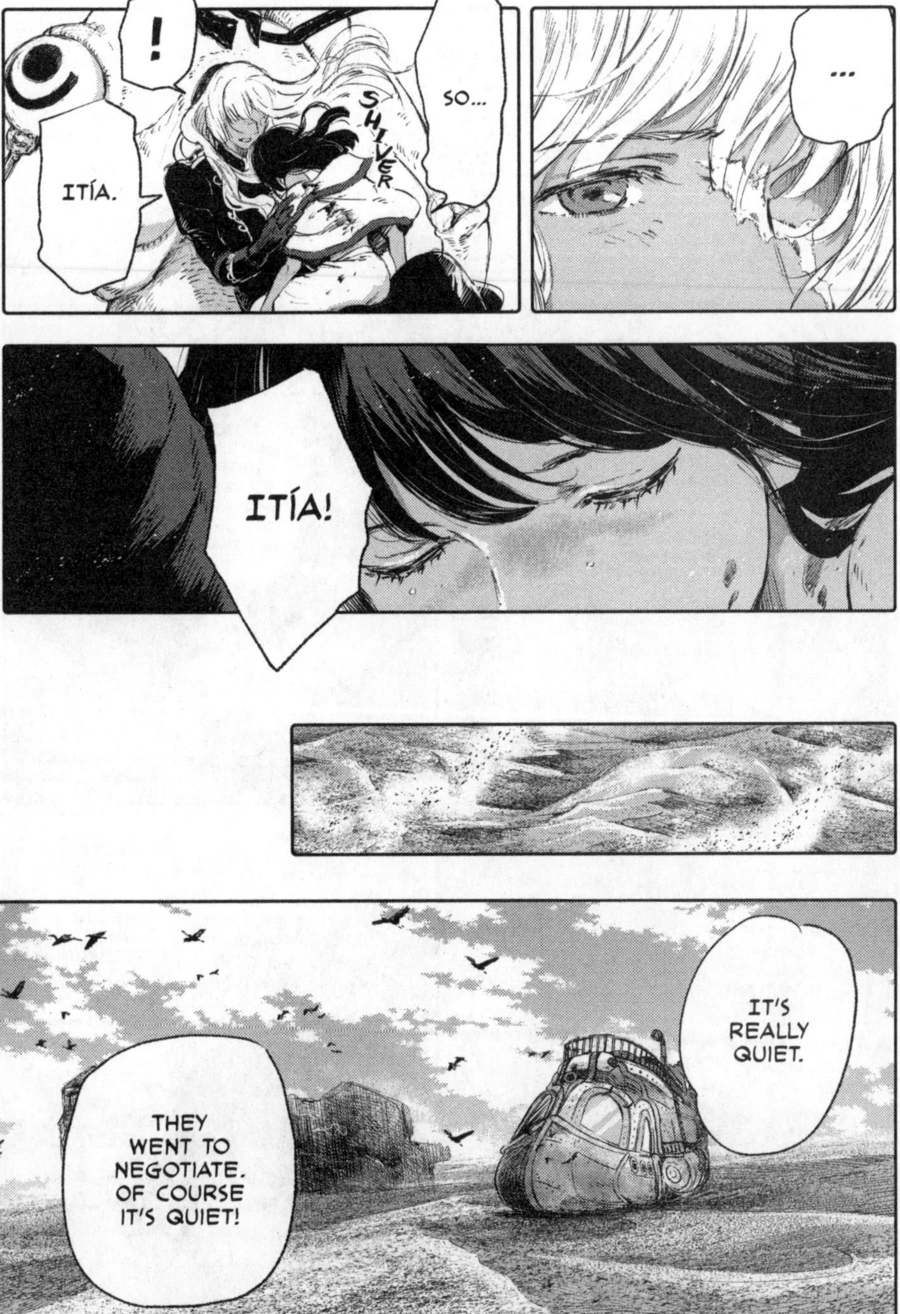
...
SO...
SHIVER
!
ITÍA.
ITÍA!
IT'S REALLY QUIET.
THEY WENT TO NEGOTIATE. OF COURSE IT'S QUIET!

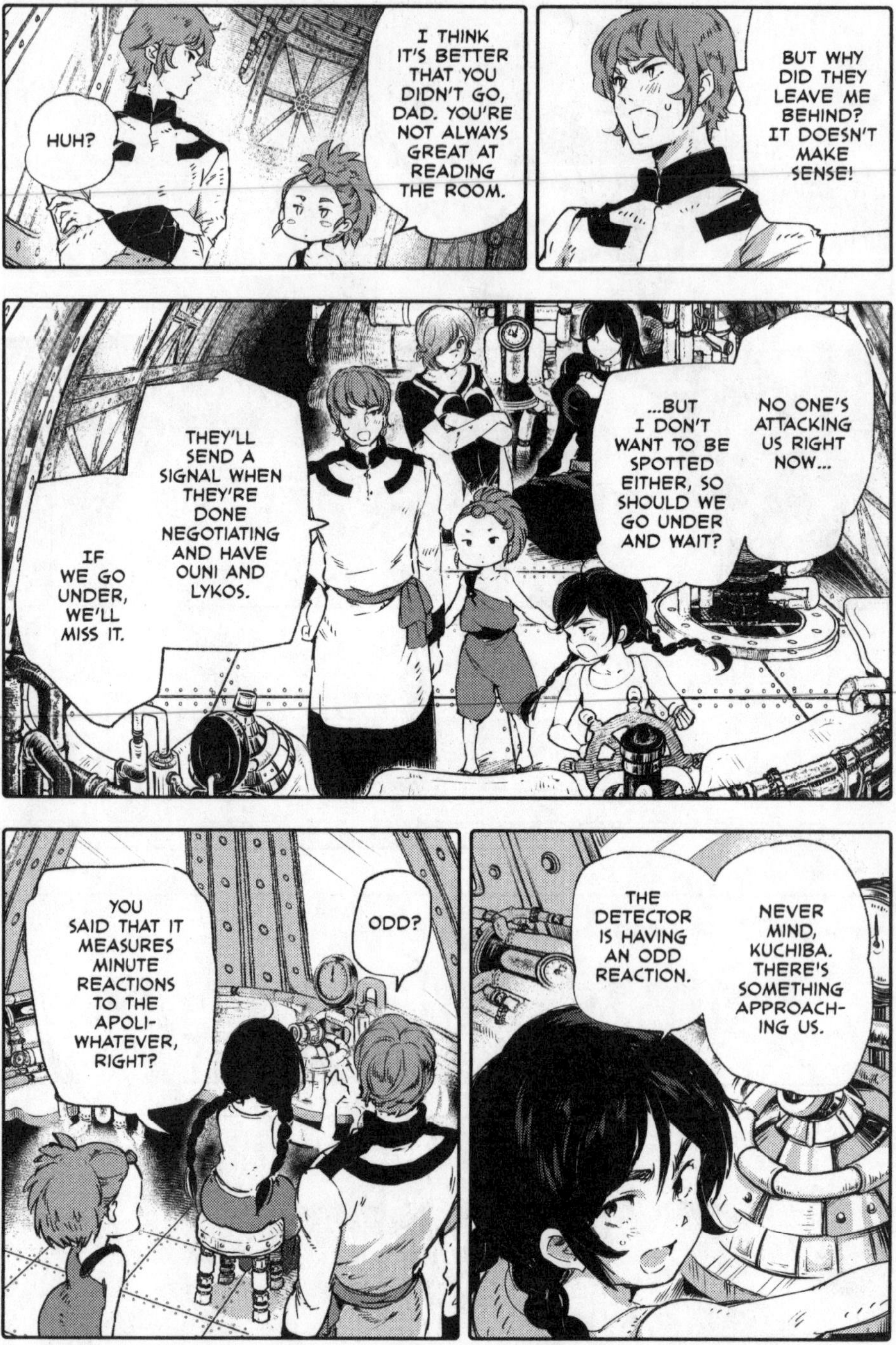
BUT WHY DID THEY LEAVE ME BEHIND? IT DOESN'T MAKE SENSE!
I THINK IT'S BETTER THAT YOU DIDN'T GO, DAD. YOU'RE NOT ALWAYS GREAT AT READING THE ROOM.
HUH?
NO ONE'S ATTACKING US RIGHT NOW...
...BUT I DON'T WANT TO BE SPOTTED EITHER, SO SHOULD WE GO UNDER AND WAIT?
THEY'LL SEND A SIGNAL WHEN THEY'RE DONE NEGOTIATING AND HAVE OUNI AND LYKOS.
IF WE GO UNDER, WE'LL MISS IT.
NEVER MIND, KUCHIBA. THERE'S SOMETHING APPROACHING US.
THE DETECTOR IS HAVING AN ODD REACTION.
ODD?
YOU SAID THAT IT MEASURES MINUTE REACTIONS TO THE APOLI-WHATEVER, RIGHT?

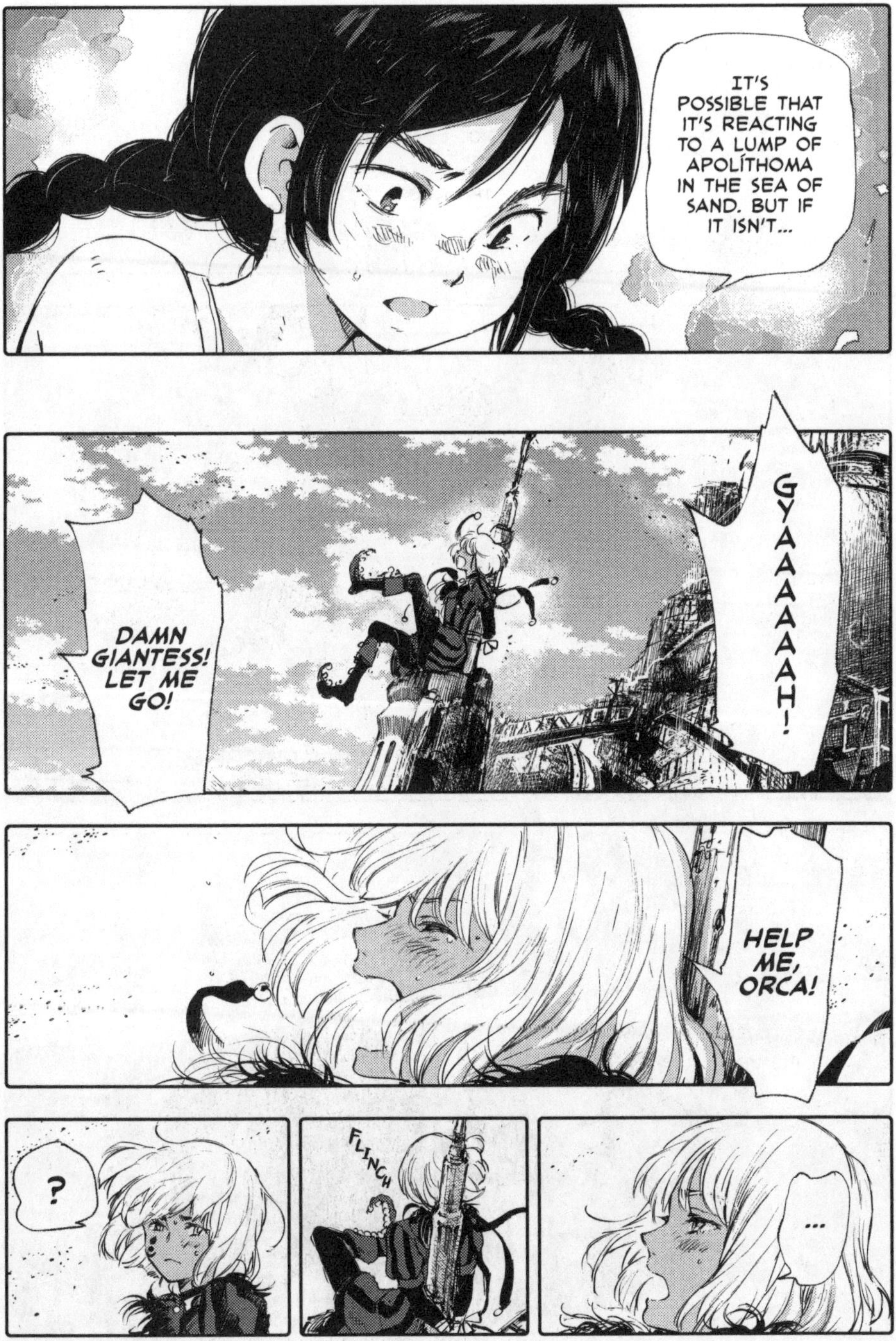
IT'S POSSIBLE THAT IT'S REACTING TO A LUMP OF APOLÍTHOMA IN THE SEA OF SAND. BUT IF IT ISN'T...
GYAAAAAAAH!
DAMN GIANTESS! LET ME GO!
HELP ME, ORCA!
...
FLINCH
?

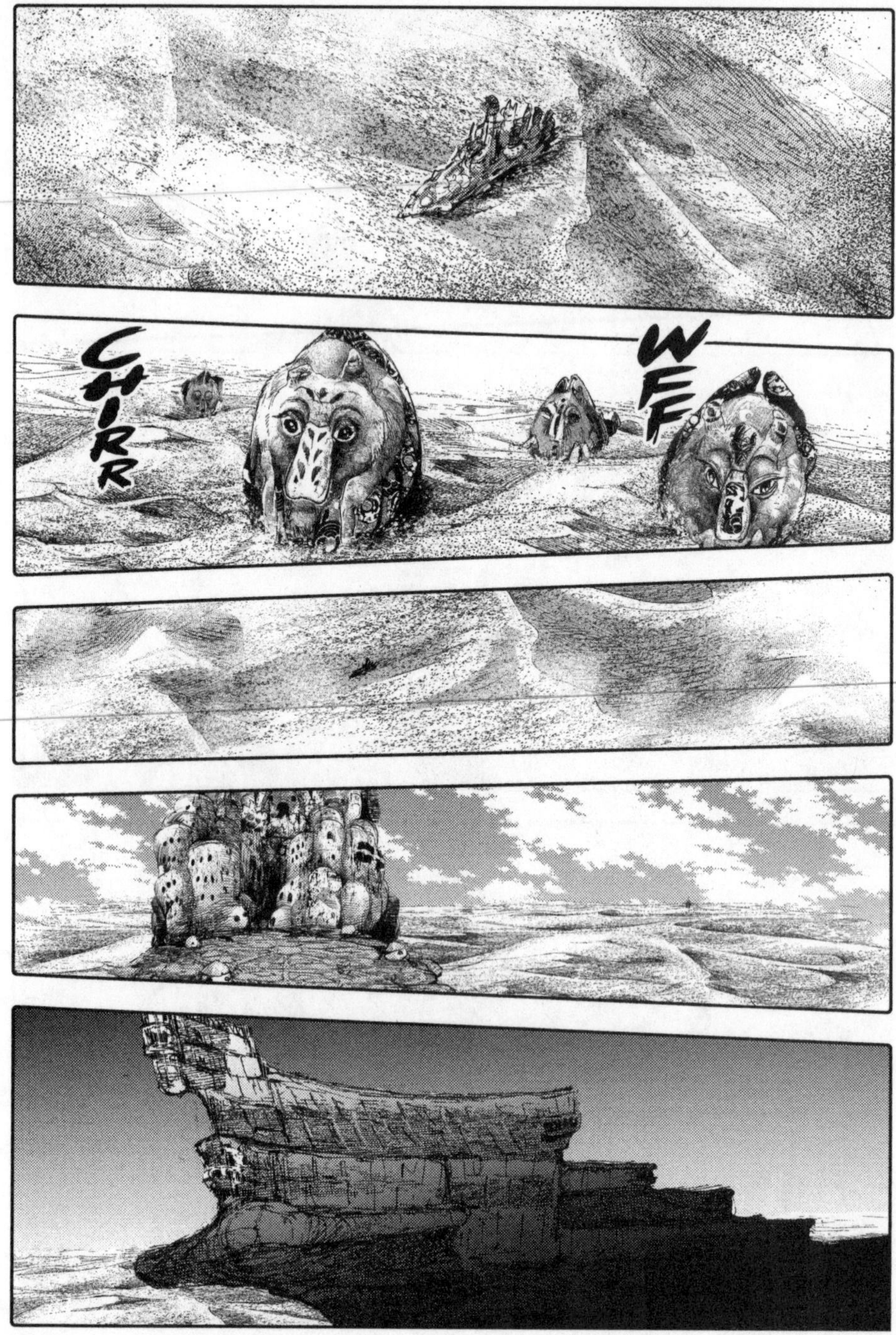
WEFF
CHIRR

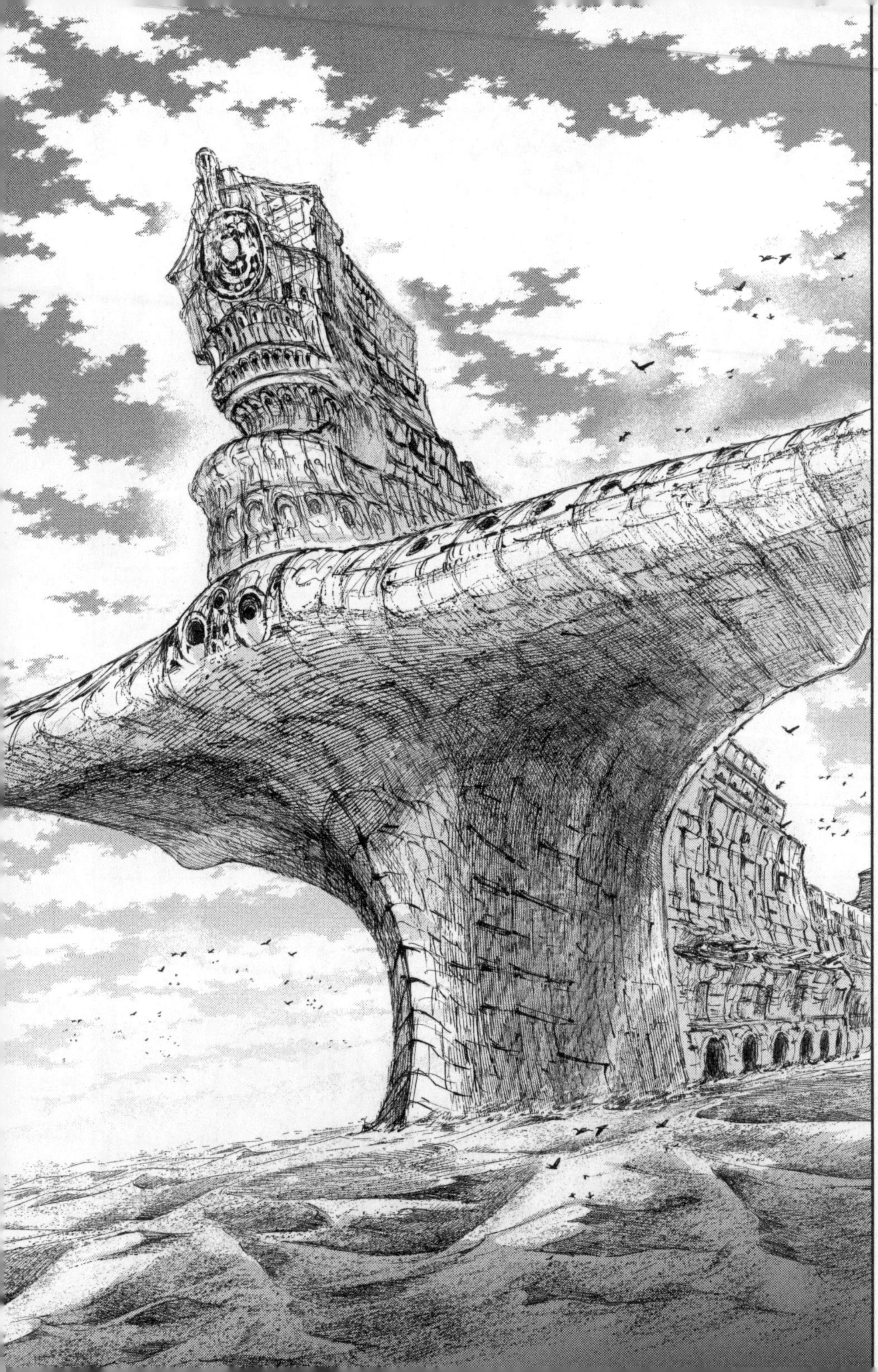

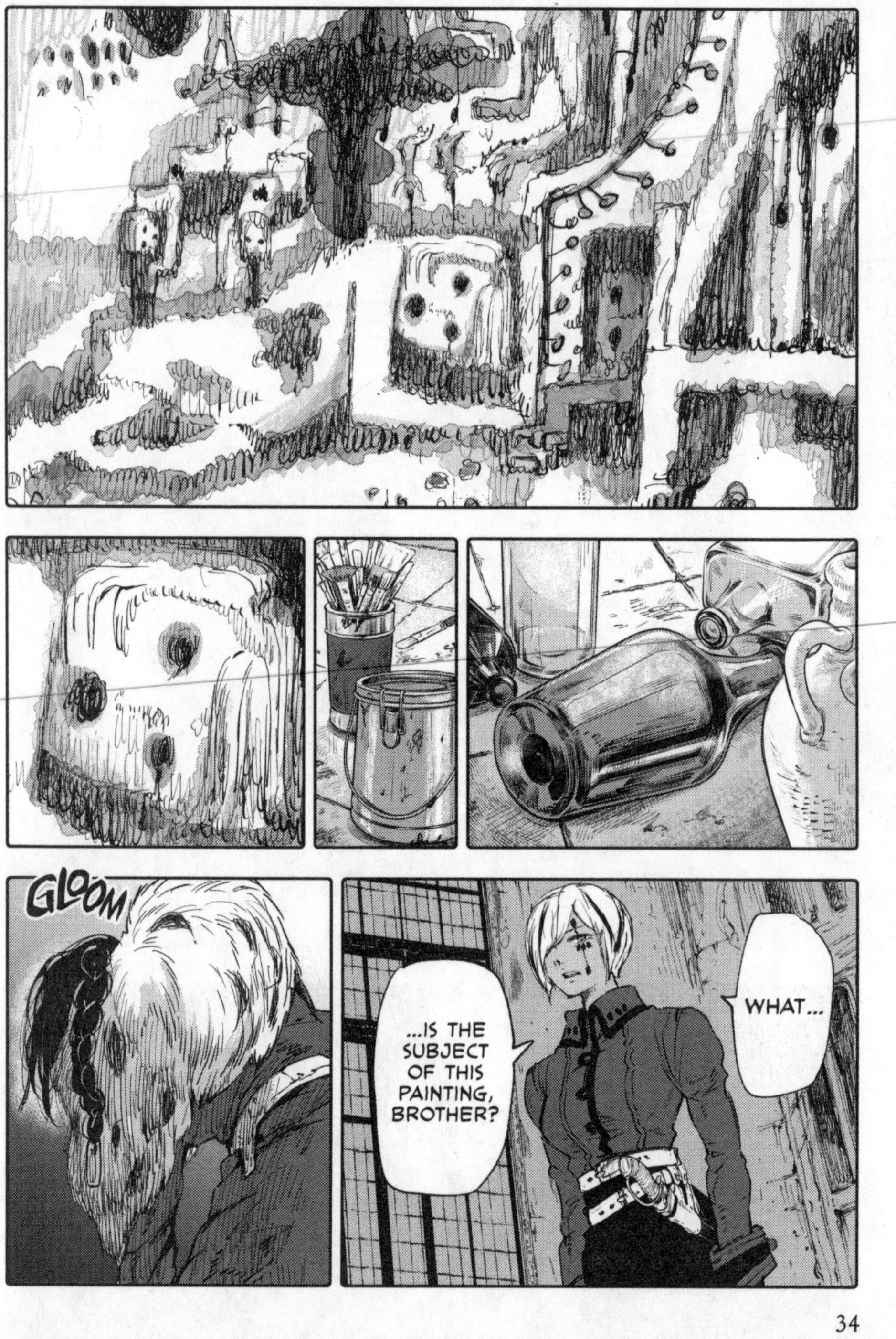
WHAT...
...IS THE SUBJECT OF THIS PAINTING, BROTHER?
GLOOM

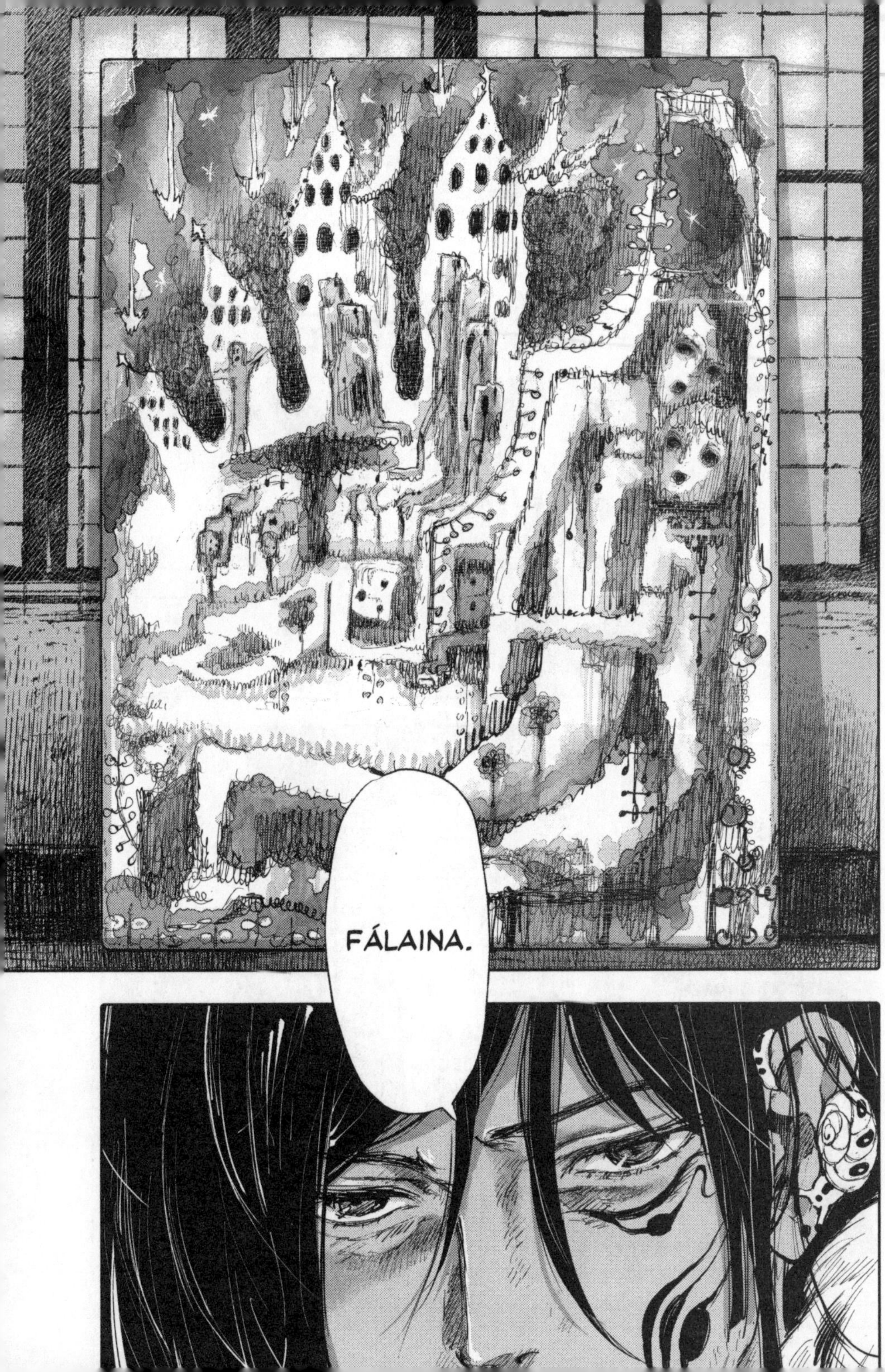
FÁLAINA.

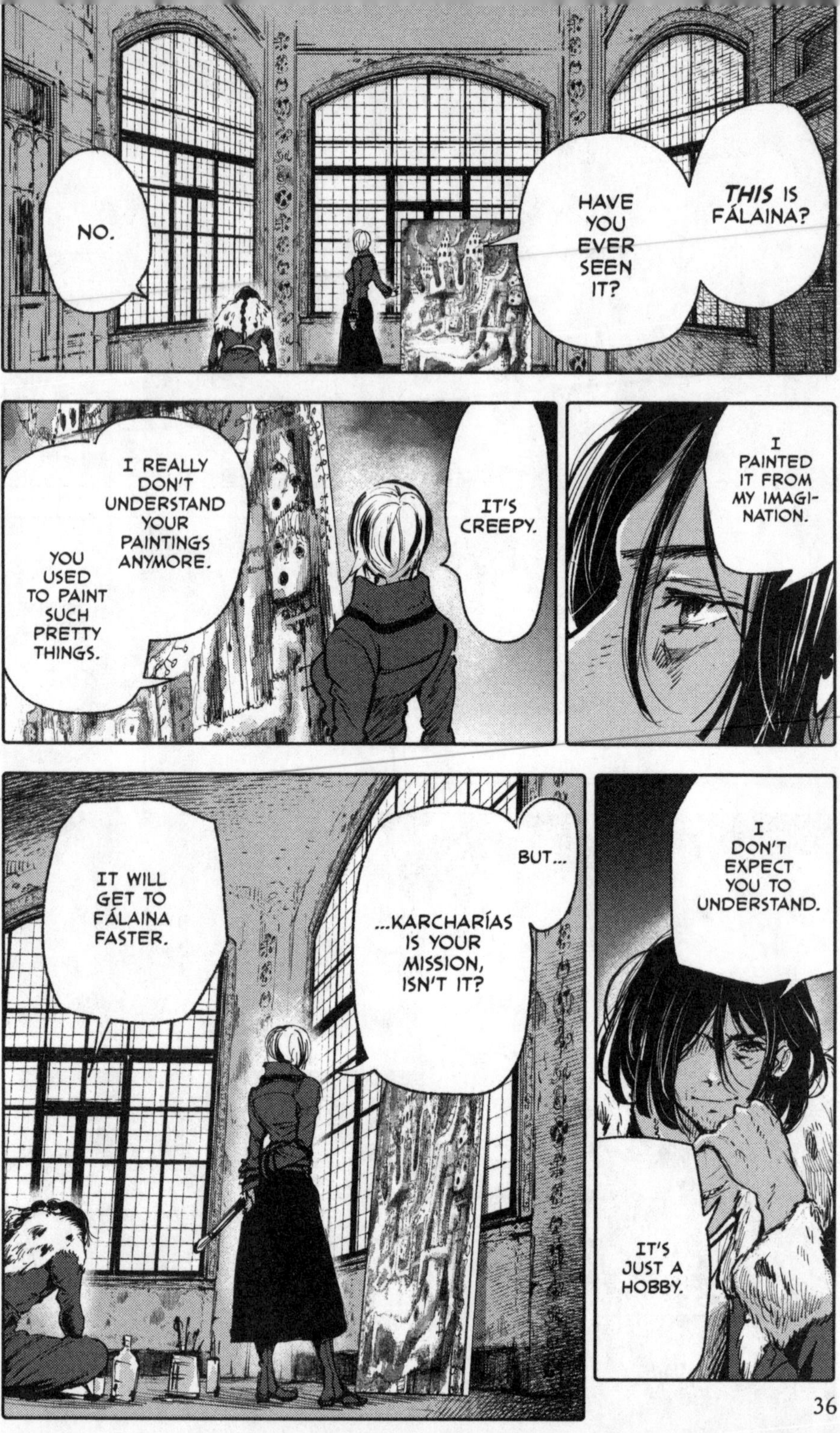
THIS IS FÁLAINA?
HAVE YOU EVER SEEN IT?
NO.
I PAINTED IT FROM MY IMAGI- NATION.
IT'S CREEPY.
I REALLY DON'T UNDERSTAND YOUR PAINTINGS ANYMORE.
YOU USED TO PAINT SUCH PRETTY THINGS.
I DON'T EXPECT YOU TO UNDERSTAND.
IT'S JUST A HOBBY.
BUT...
...KARCHARÍAS IS YOUR MISSION, ISN'T IT?
IT WILL GET TO FÁLAINA FASTER.

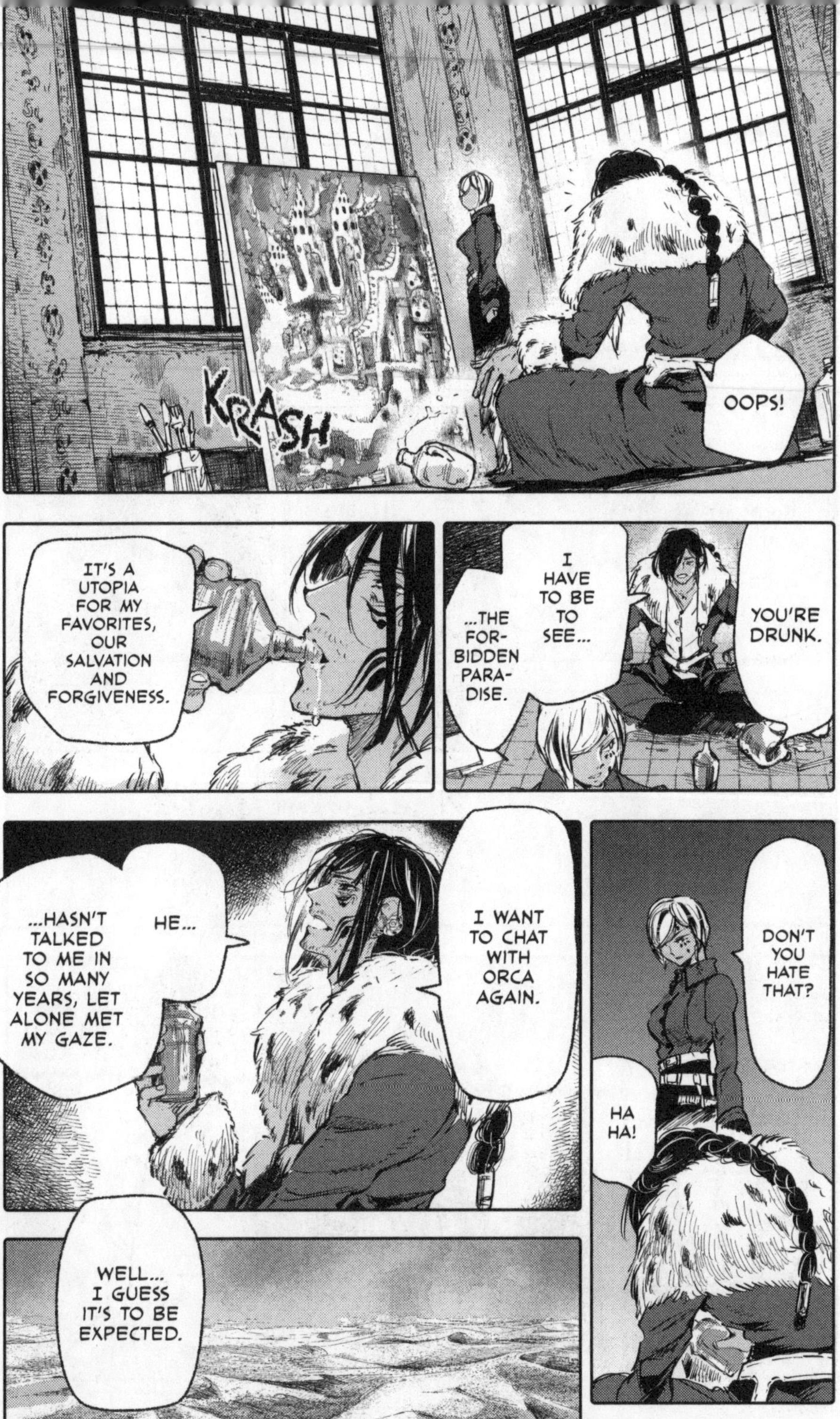
OOPS!
KRASH
YOU'RE DRUNK.
I HAVE TO BE TO SEE...
...THE FORBIDDEN PARADISE.
IT'S A UTOPIA FOR MY FAVORITES, OUR SALVATION AND FORGIVENESS.
DON'T YOU HATE THAT?
HA HA!
I WANT TO CHAT WITH ORCA AGAIN.
HE...
...HASN'T TALKED TO ME IN SO MANY YEARS, LET ALONE MET MY GAZE.
WELL... I GUESS IT'S TO BE EXPECTED.

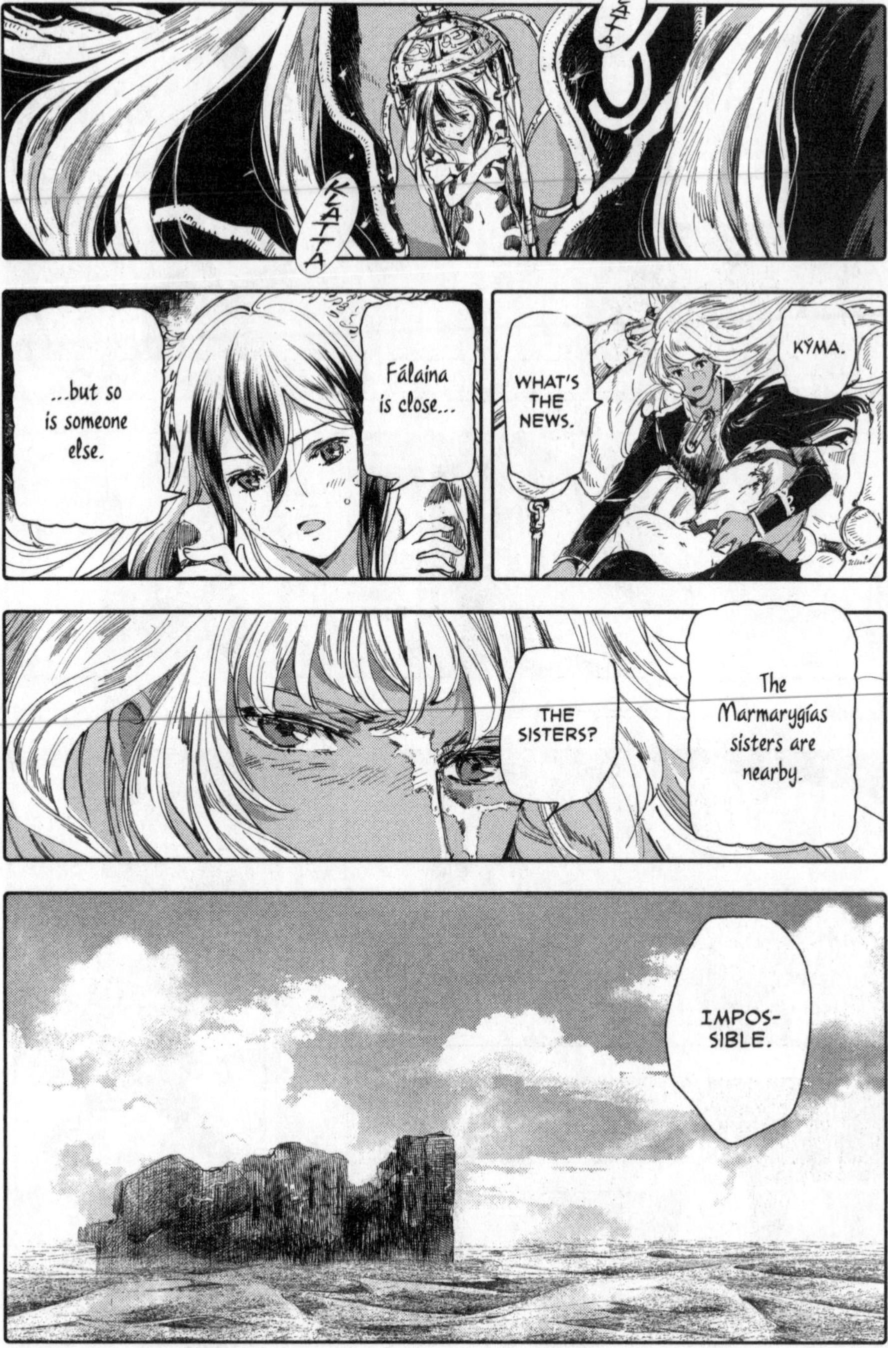
KLATTA
KLATTA
KÝMA.
WHAT'S THE NEWS.
Fálaina is close...
...but so is someone else.
The Marmarygías sisters are nearby.
THE SISTERS?
IMPOS-SIBLE.

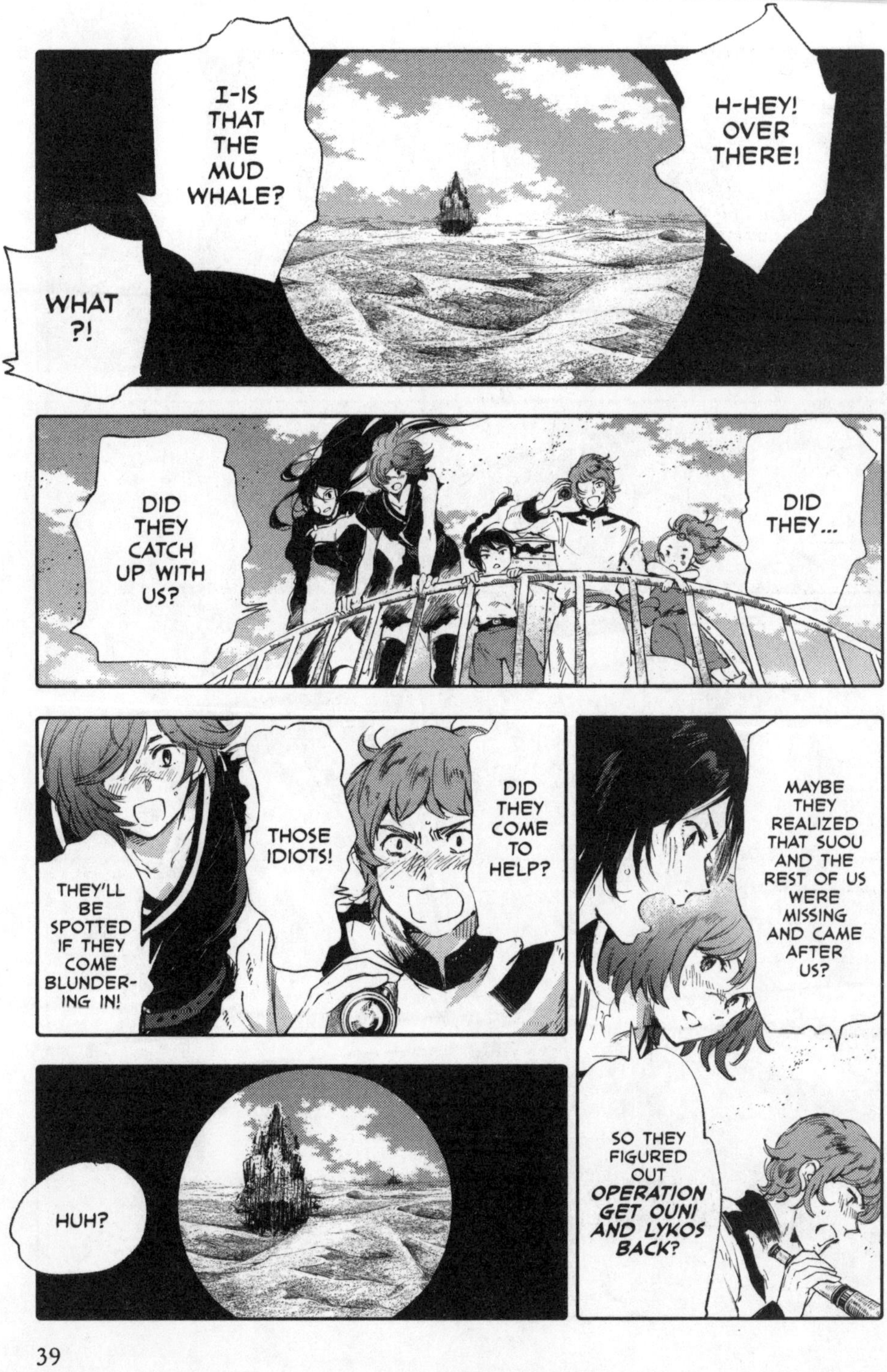
H-HEY! OVER THERE!
I-IS THAT THE MUD WHALE?
WHAT?!
DID THEY...
DID THEY CATCH UP WITH US?
MAYBE THEY REALIZED THAT SUOU AND THE REST OF US WERE MISSING AND CAME AFTER US?
SO THEY FIGURED OUT *OPERATION GET OUNI AND LYKOS BACK?*
DID THEY COME TO HELP?
THOSE IDIOTS!
THEY'LL BE SPOTTED IF THEY COME BLUNDERING IN!
HUH?

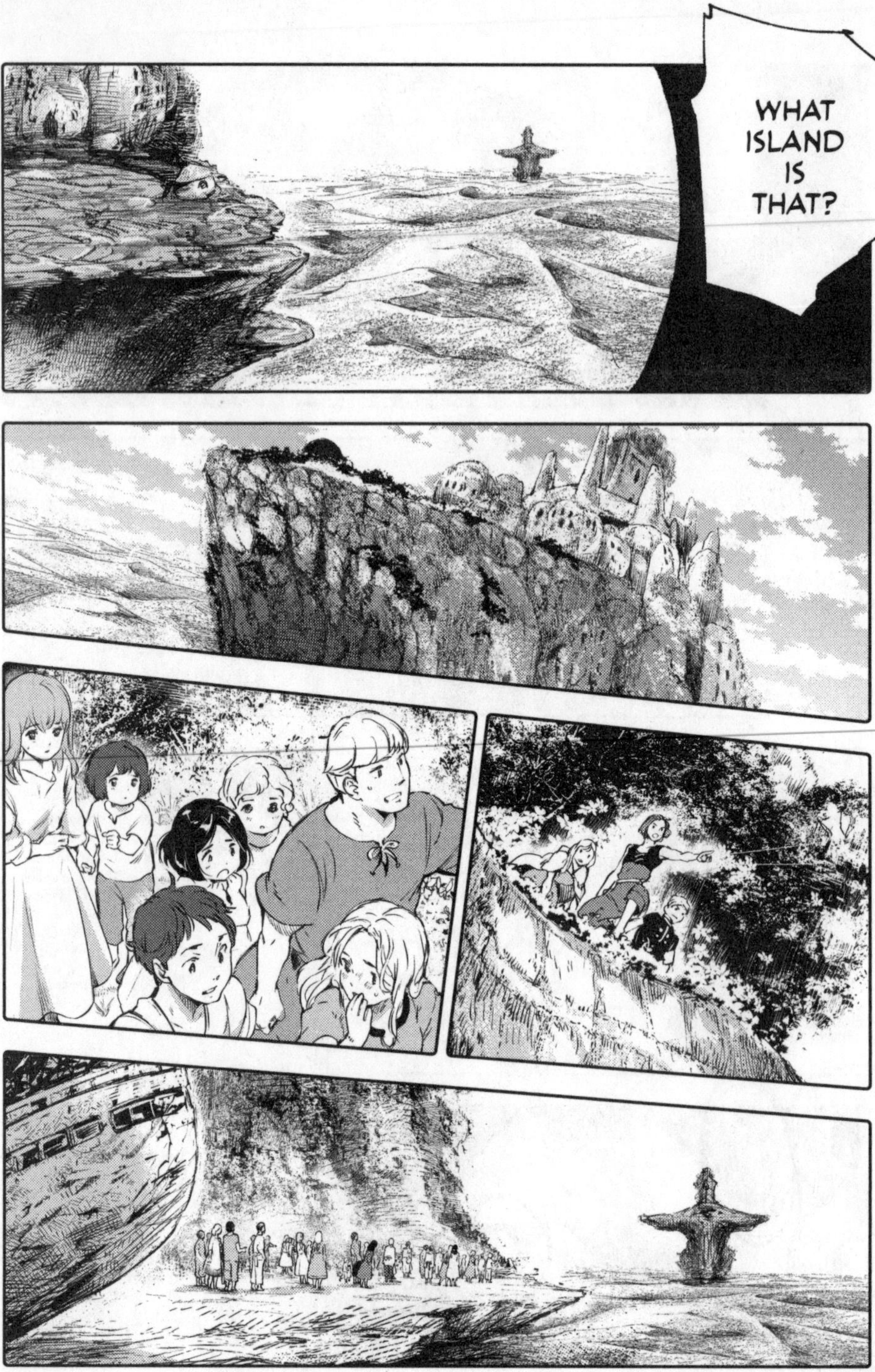
WHAT ISLAND IS THAT?

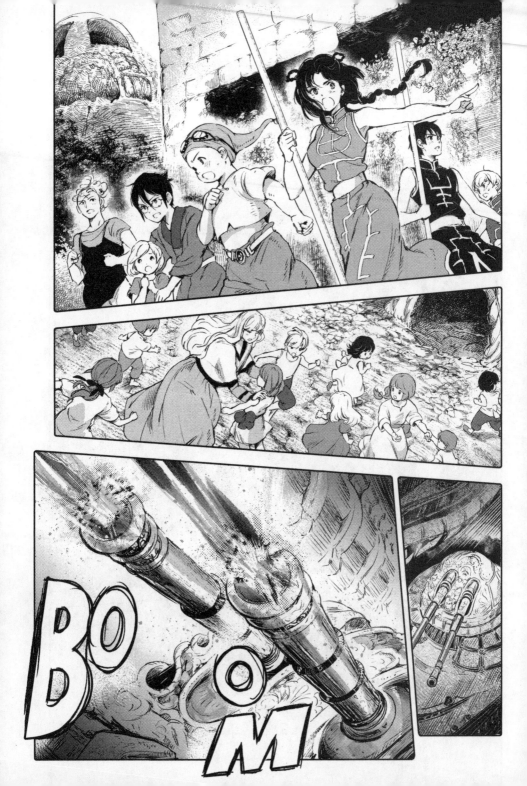

BOOM

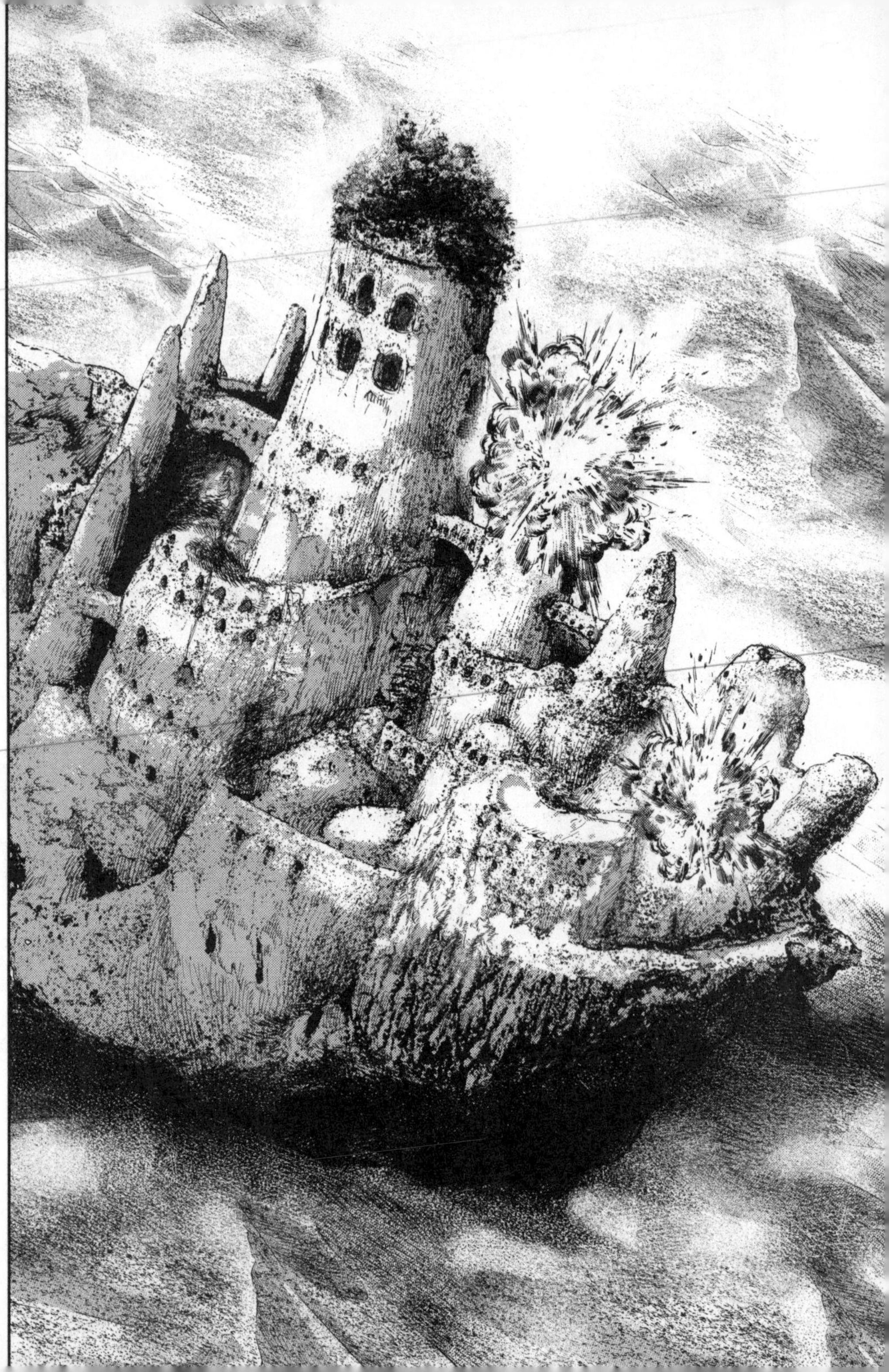

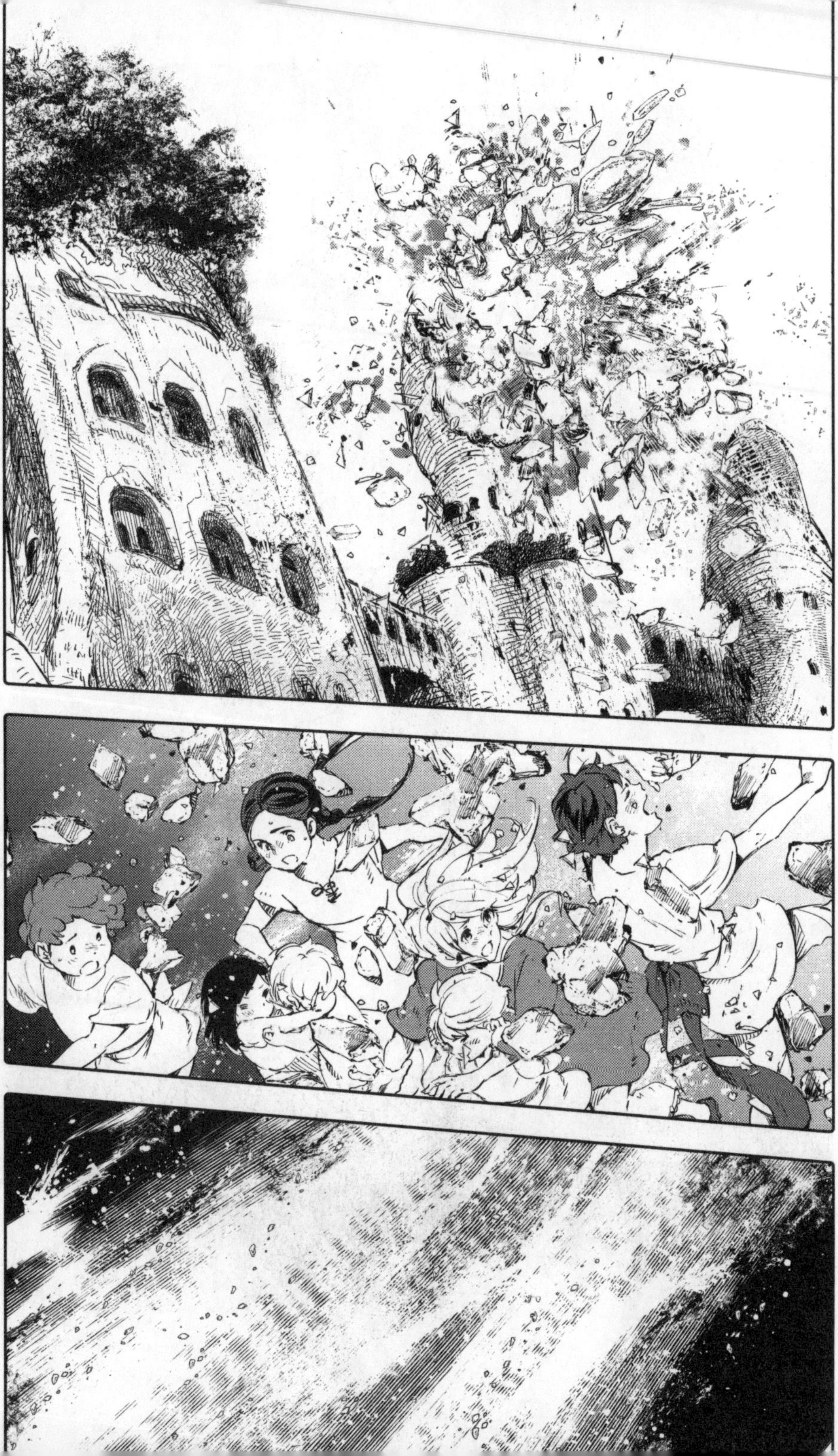

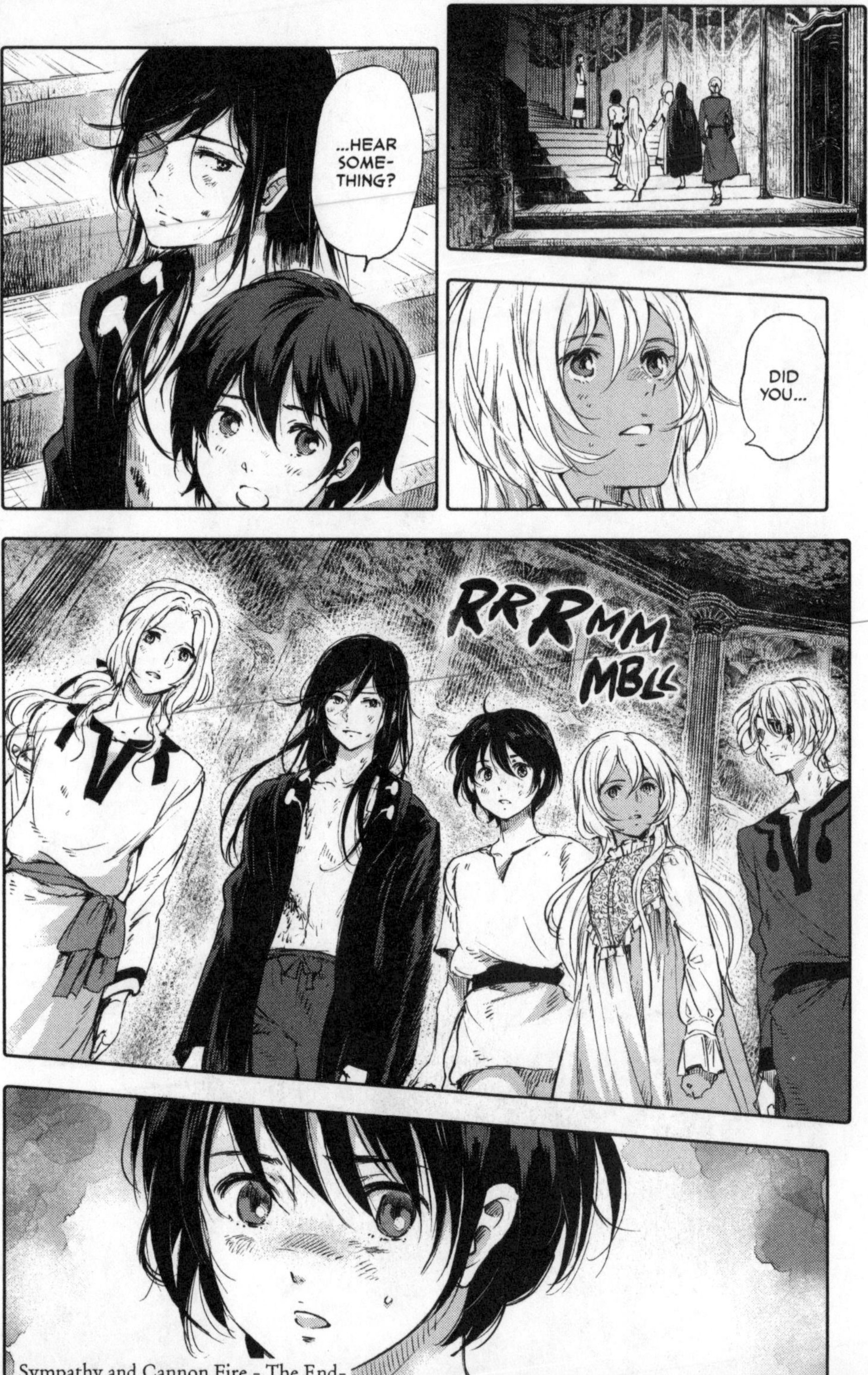
DID YOU...
...HEAR SOMETHING?
RRRMM MBLL
Sympathy and Cannon Fire - The End-

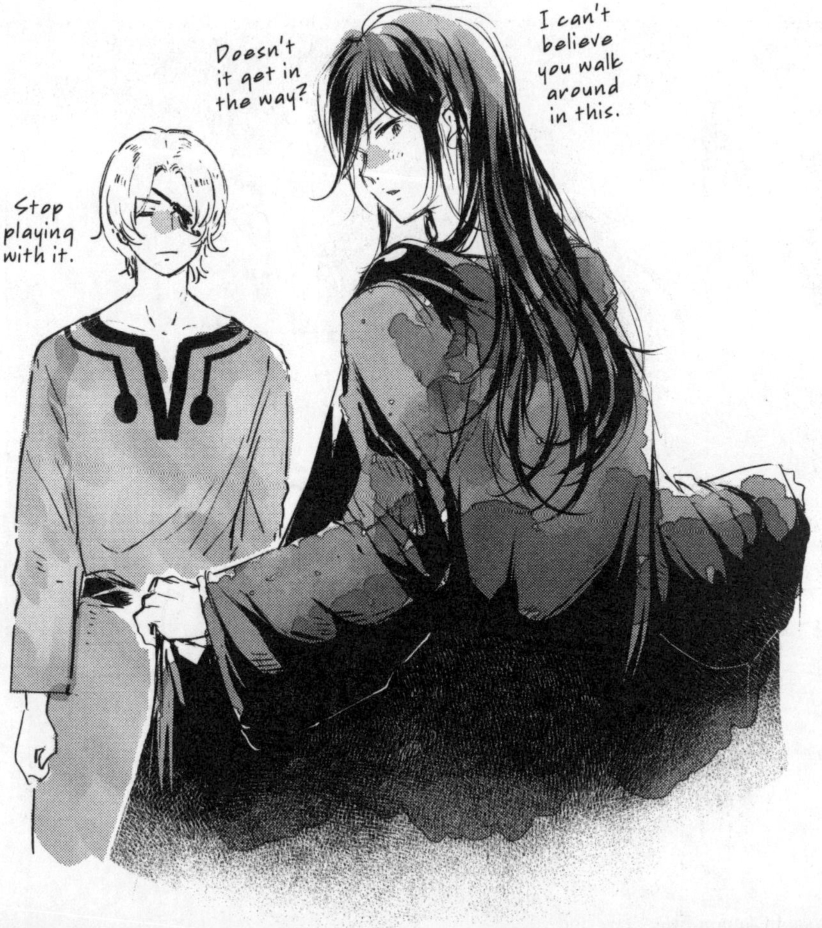
I can't believe you walk around in this.
Doesn't it get in the way?
Stop playing with it.

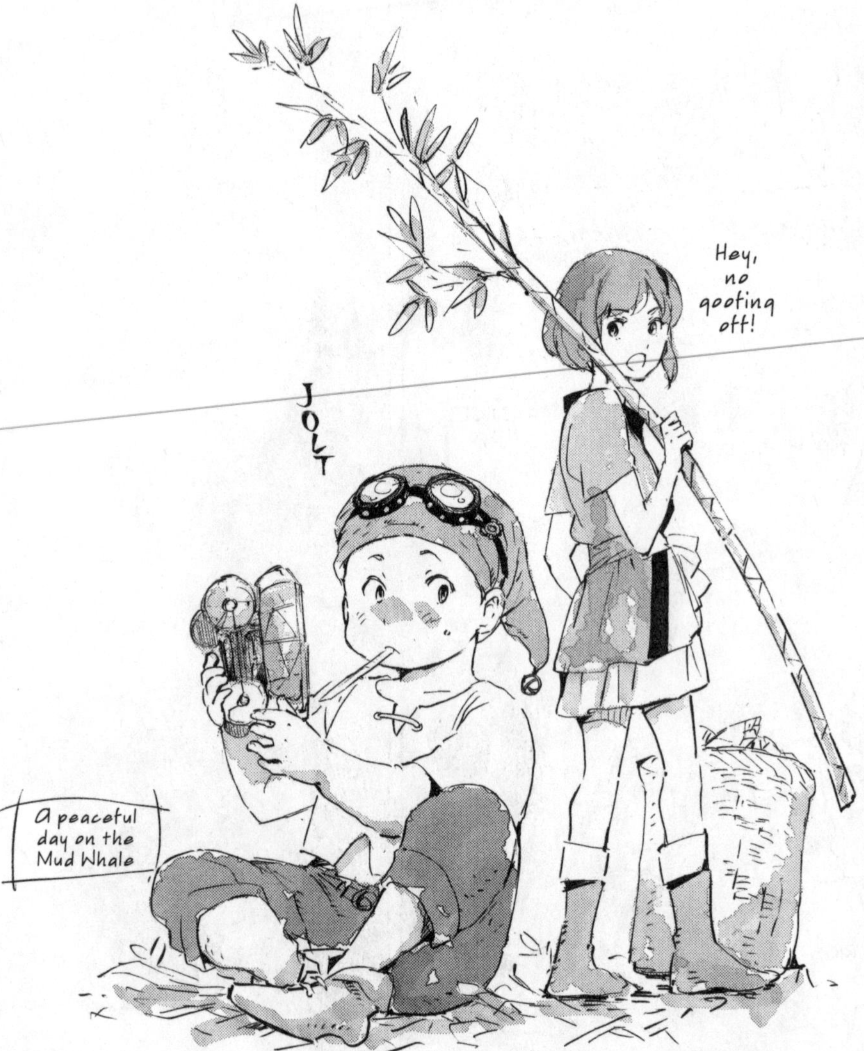
Hey, no goofing off!
JOLT
A peaceful day on the Mud Whale

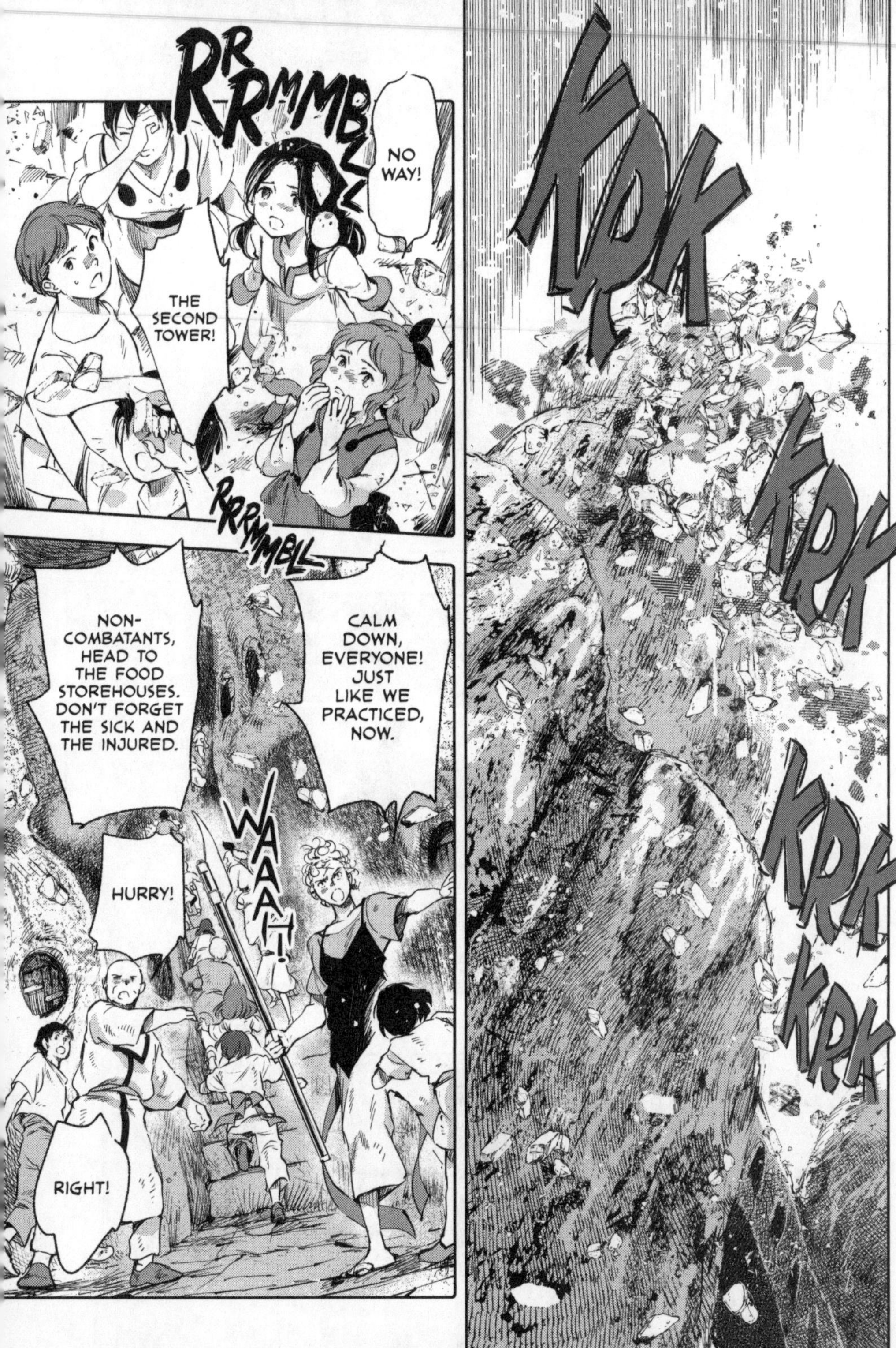
KRK
KRK
KRK
KRK
KRK
RRRRMMBLL
NO WAY!
THE SECOND TOWER!
RRRMMBLL
CALM DOWN, EVERYONE! JUST LIKE WE PRACTICED, NOW.
NON-COMBATANTS, HEAD TO THE FOOD STOREHOUSES. DON'T FORGET THE SICK AND THE INJURED.
WAAAH!
HURRY!
RIGHT!

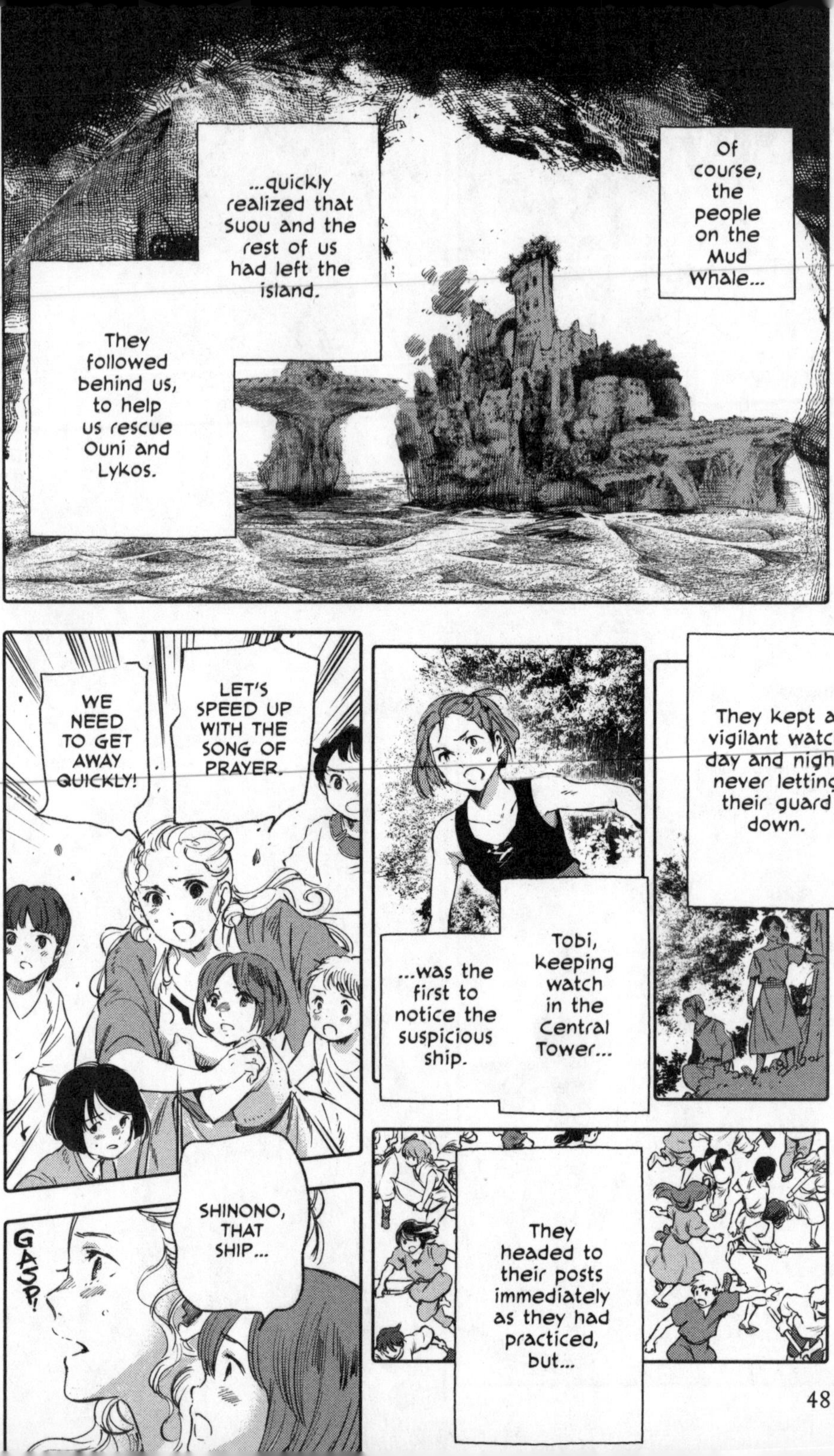
Of course, the people on the Mud Whale...
...quickly realized that Suou and the rest of us had left the island.
They followed behind us, to help us rescue Ouni and Lykos.
They kept a vigilant watch day and night, never letting their guard down.
Tobi, keeping watch in the Central Tower...
...was the first to notice the suspicious ship.
They headed to their posts immediately as they had practiced, but...
LET'S SPEED UP WITH THE SONG OF PRAYER.
WE NEED TO GET AWAY QUICKLY!
SHINONO, THAT SHIP...
GASP!

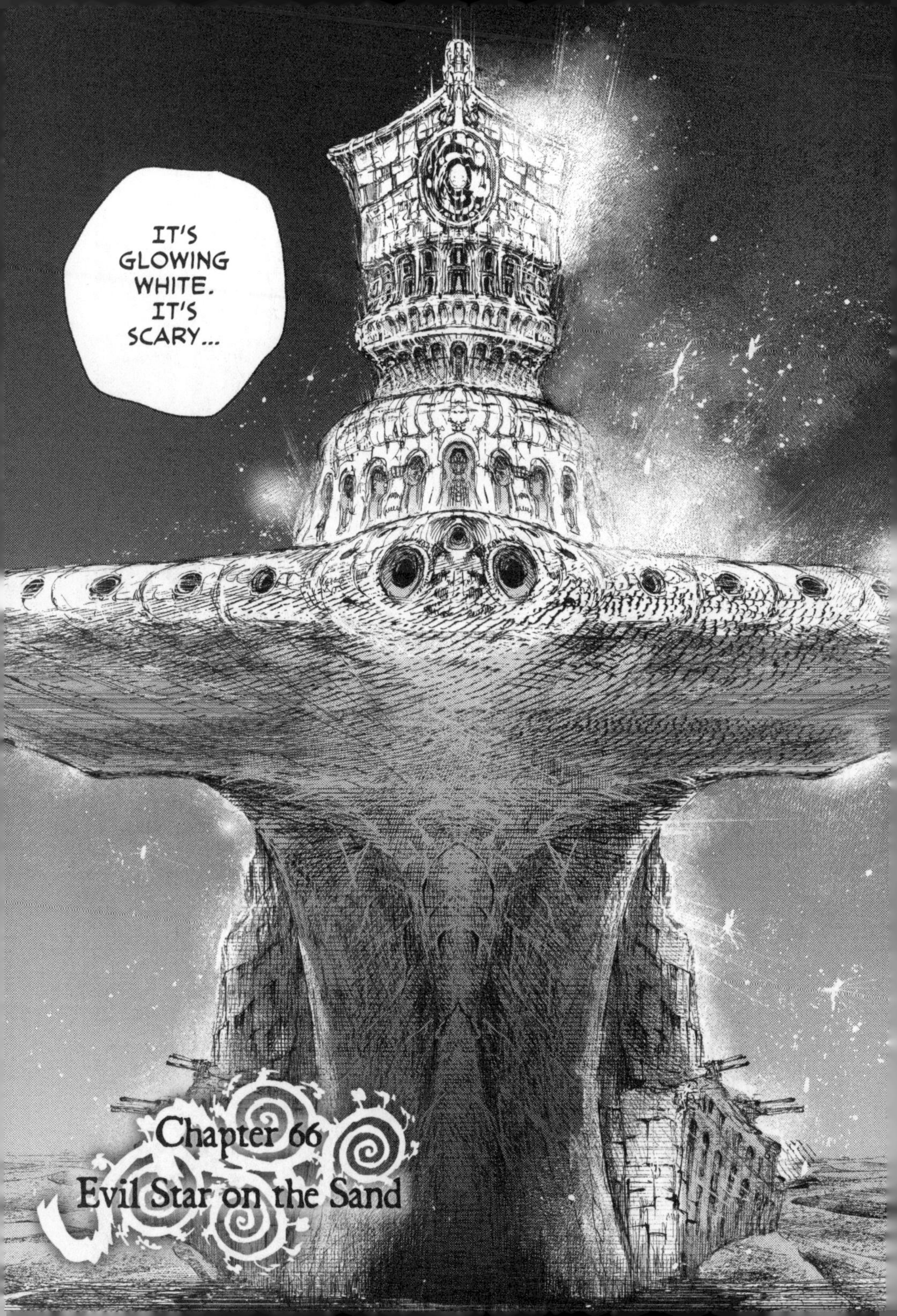
IT'S GLOWING WHITE. IT'S SCARY...
Chapter 66
Evil Star on the Sand

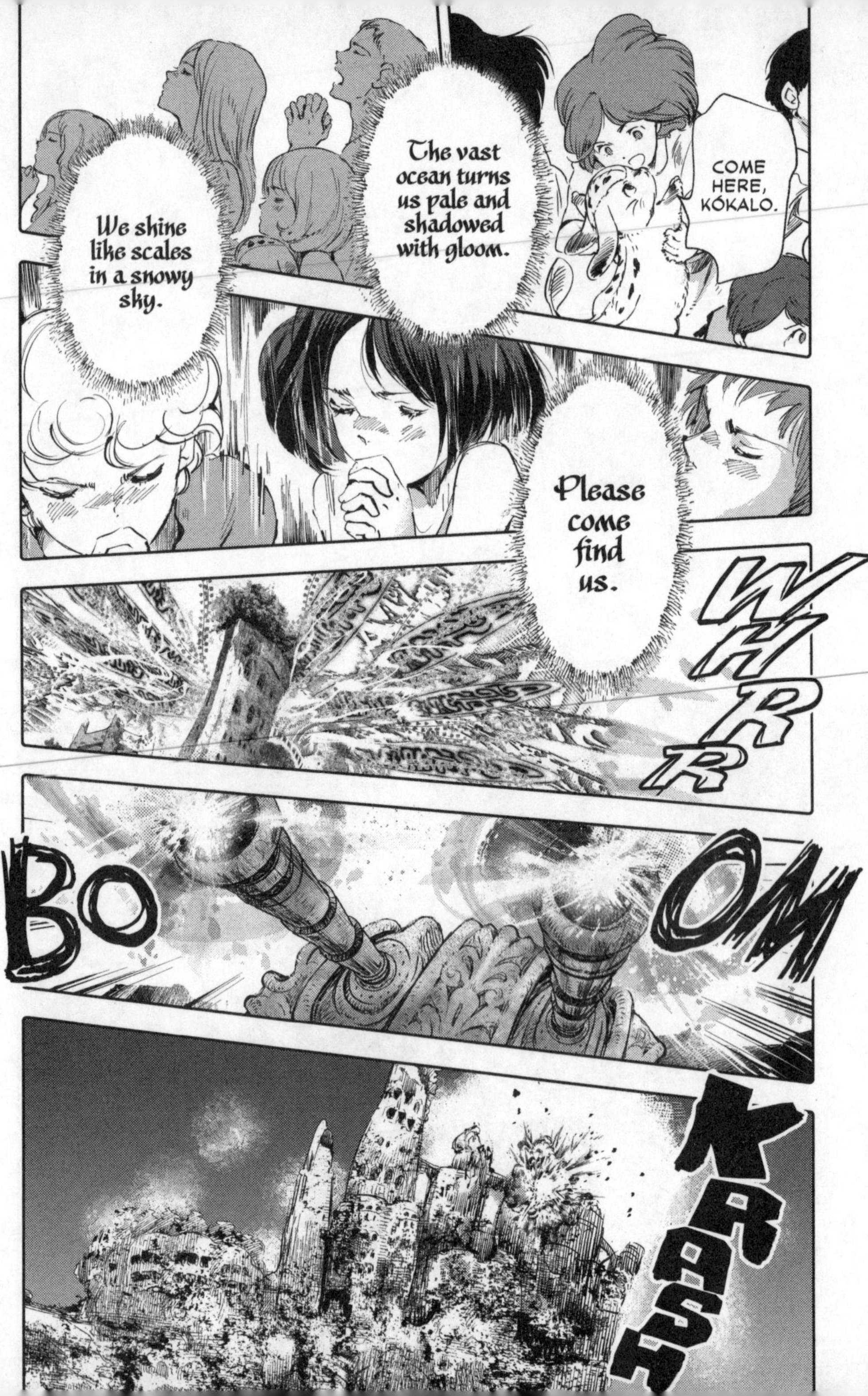
COME HERE, KÓKALO.
The vast ocean turns us pale and shadowed with gloom.
We shine like scales in a snowy sky.
Please come find us.
WHRRR
BOOM
KRASH

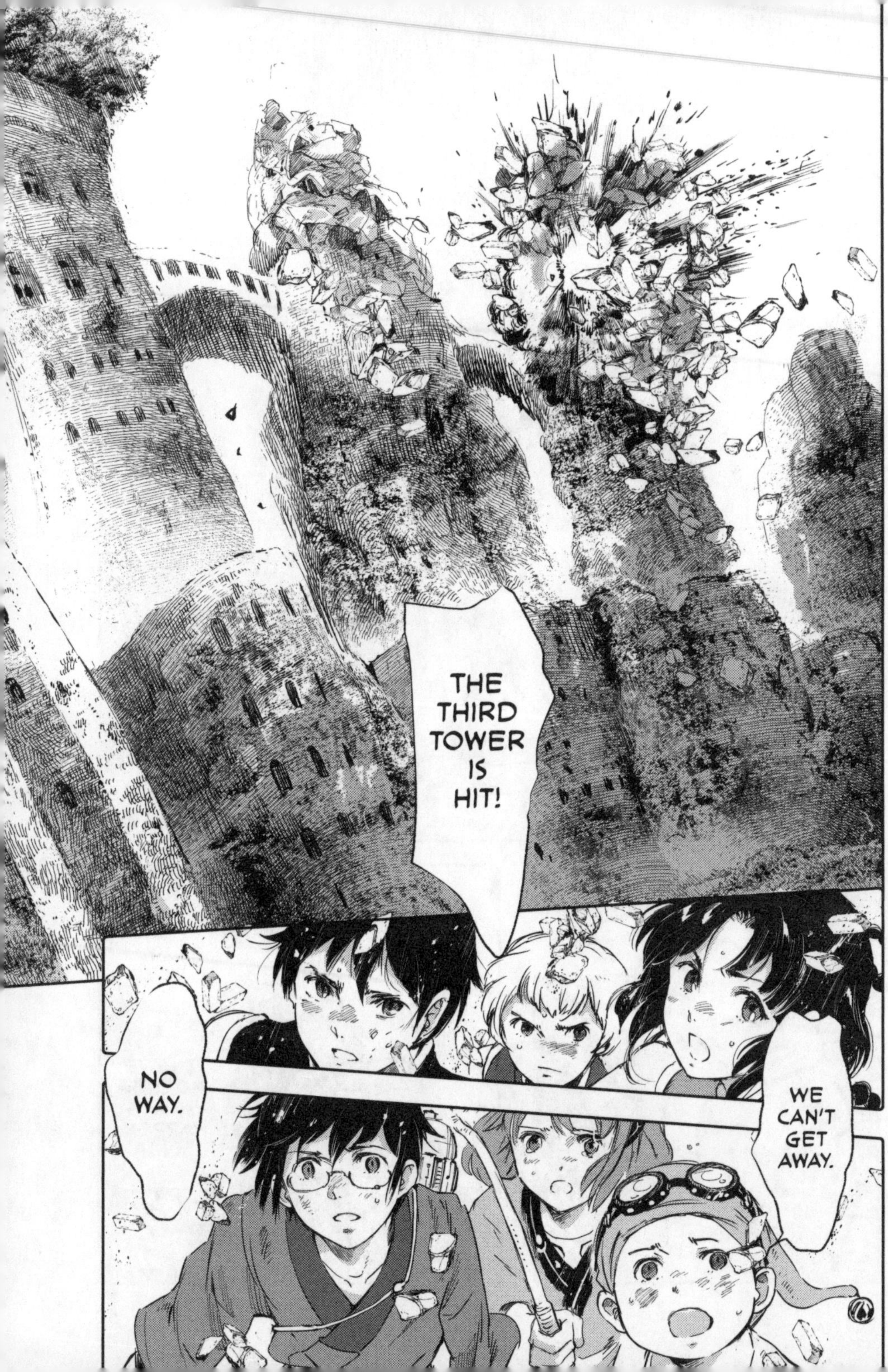
THE THIRD TOWER IS HIT!
WE CAN'T GET AWAY.
NO WAY.

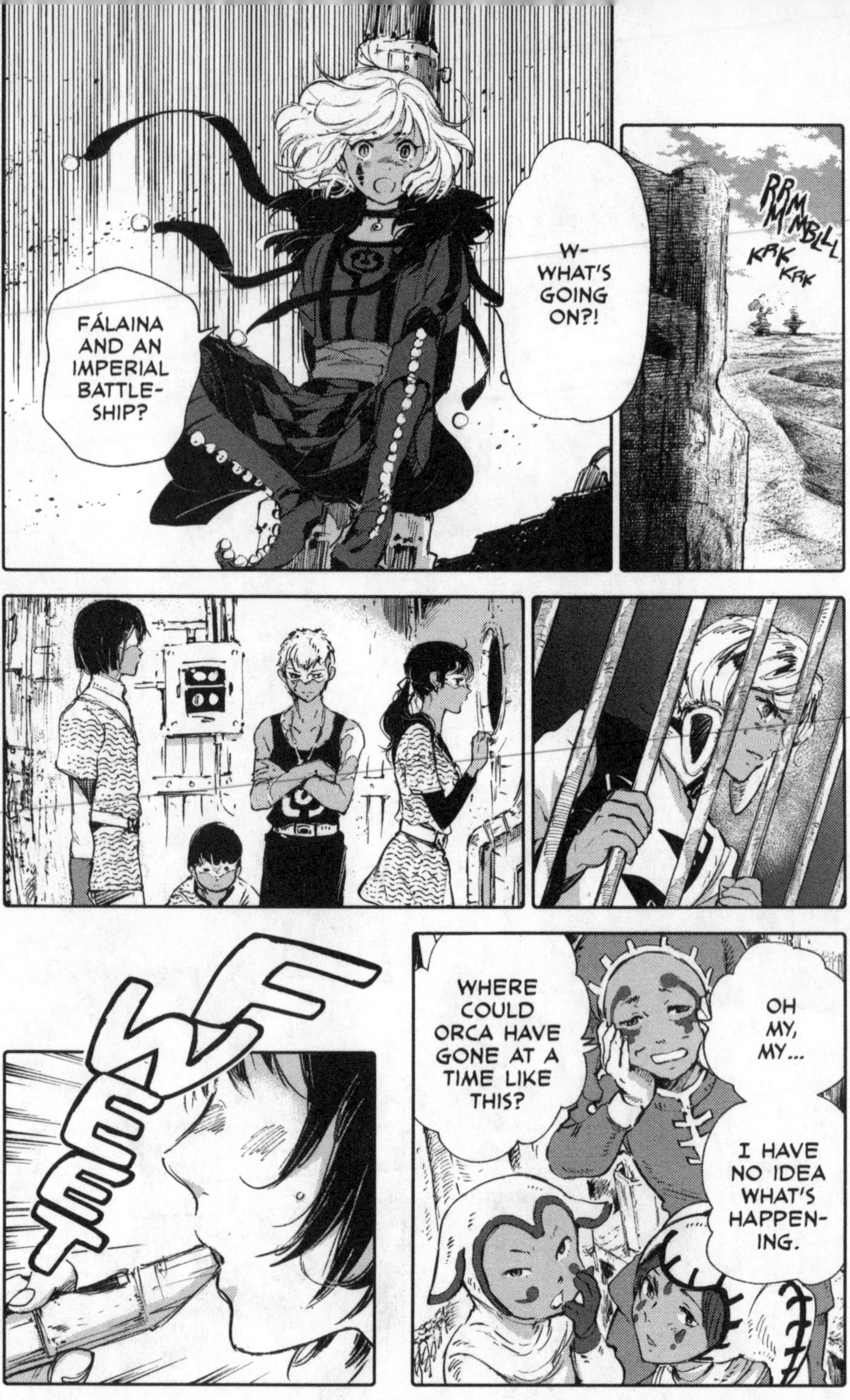
RRMMMBLLL
KRK KRK
W-WHAT'S GOING ON?!
FÁLAINA AND AN IMPERIAL BATTLESHIP?
OH MY, MY...
WHERE COULD ORCA HAVE GONE AT A TIME LIKE THIS?
I HAVE NO IDEA WHAT'S HAPPENING.

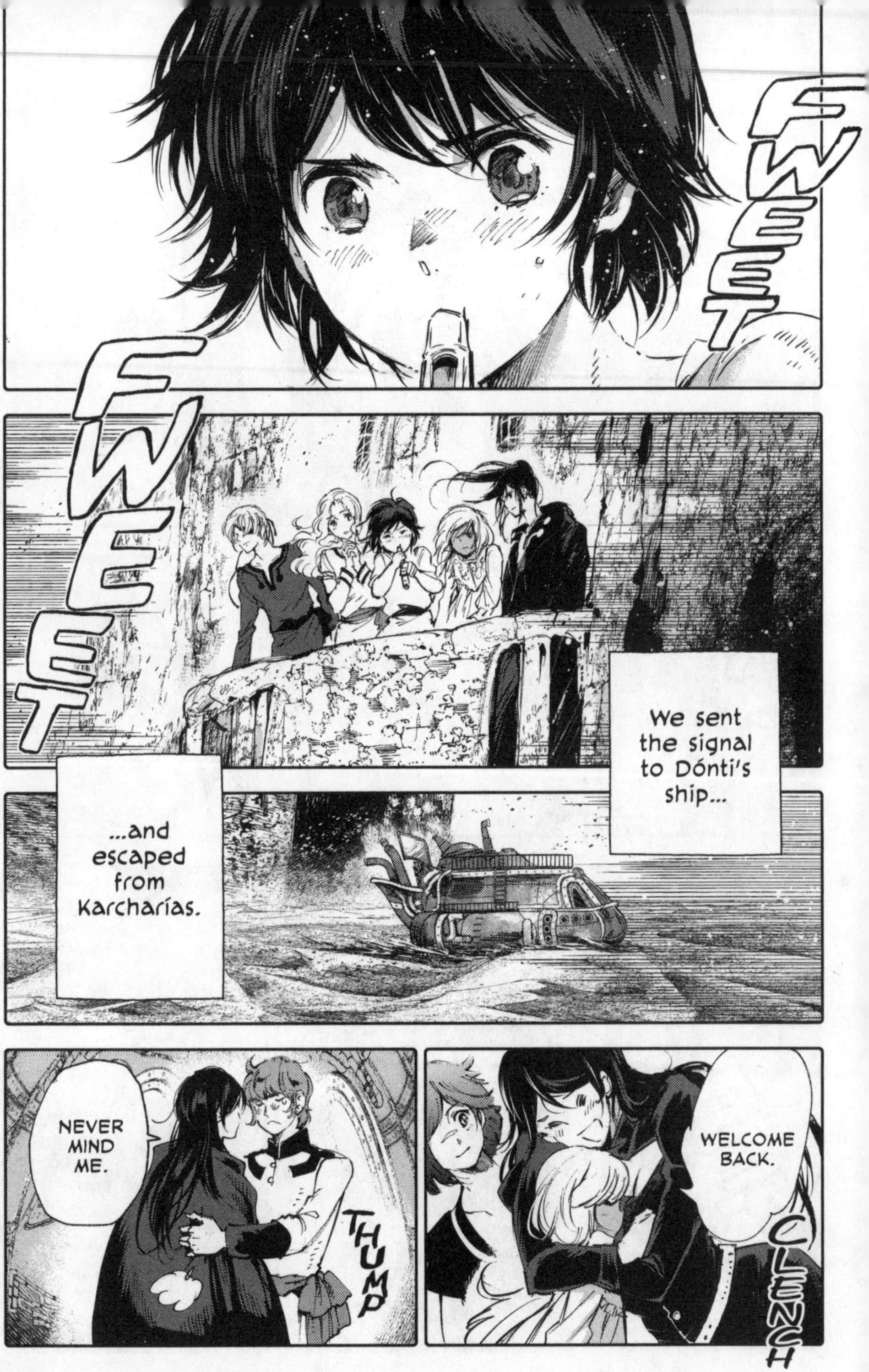
FWEET
FWEET
We sent the signal to Dónti's ship...
...and escaped from Karcharías.
WELCOME BACK.
CLENCH
NEVER MIND ME.
THUMP

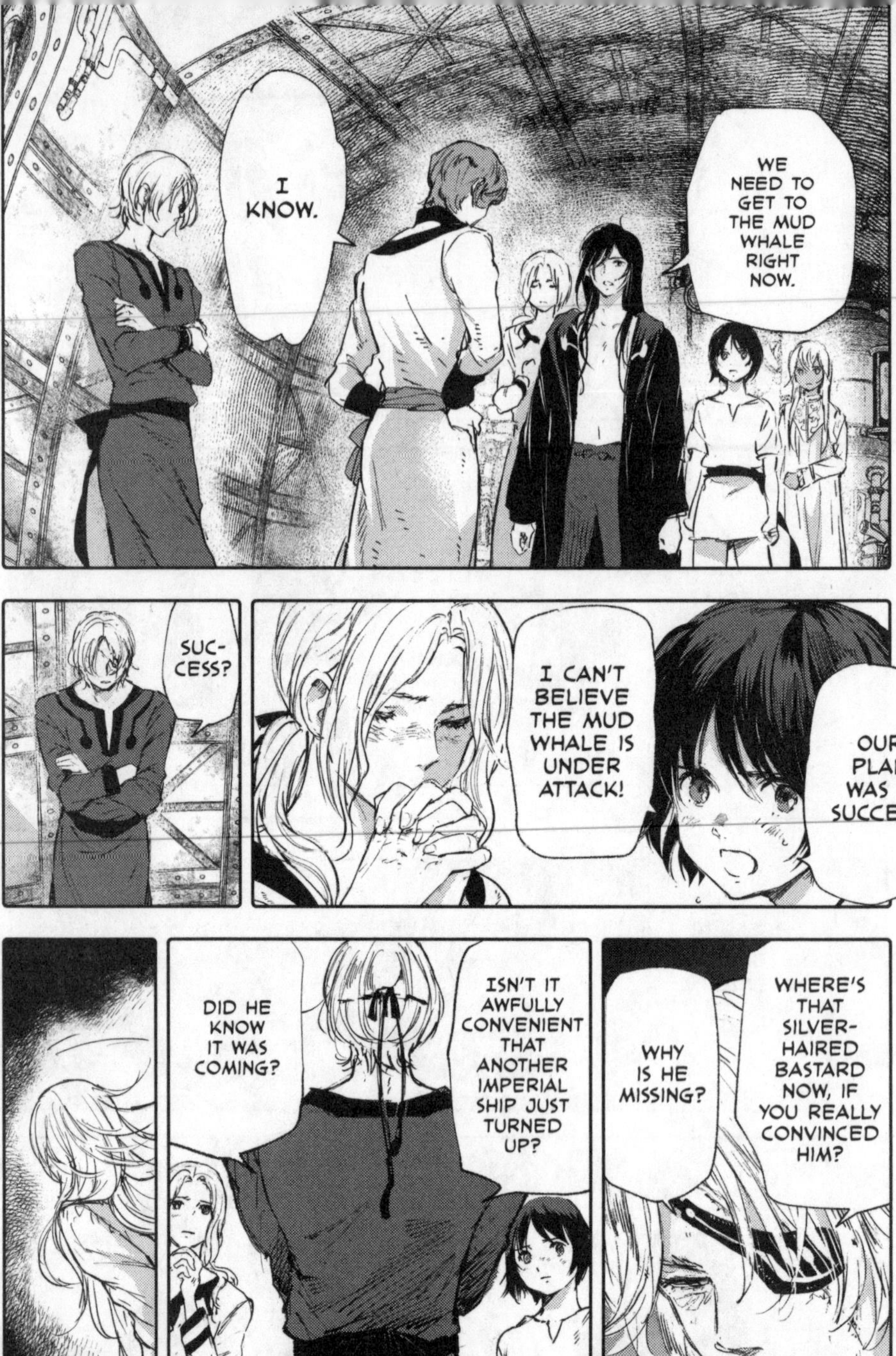
WE NEED TO GET TO THE MUD WHALE RIGHT NOW.
I KNOW.
OUR PLAN WAS A SUCCESS.
I CAN'T BELIEVE THE MUD WHALE IS UNDER ATTACK!
SUC-CESS?
WHERE'S THAT SILVER-HAIRED BASTARD NOW, IF YOU REALLY CONVINCED HIM?
WHY IS HE MISSING?
ISN'T IT AWFULLY CONVENIENT THAT ANOTHER IMPERIAL SHIP JUST TURNED UP?
DID HE KNOW IT WAS COMING?

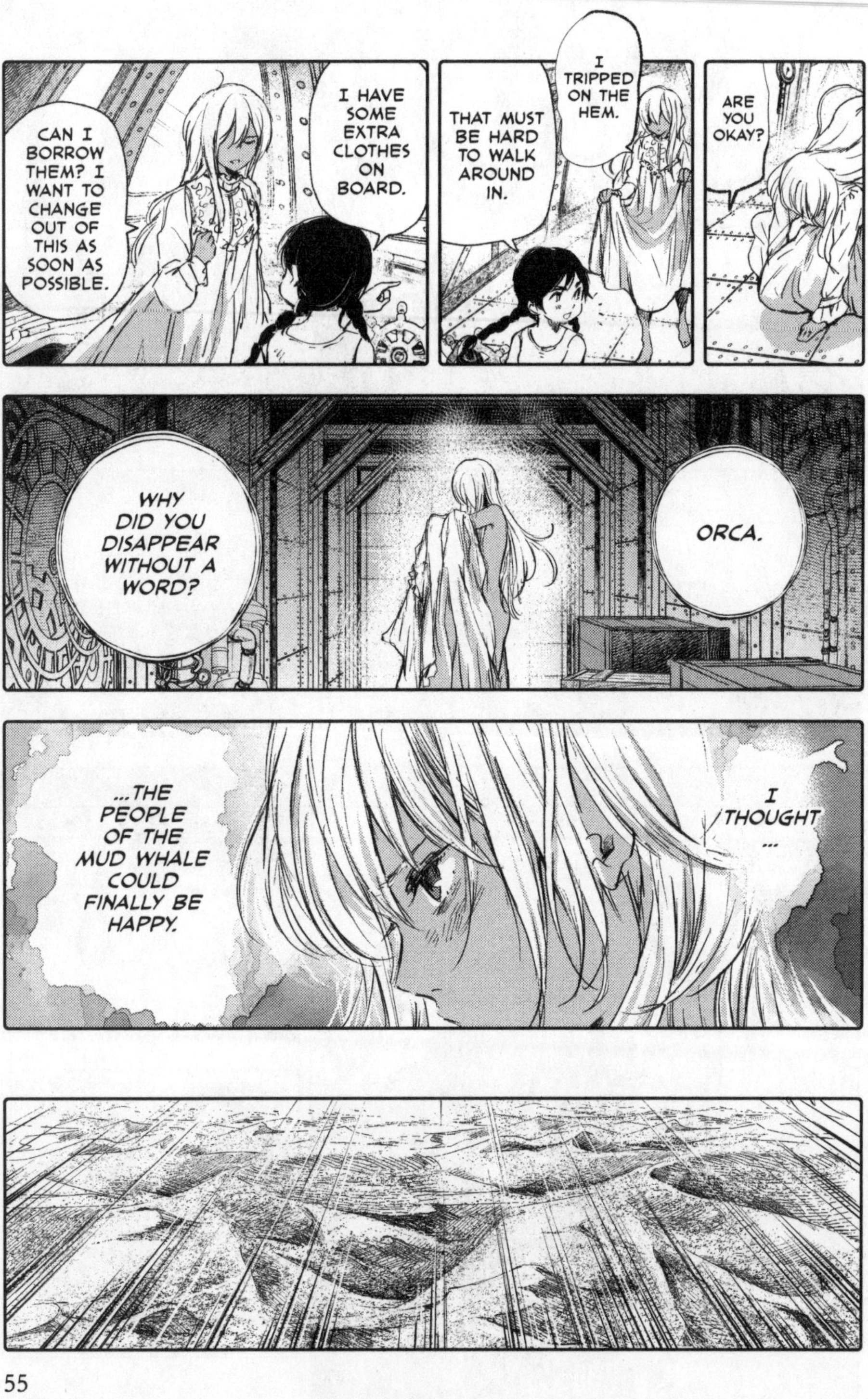
ARE YOU OKAY?
I TRIPPED ON THE HEM.
THAT MUST BE HARD TO WALK AROUND IN.
I HAVE SOME EXTRA CLOTHES ON BOARD.
CAN I BORROW THEM? I WANT TO CHANGE OUT OF THIS AS SOON AS POSSIBLE.
ORCA.
WHY DID YOU DISAPPEAR WITHOUT A WORD?
I THOUGHT...
...THE PEOPLE OF THE MUD WHALE COULD FINALLY BE HAPPY.

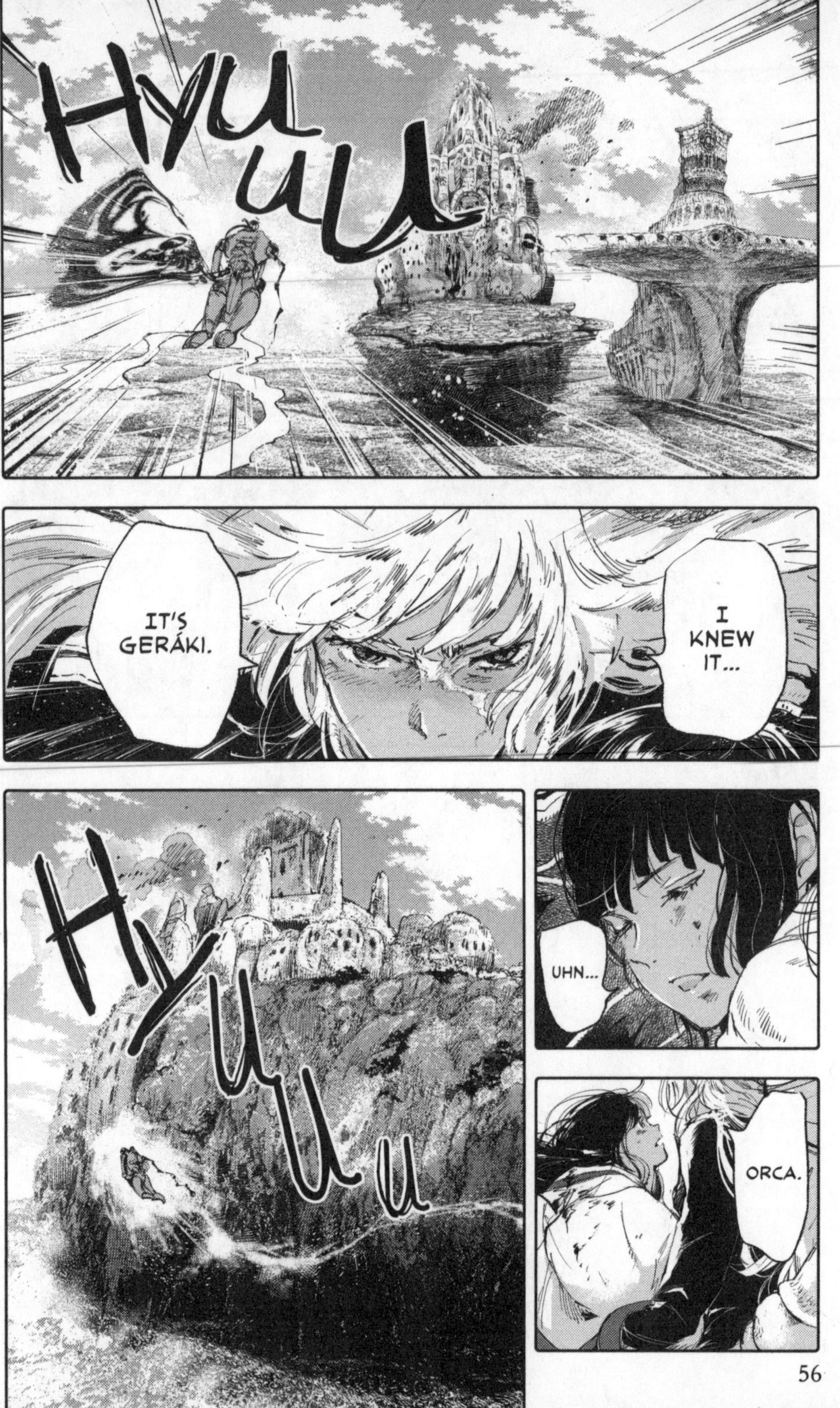
HYUUU
I KNEW IT...
IT'S GERÁKI.
UHN...
ORCA.
HYUUUU

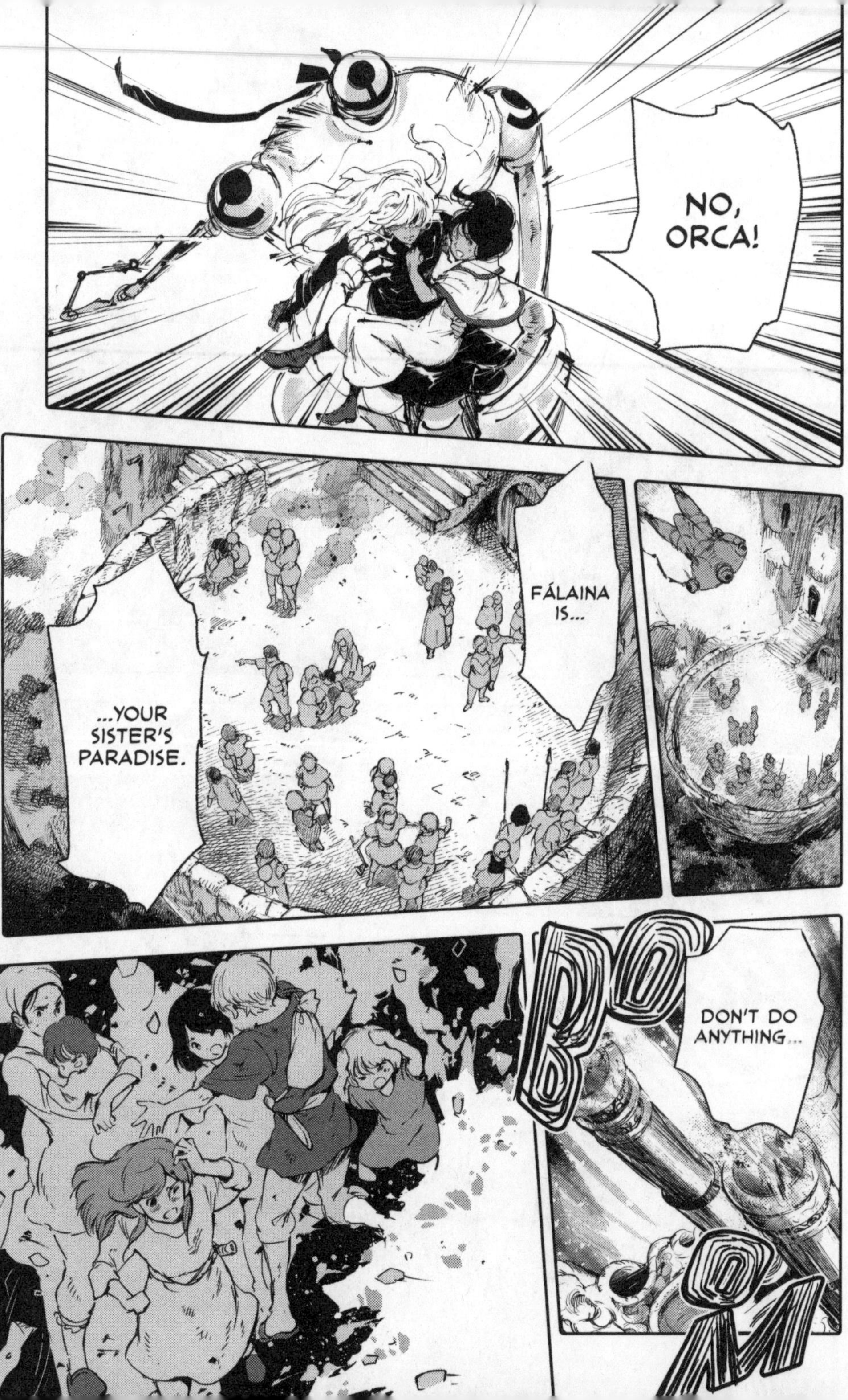
NO, ORCA!
FÁLAINA IS...
...YOUR SISTER'S PARADISE.
DON'T DO ANYTHING...
BOOM

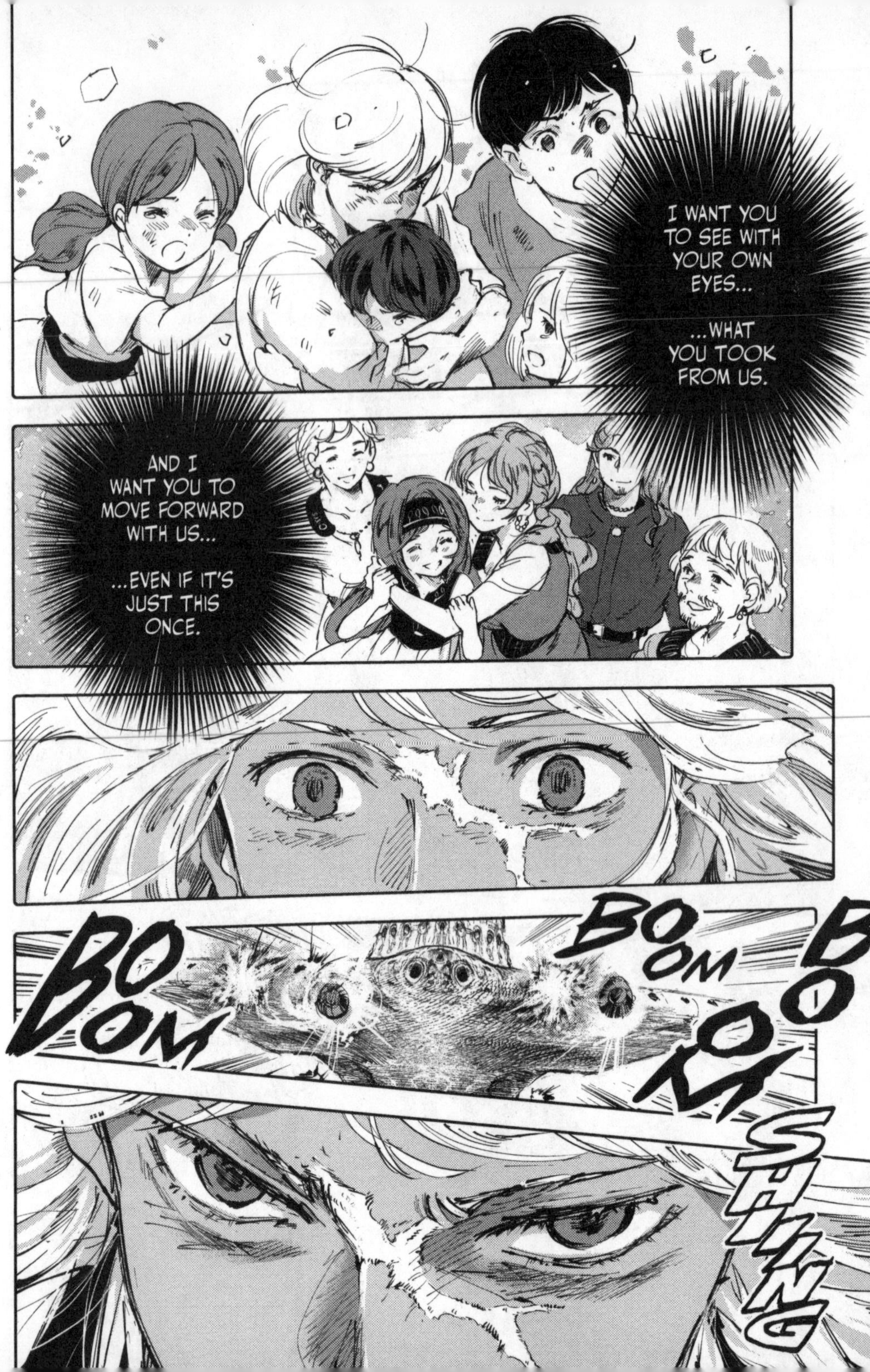
I WANT YOU TO SEE WITH YOUR OWN EYES...
...WHAT YOU TOOK FROM US.
AND I WANT YOU TO MOVE FORWARD WITH US...
...EVEN IF IT'S JUST THIS ONCE.
BOOM
BOOM
BOOM
SHING

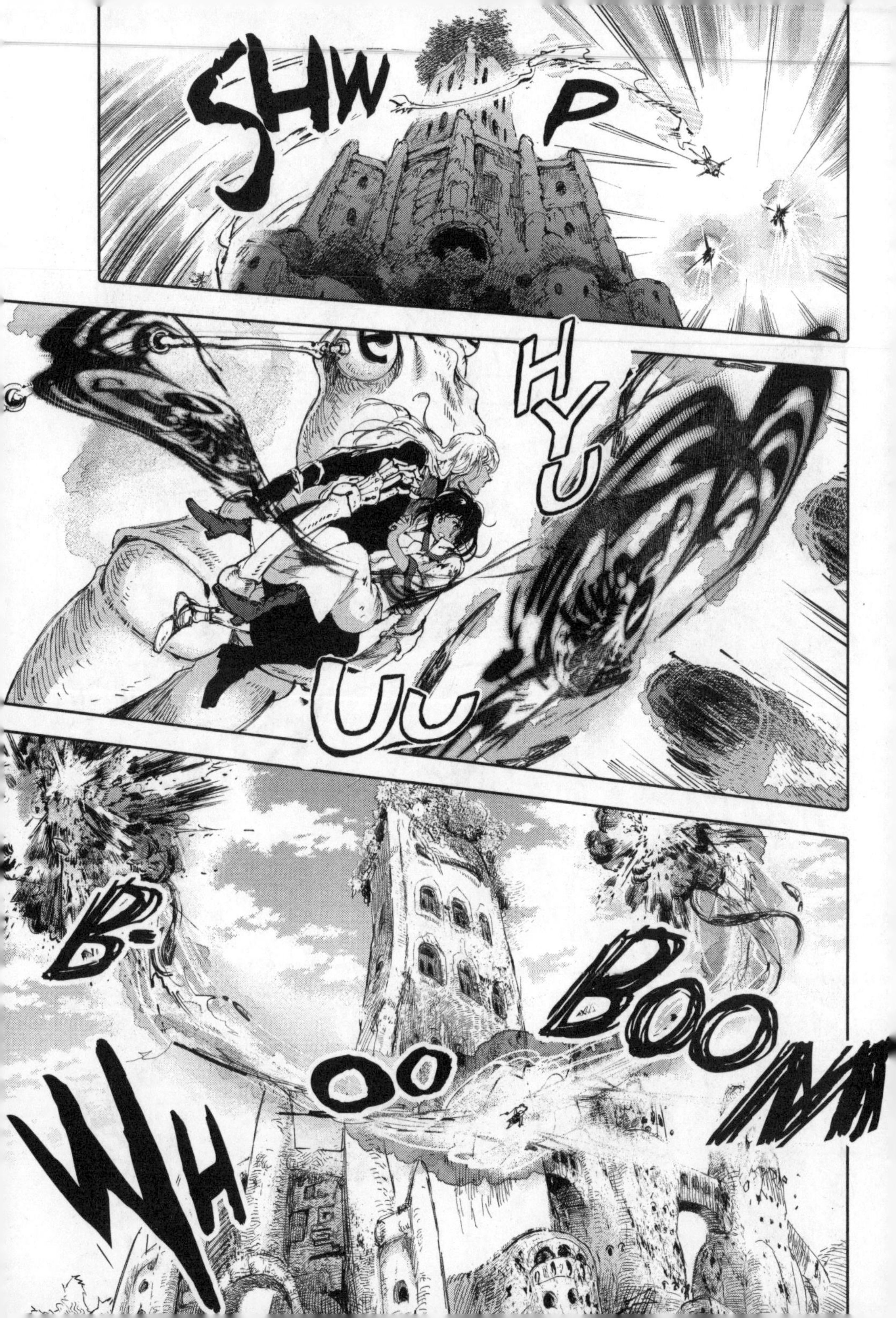
SHWP
HYUUU
B-BOOM
WHOO

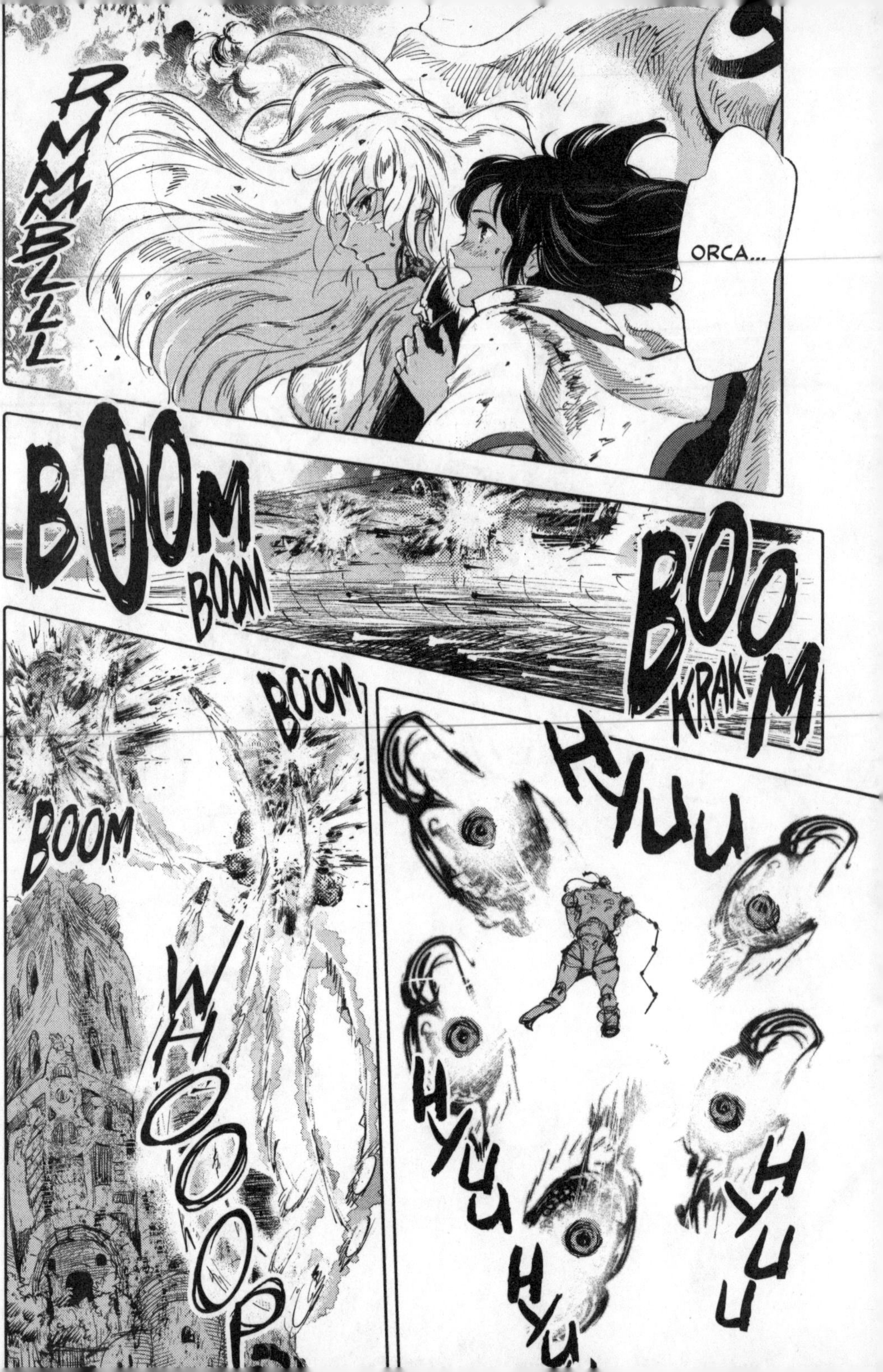
ORCA...
RMMMBLLL
BOOM
BOOM
BOOM
KRAK
HYUU
HYUU
HYUU
HYU...
BOOM
BOOM
WHOOOOP

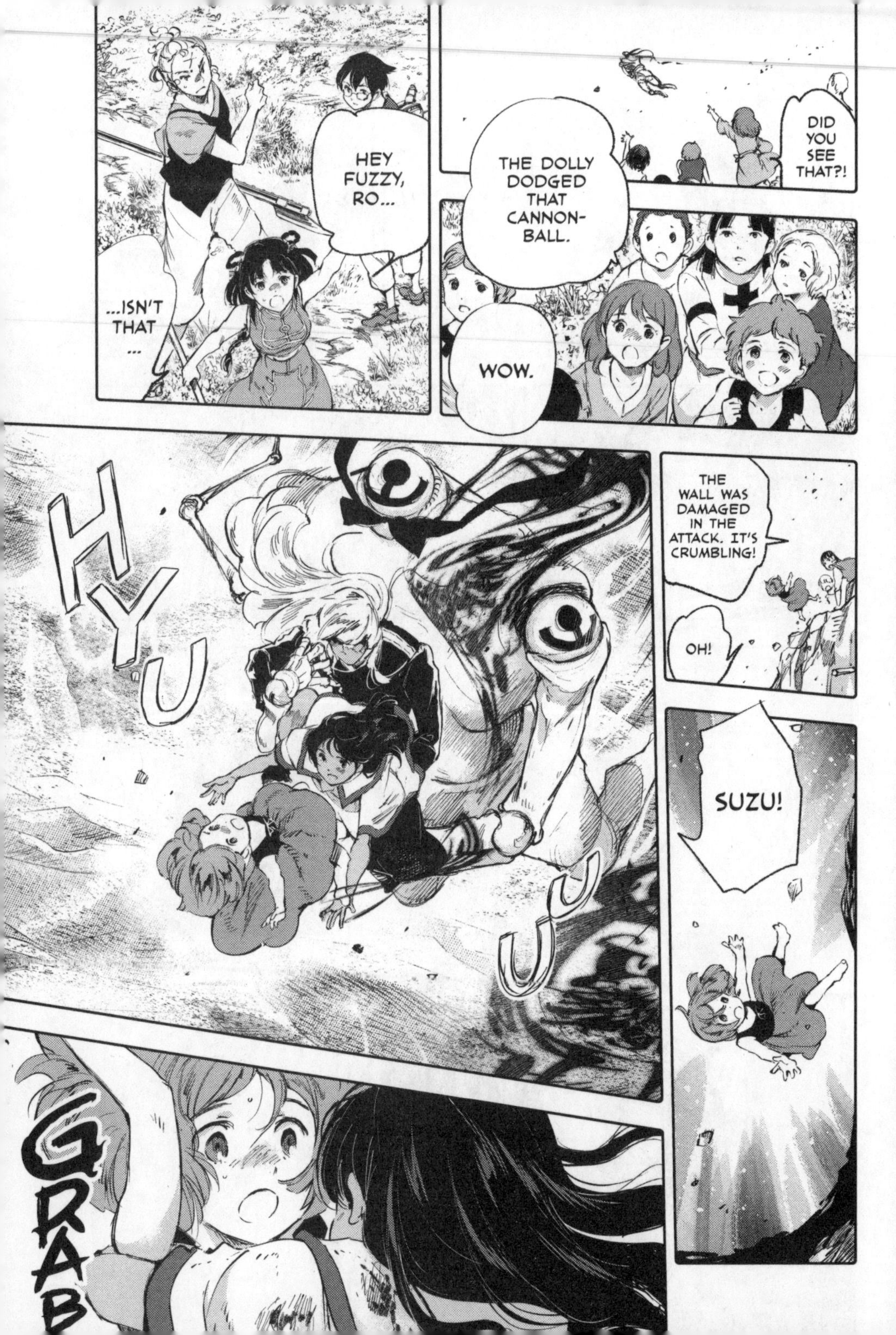
DID YOU SEE THAT?!
THE DOLLY DODGED THAT CANNON-BALL.
WOW.
HEY FUZZY, RO...
...ISN'T THAT ...
THE WALL WAS DAMAGED IN THE ATTACK. IT'S CRUMBLING!
OH!
SUZU!
HYUUUU
GRAB

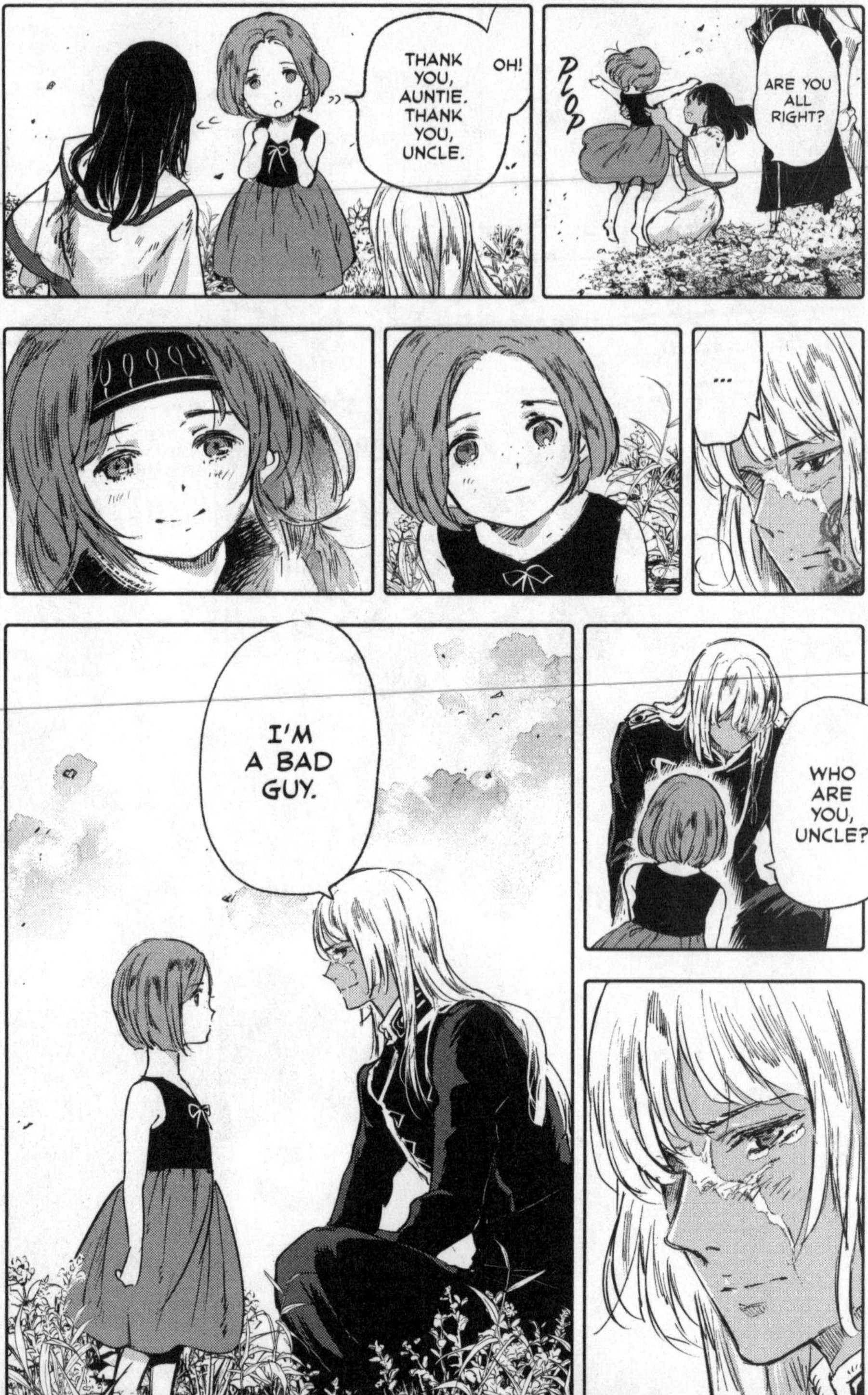
ARE YOU ALL RIGHT?
PLOP
OH!
THANK YOU, AUNTIE. THANK YOU, UNCLE.
...
WHO ARE YOU, UNCLE?
I'M A BAD GUY.

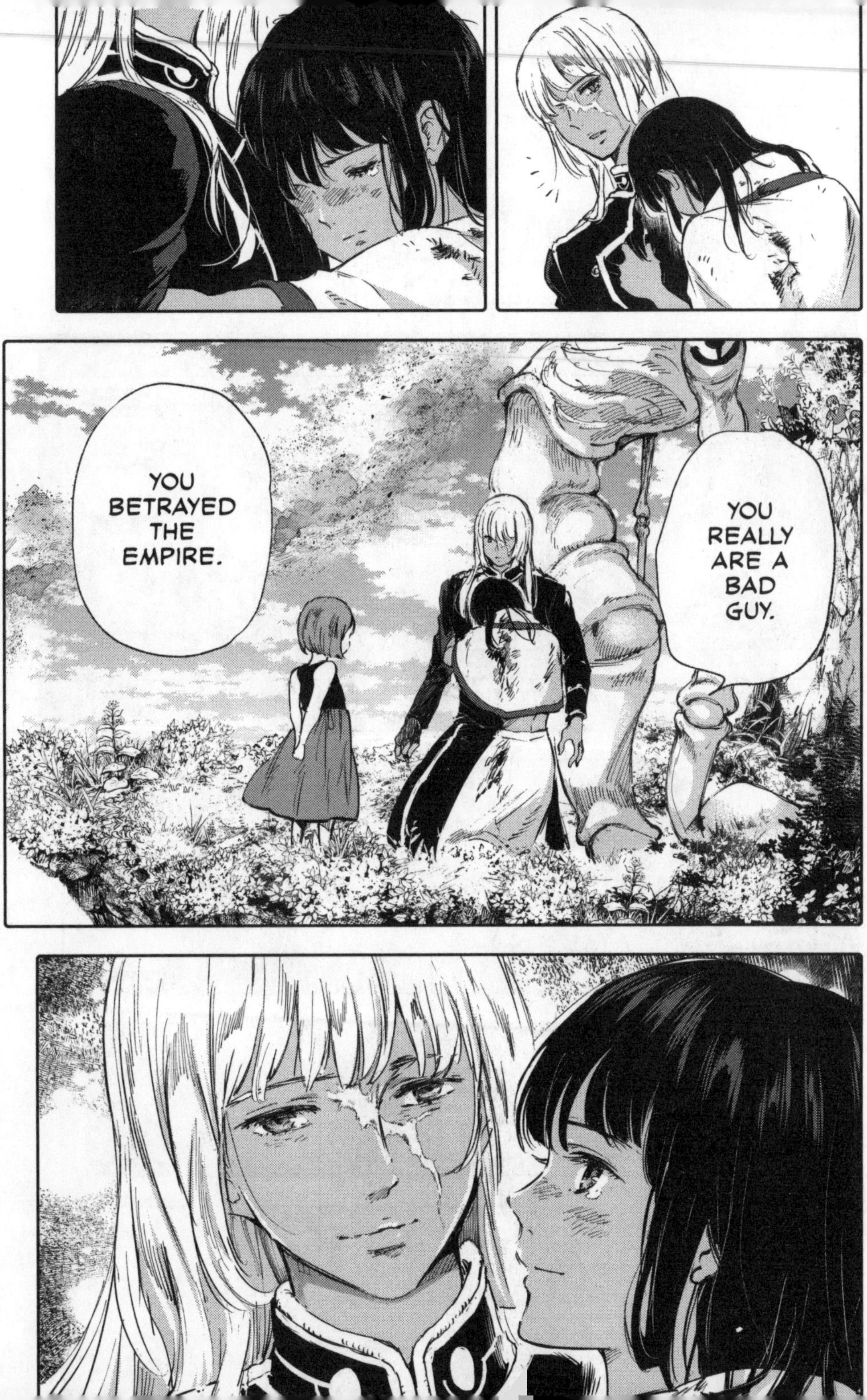
YOU REALLY ARE A BAD GUY.
YOU BETRAYED THE EMPIRE.

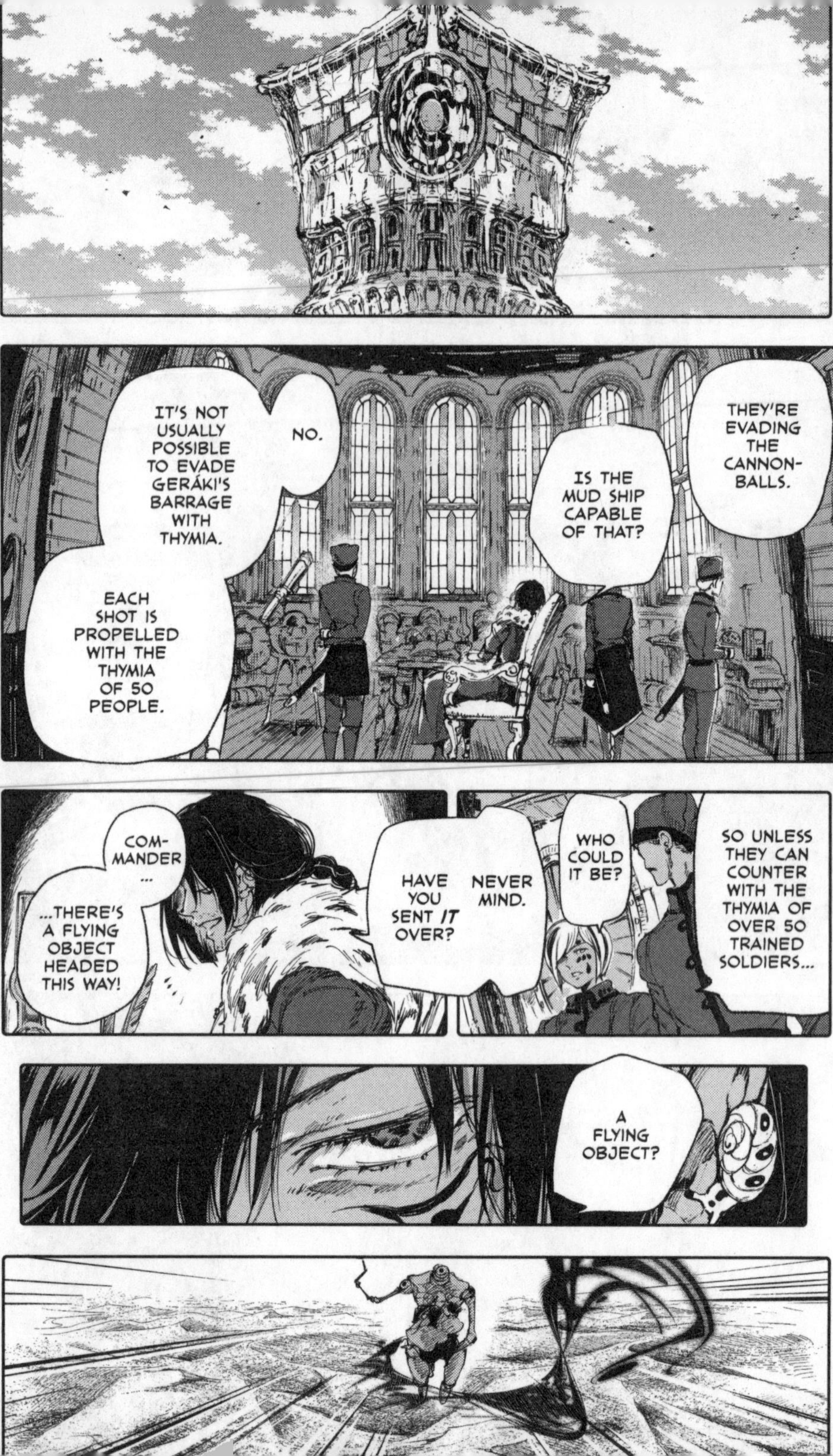
THEY'RE EVADING THE CANNON-BALLS.
IS THE MUD SHIP CAPABLE OF THAT?
NO.
IT'S NOT USUALLY POSSIBLE TO EVADE GERÁKI'S BARRAGE WITH THYMIA.
EACH SHOT IS PROPELLED WITH THE THYMIA OF 50 PEOPLE.
SO UNLESS THEY CAN COUNTER WITH THE THYMIA OF OVER 50 TRAINED SOLDIERS...
WHO COULD IT BE?
NEVER MIND.
HAVE YOU SENT *IT* OVER?
COM-MANDER...
...THERE'S A FLYING OBJECT HEADED THIS WAY!
A FLYING OBJECT?

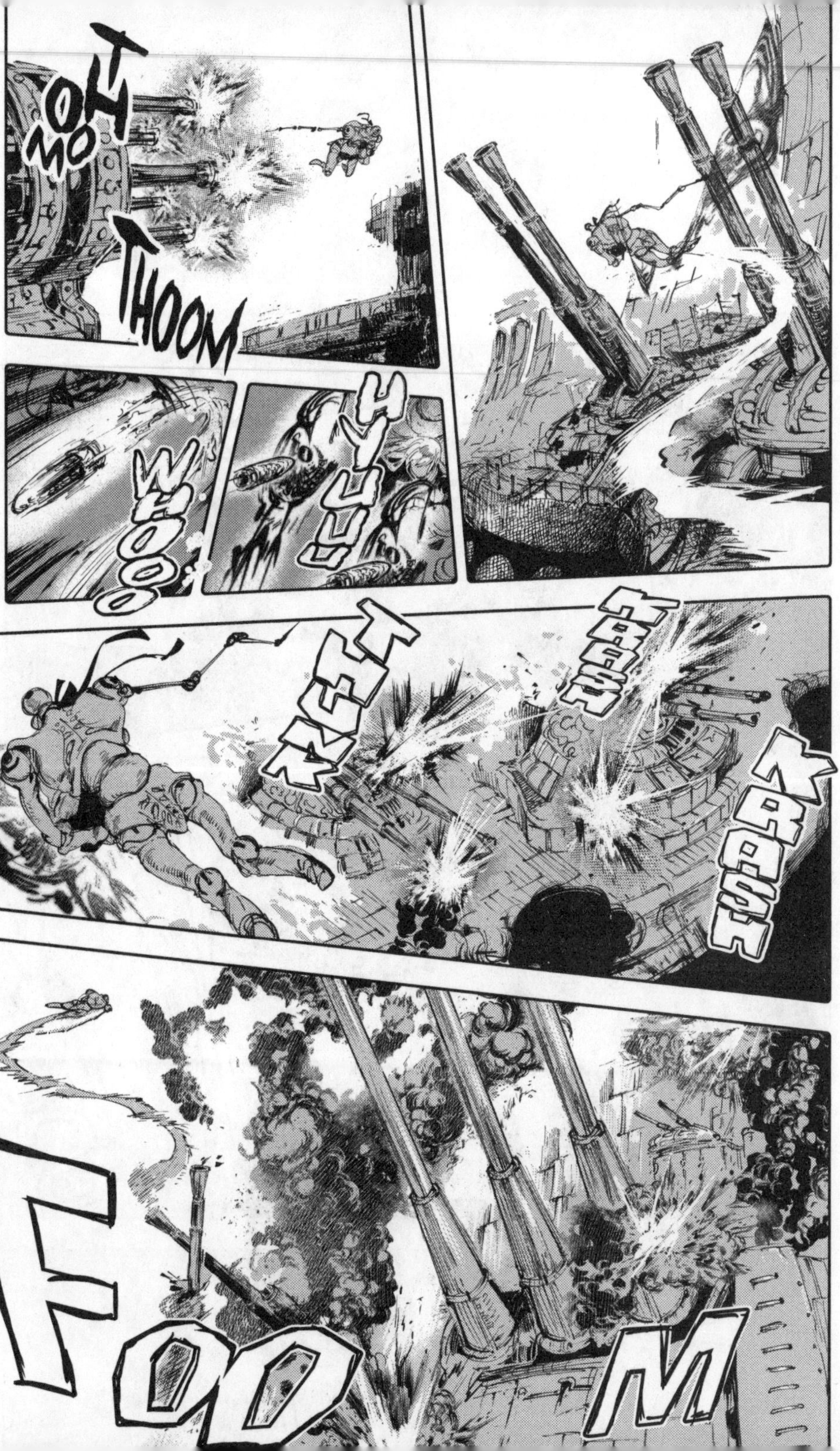
THOOM
THOOM
HYUUU
WHOOOO
KRASH
KRASH
THUNK
FOOM

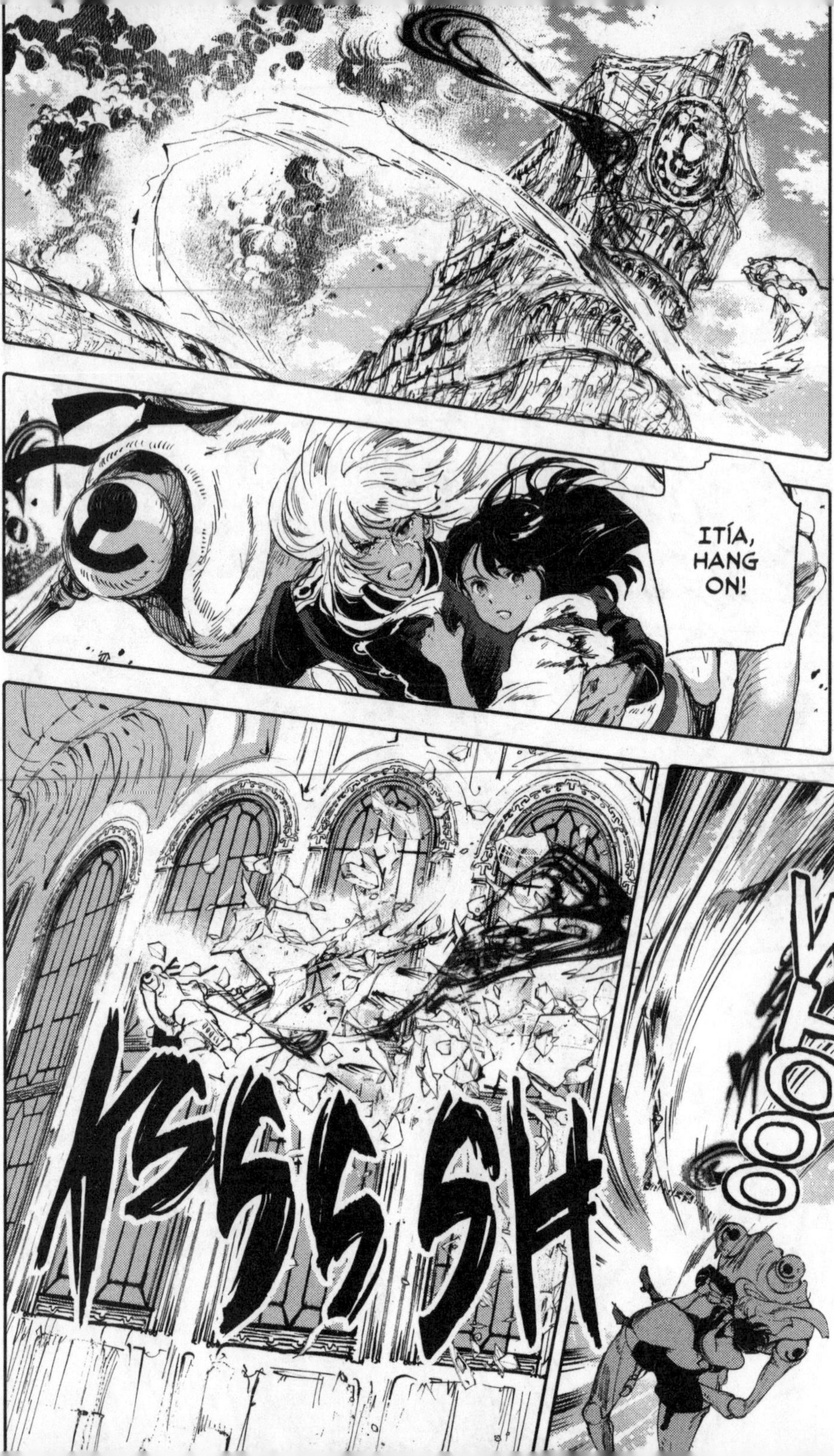
ITÍA, HANG ON!
WHOOOO
KSSSH

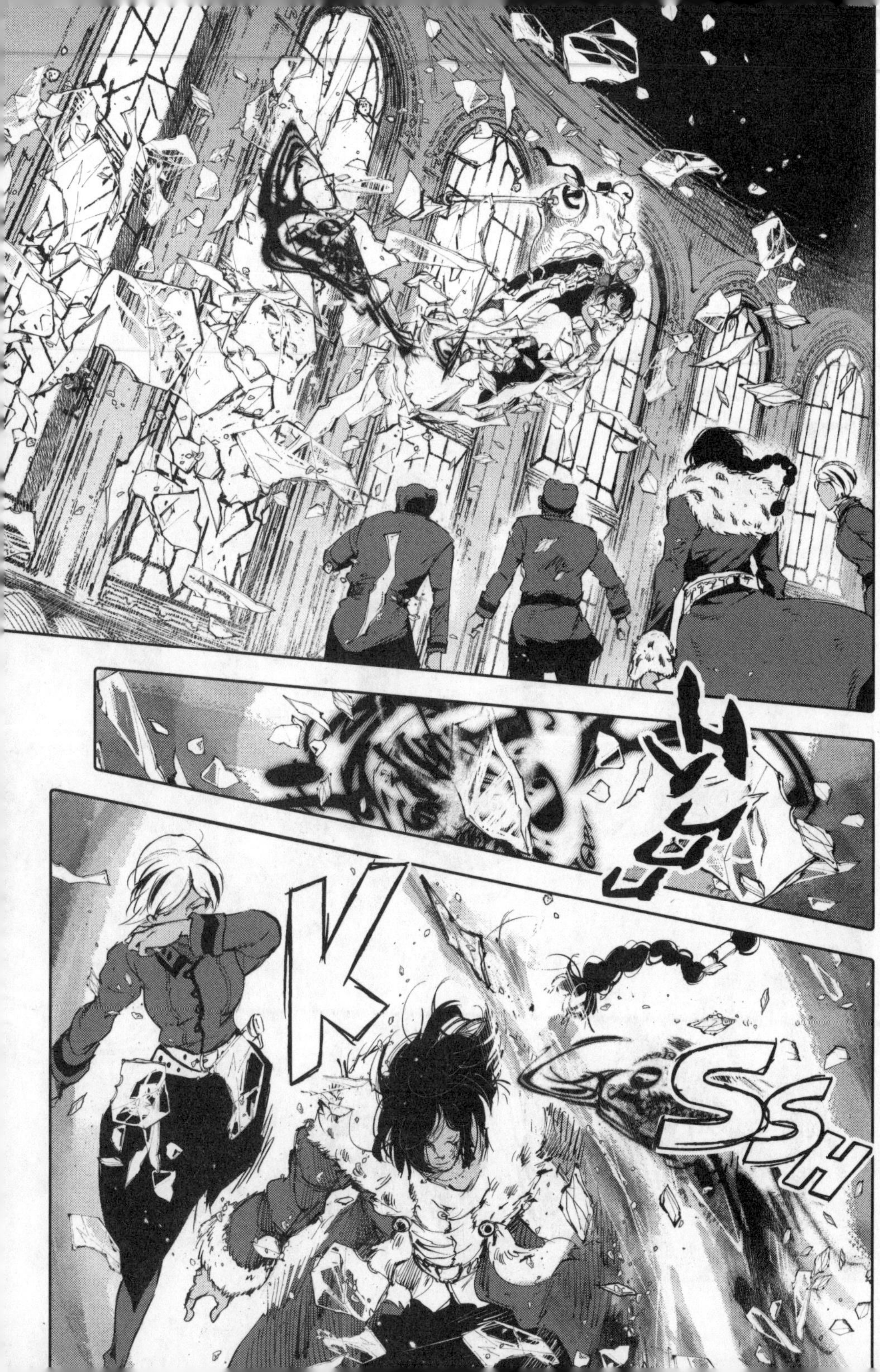
K
SSH

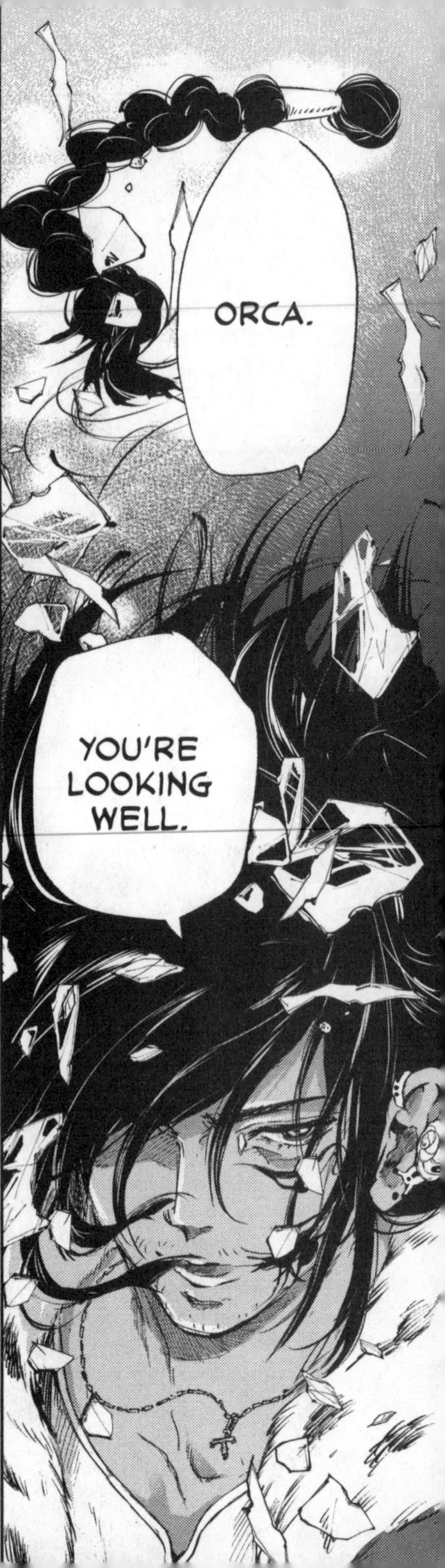
ORCA.
YOU'RE LOOKING WELL.

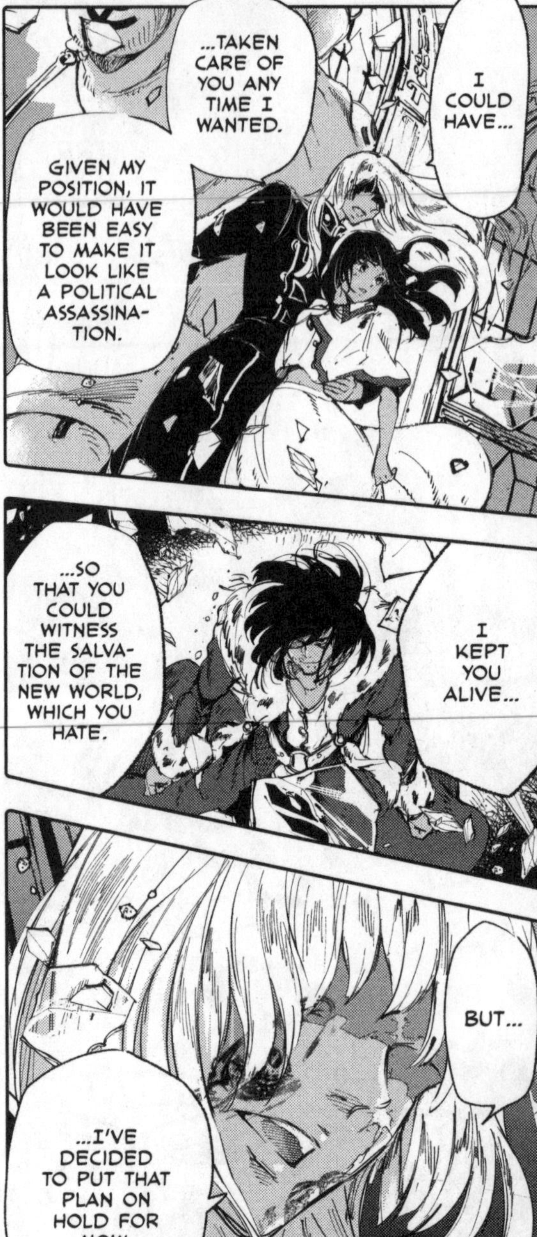
I COULD HAVE...
...TAKEN CARE OF YOU ANY TIME I WANTED.
GIVEN MY POSITION, IT WOULD HAVE BEEN EASY TO MAKE IT LOOK LIKE A POLITICAL ASSASSINATION.
I KEPT YOU ALIVE...
...SO THAT YOU COULD WITNESS THE SALVATION OF THE NEW WORLD, WHICH YOU HATE.
BUT...
...I'VE DECIDED TO PUT THAT PLAN ON HOLD FOR NOW.

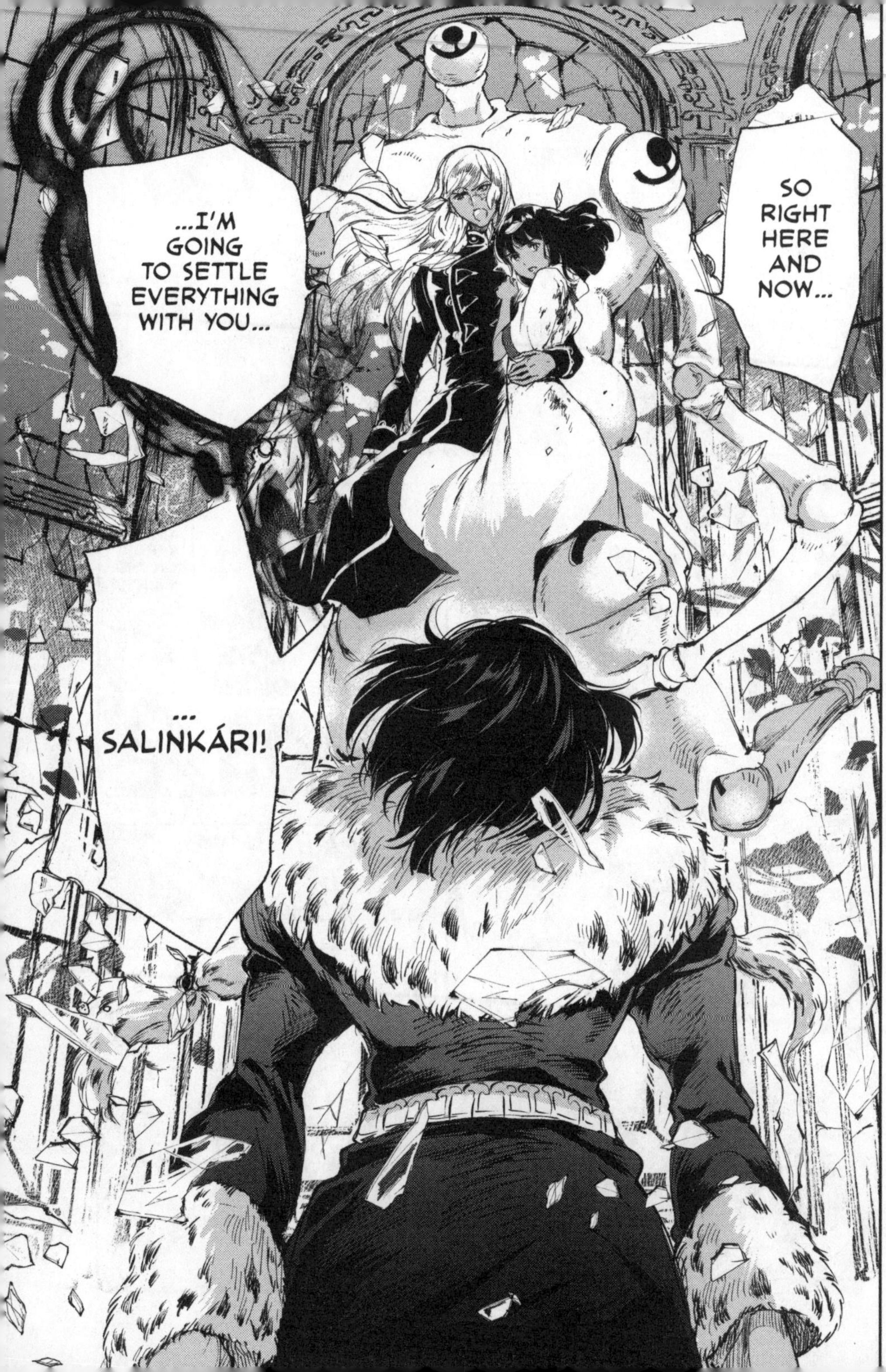
SO RIGHT HERE AND NOW...
...I'M GOING TO SETTLE EVERYTHING WITH YOU...
... SALINKÁRI!

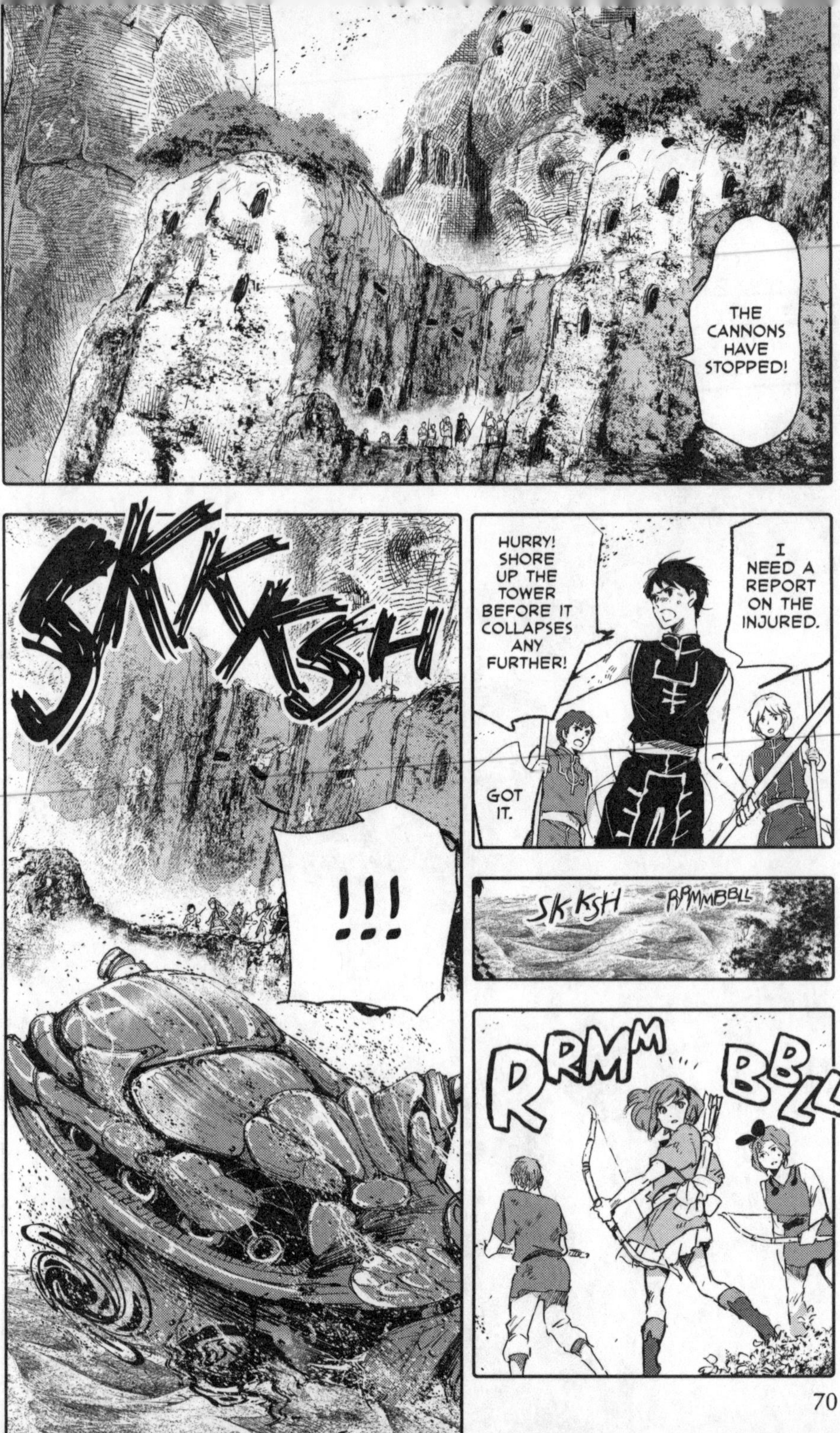
THE CANNONS HAVE STOPPED!
I NEED A REPORT ON THE INJURED.
HURRY! SHORE UP THE TOWER BEFORE IT COLLAPSES ANY FURTHER!
GOT IT.
SK KSH
RRMMBBLL
RRMM BBLL
SKKKSH
!!!

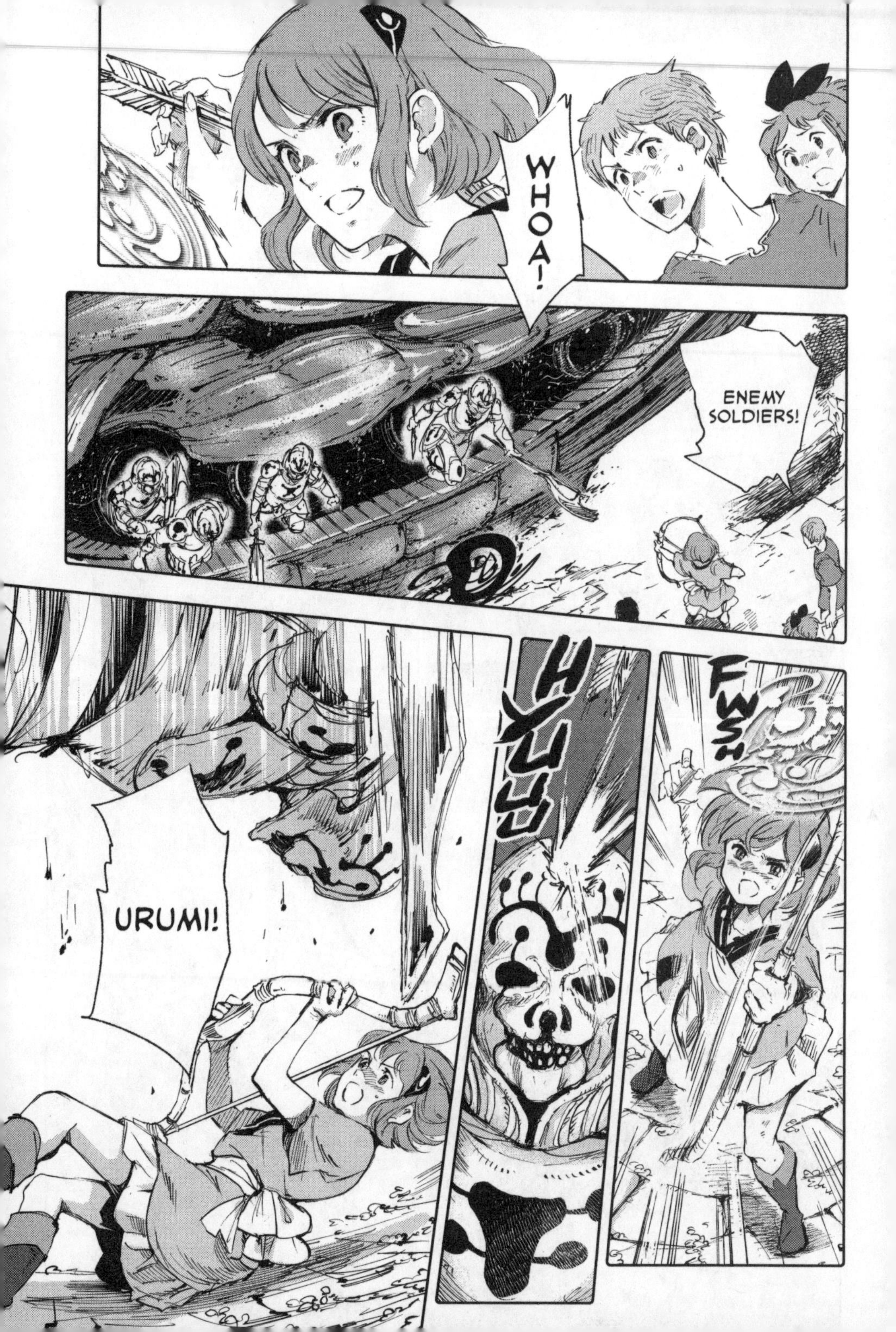
WHOA!
ENEMY SOLDIERS!
FWSH
HYUUU
URUMI!

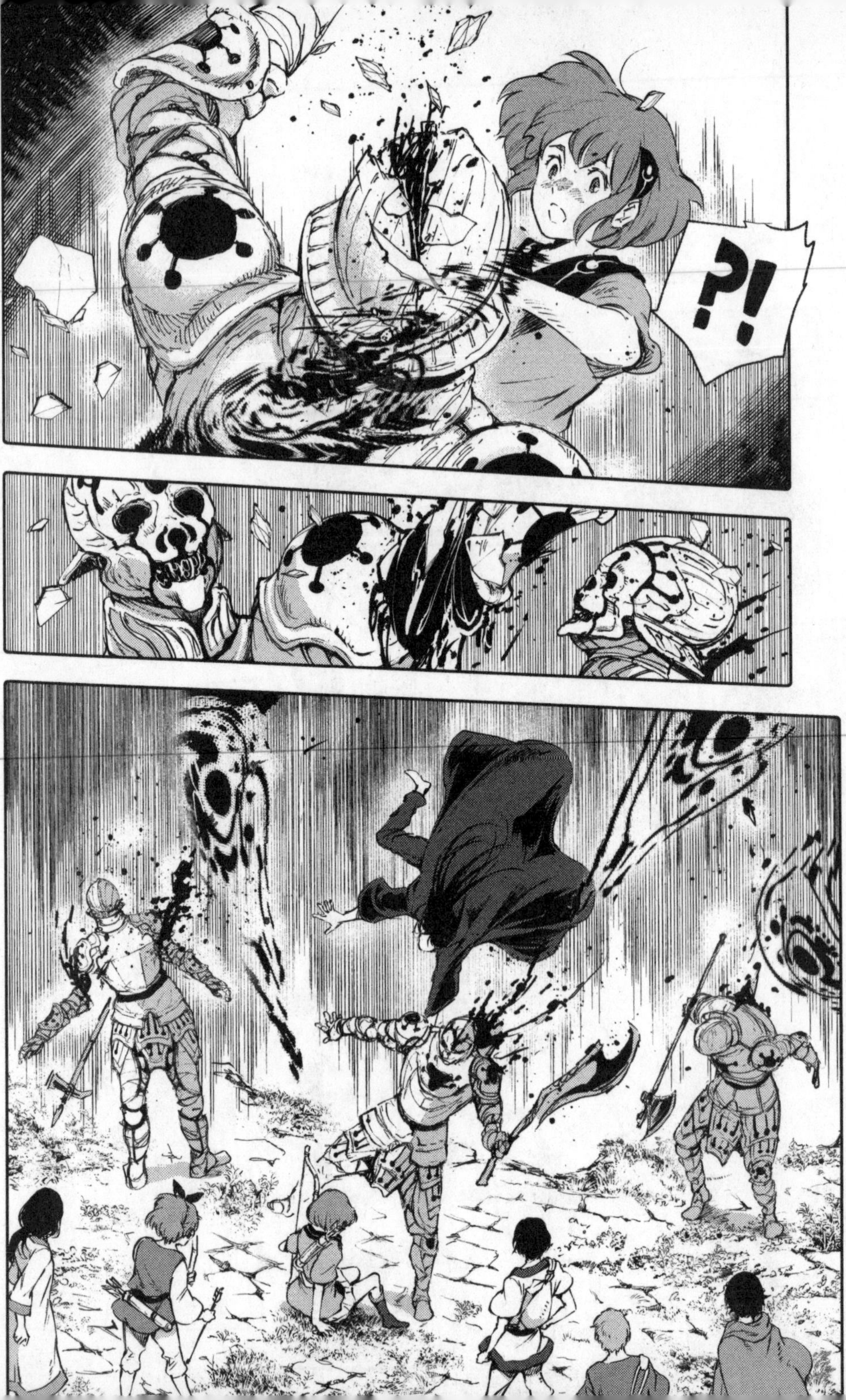
?!

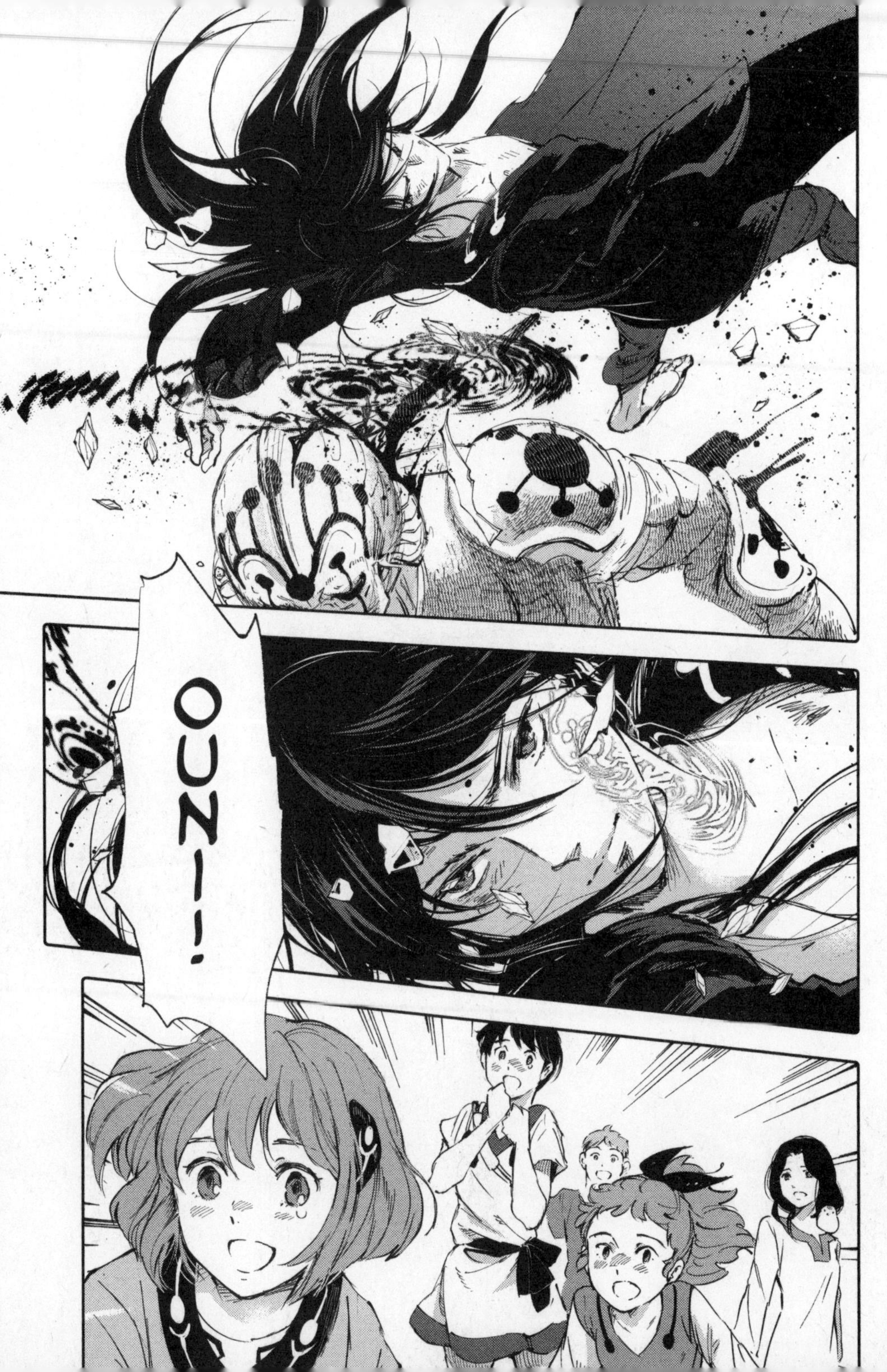
OUN!!!

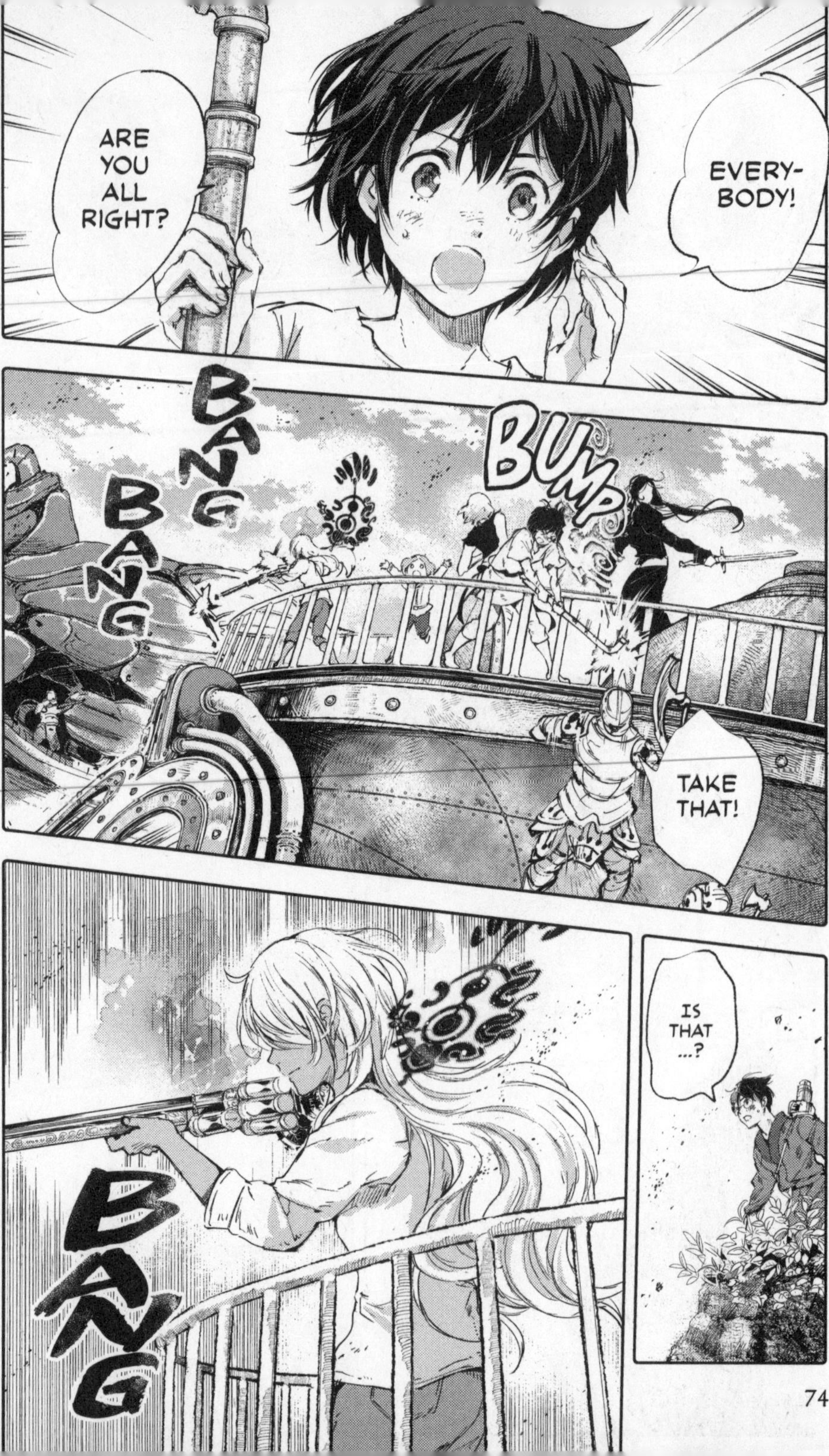
EVERY-BODY!
ARE YOU ALL RIGHT?
BUMP
BANG
BANG
TAKE THAT!
IS THAT ...?
BANG

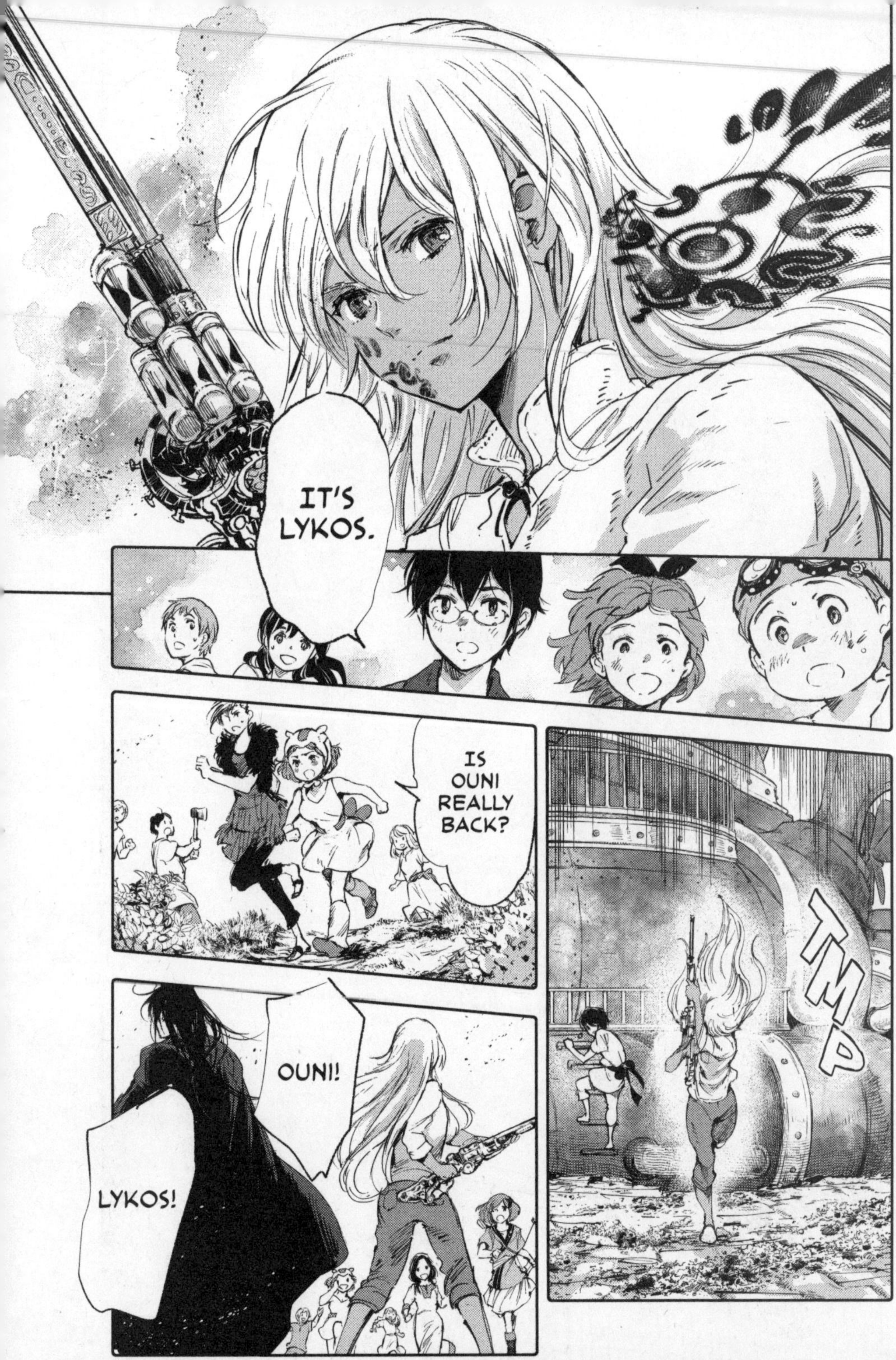
IT'S LYKOS.
TMP
IS OUNI REALLY BACK?
OUNI!
LYKOS!

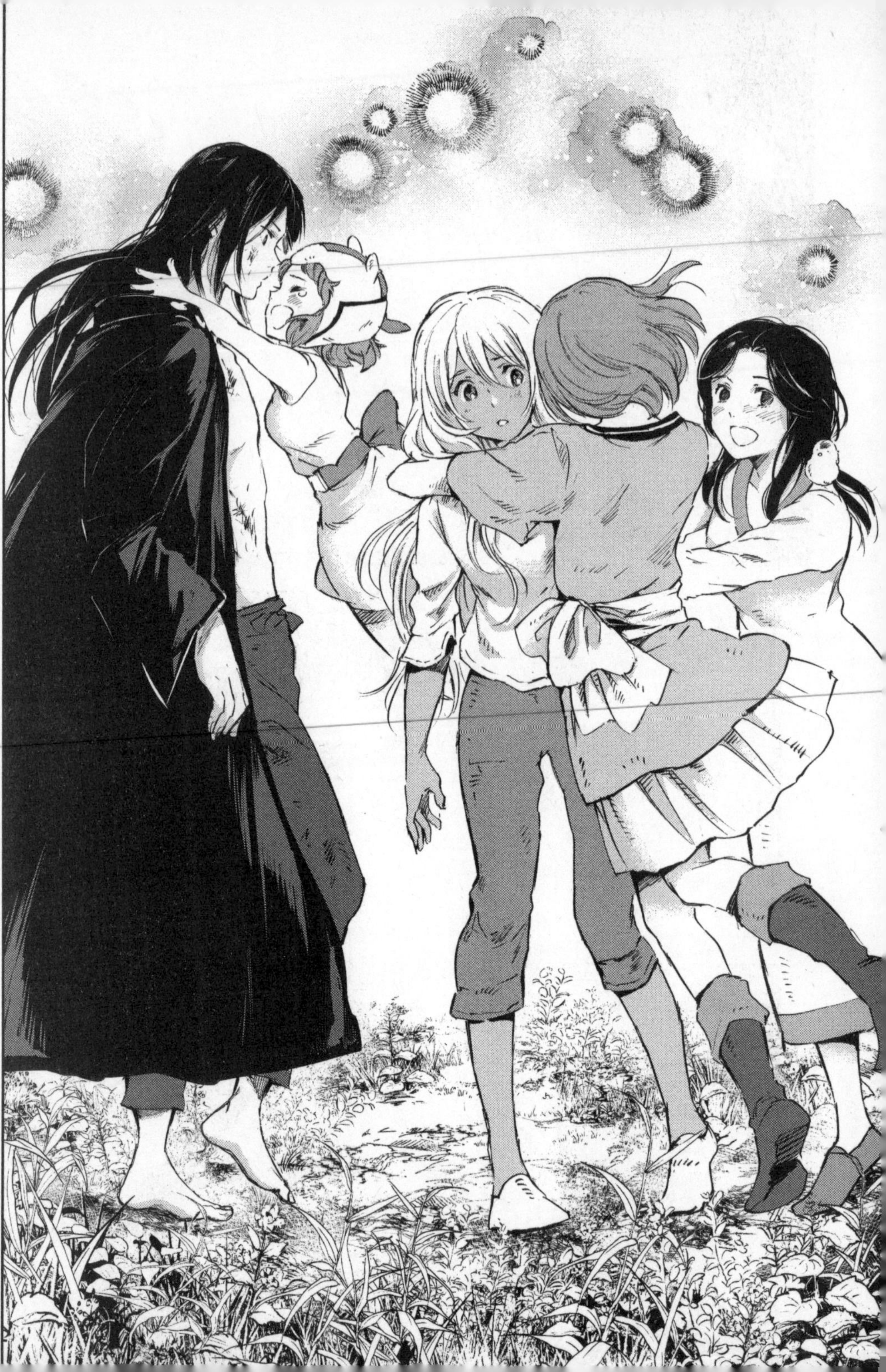

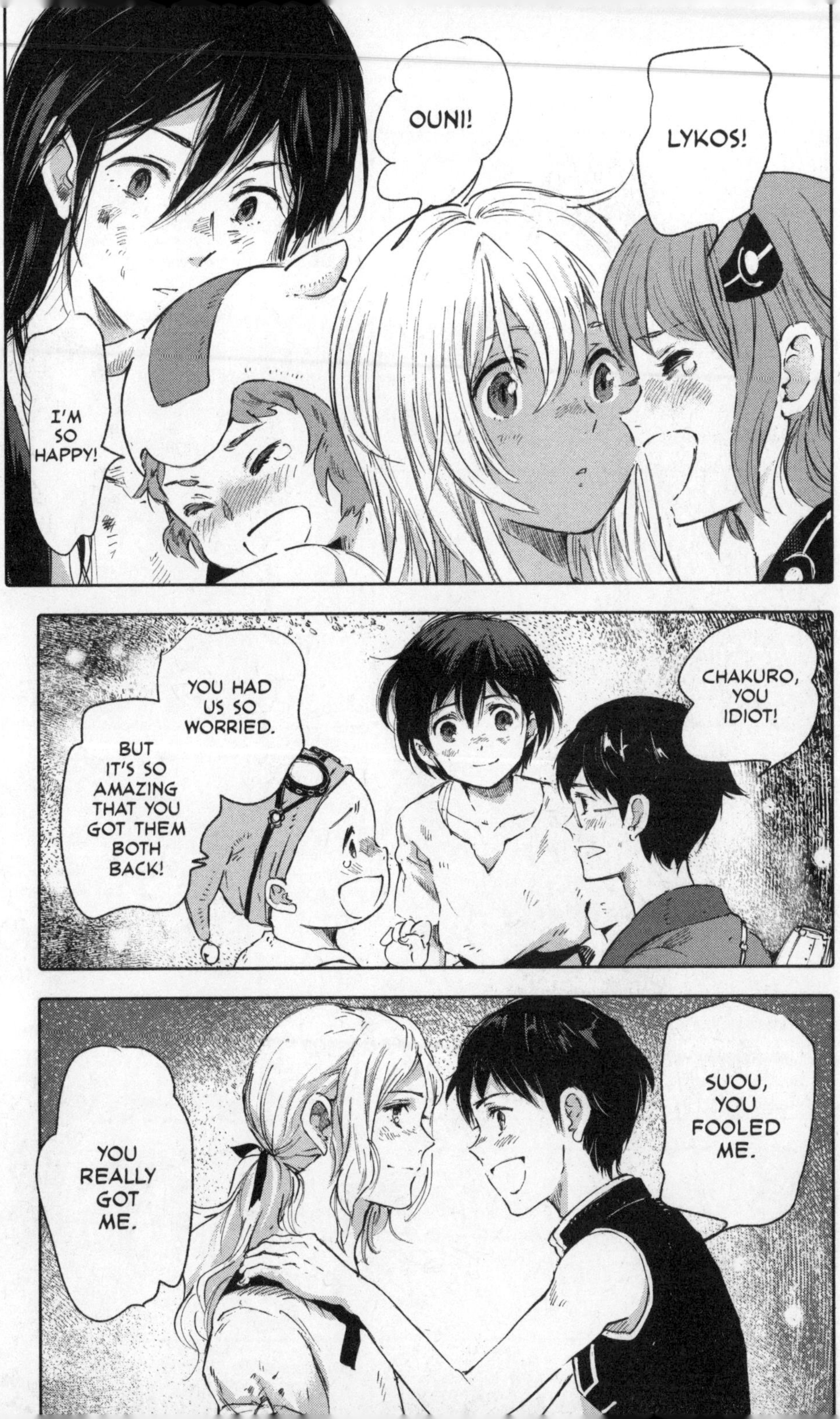
LYKOS!
OUNI!
I'M SO HAPPY!
CHAKURO, YOU IDIOT!
YOU HAD US SO WORRIED.
BUT IT'S SO AMAZING THAT YOU GOT THEM BOTH BACK!
SUOU, YOU FOOLED ME.
YOU REALLY GOT ME.

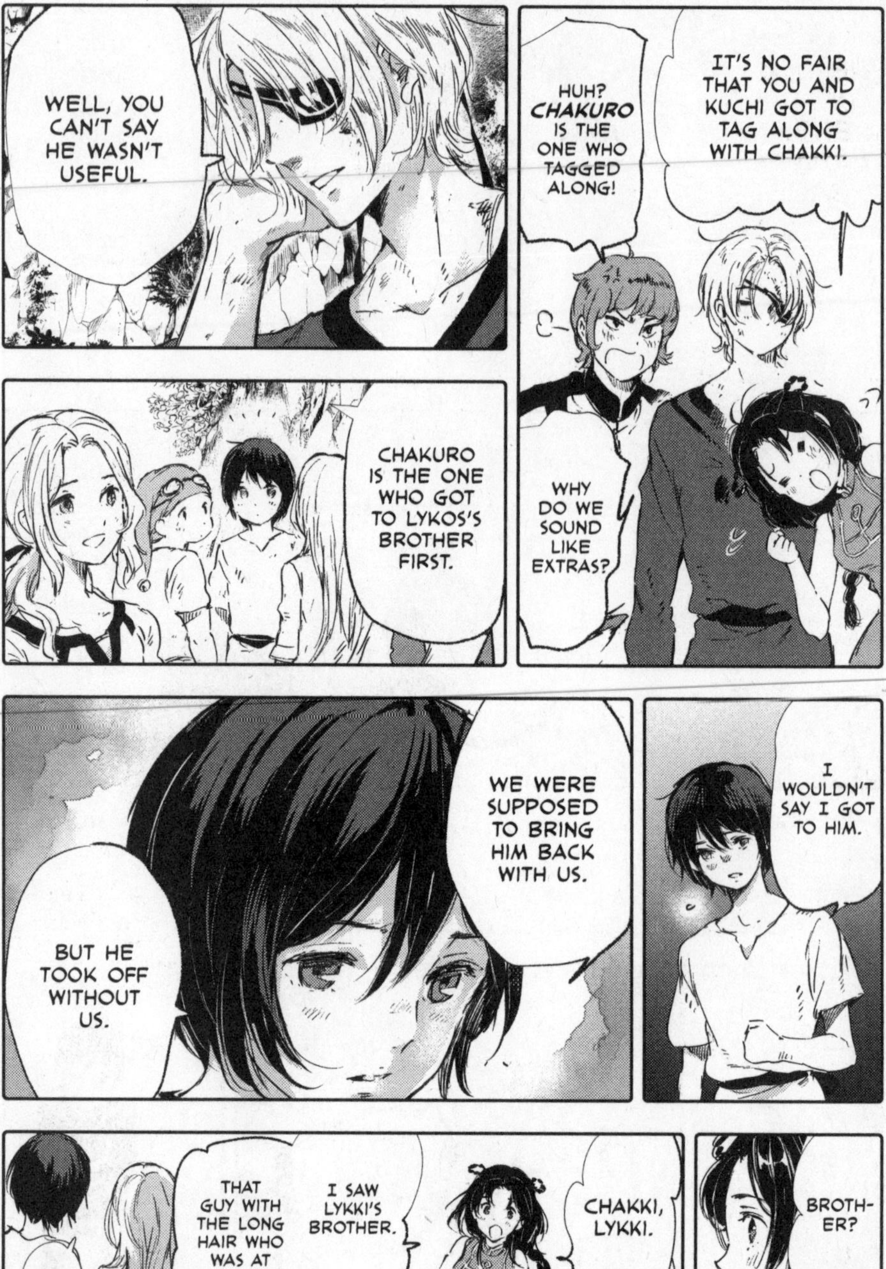
IT'S NO FAIR THAT YOU AND KUCHI GOT TO TAG ALONG WITH CHAKKI.
HUH? *CHAKURO* IS THE ONE WHO TAGGED ALONG!
WHY DO WE SOUND LIKE EXTRAS?
WELL, YOU CAN'T SAY HE WASN'T USEFUL.
CHAKURO IS THE ONE WHO GOT TO LYKOS'S BROTHER FIRST.
I WOULDN'T SAY I GOT TO HIM.
WE WERE SUPPOSED TO BRING HIM BACK WITH US.
BUT HE TOOK OFF WITHOUT US.
BROTH-ER?
CHAKKI, LYKKI.
I SAW LYKKI'S BROTHER.
THAT GUY WITH THE LONG HAIR WHO WAS AT AMONLOGIA.
HUH?

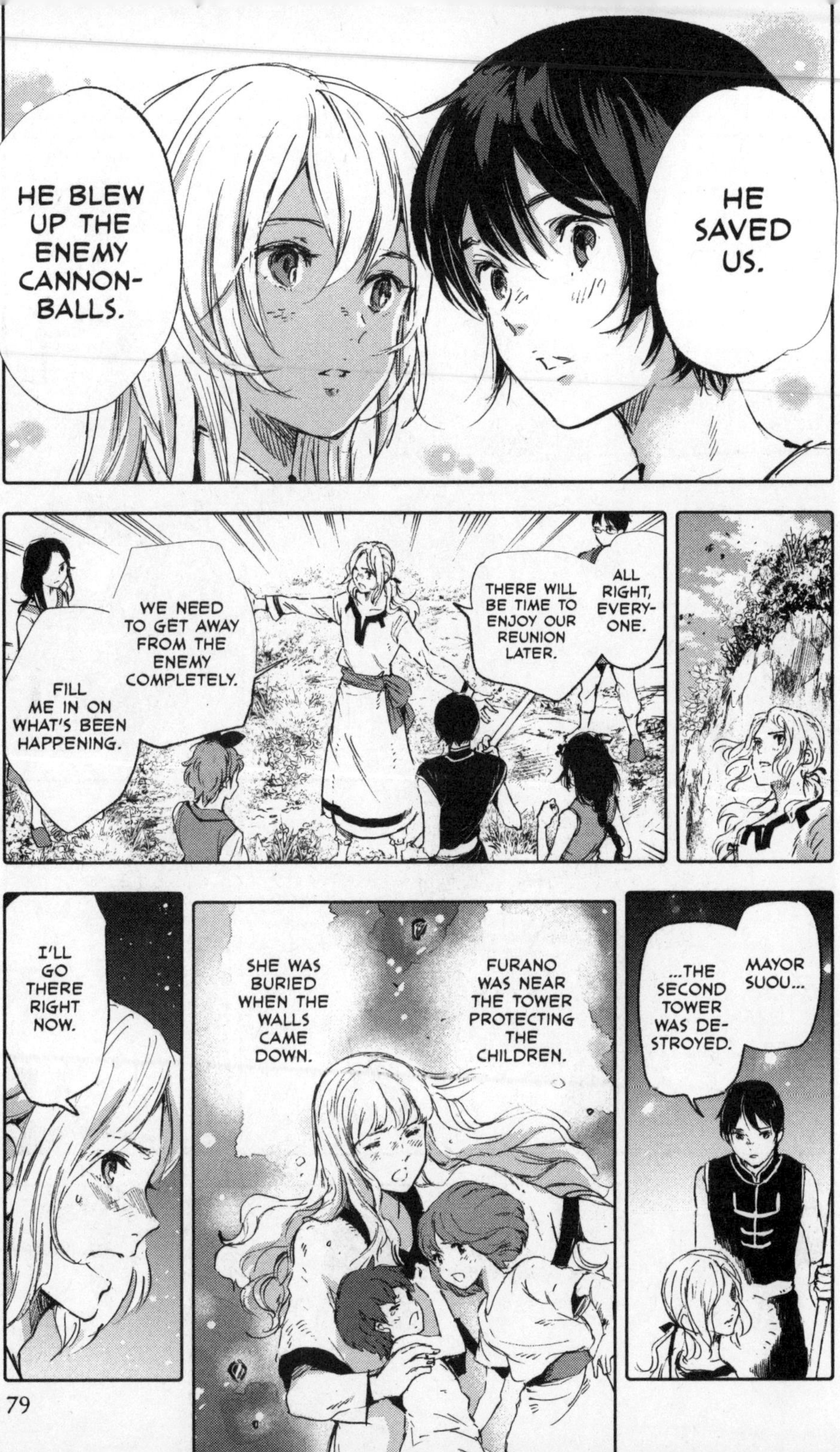
HE SAVED US.
HE BLEW UP THE ENEMY CANNON-BALLS.
ALL RIGHT, EVERY-ONE.
THERE WILL BE TIME TO ENJOY OUR REUNION LATER.
WE NEED TO GET AWAY FROM THE ENEMY COMPLETELY.
FILL ME IN ON WHAT'S BEEN HAPPENING.
MAYOR SUOU...
...THE SECOND TOWER WAS DE-STROYED.
FURANO WAS NEAR THE TOWER PROTECTING THE CHILDREN.
SHE WAS BURIED WHEN THE WALLS CAME DOWN.
I'LL GO THERE RIGHT NOW.

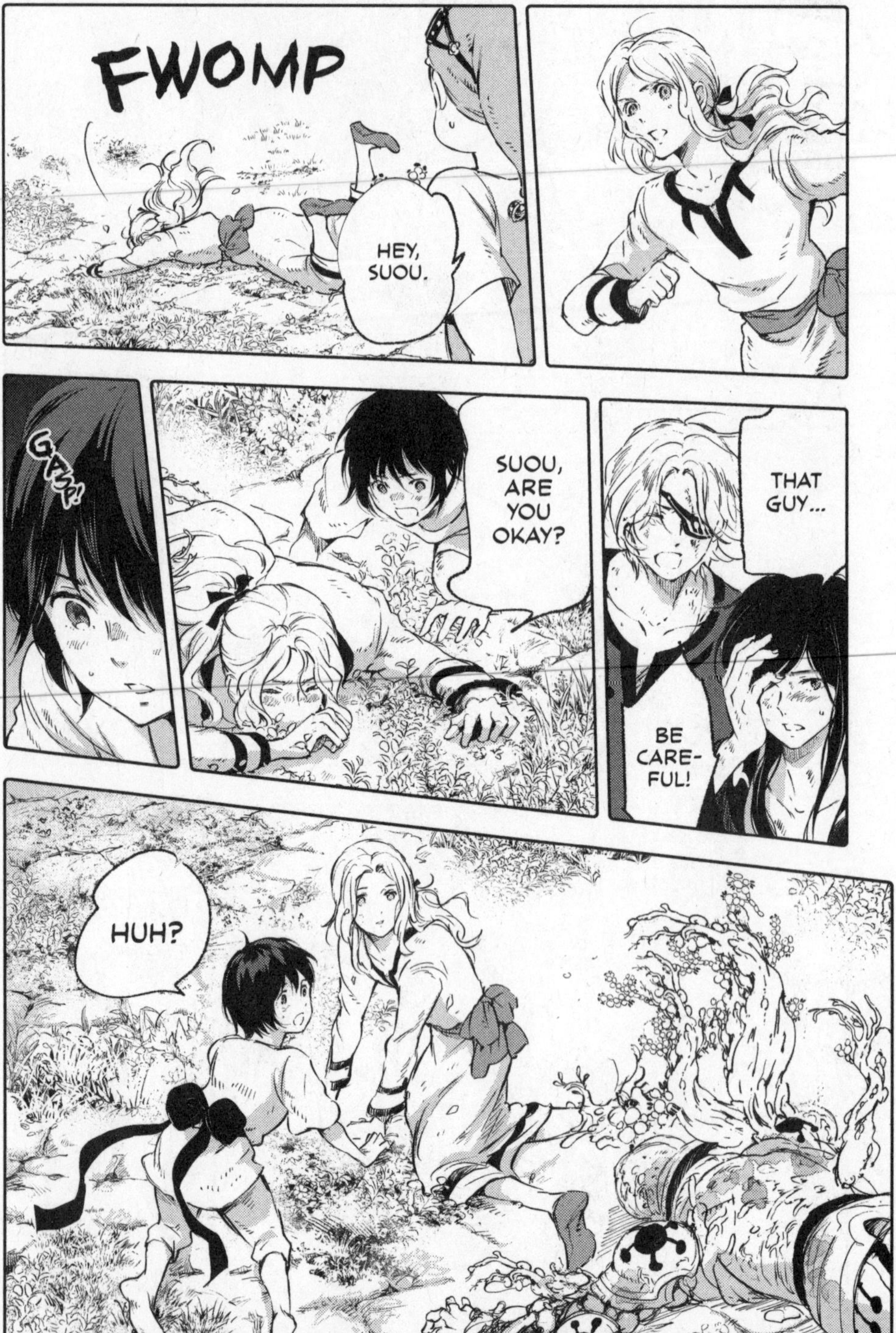
FWOMP
HEY, SUOU.
THAT GUY...
BE CAREFUL!
SUOU, ARE YOU OKAY?
GASP!
HUH?

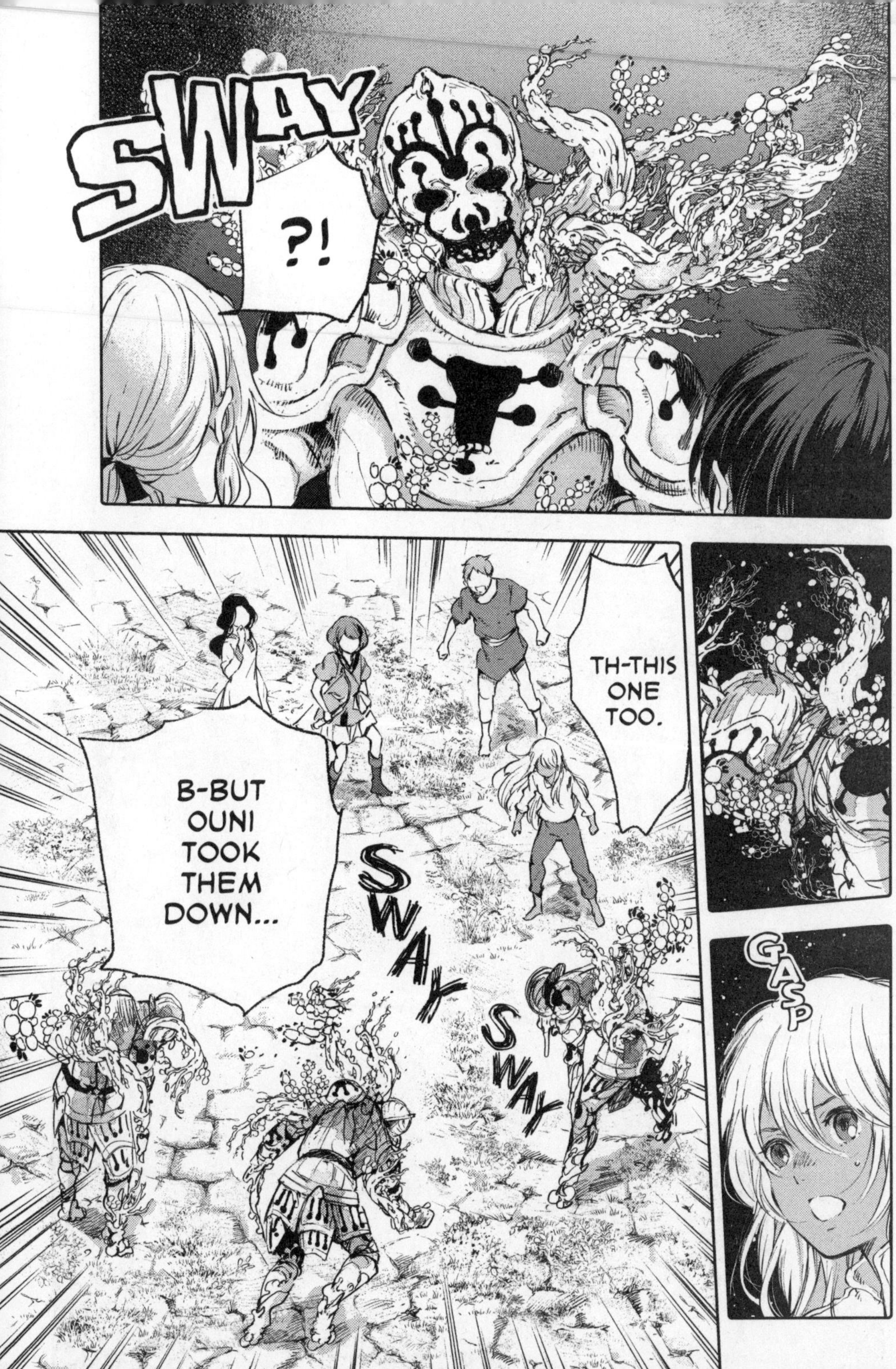
SWAY
?!
GASP
TH-THIS ONE TOO.
B-BUT OUNI TOOK THEM DOWN...
SWAY
SWAY

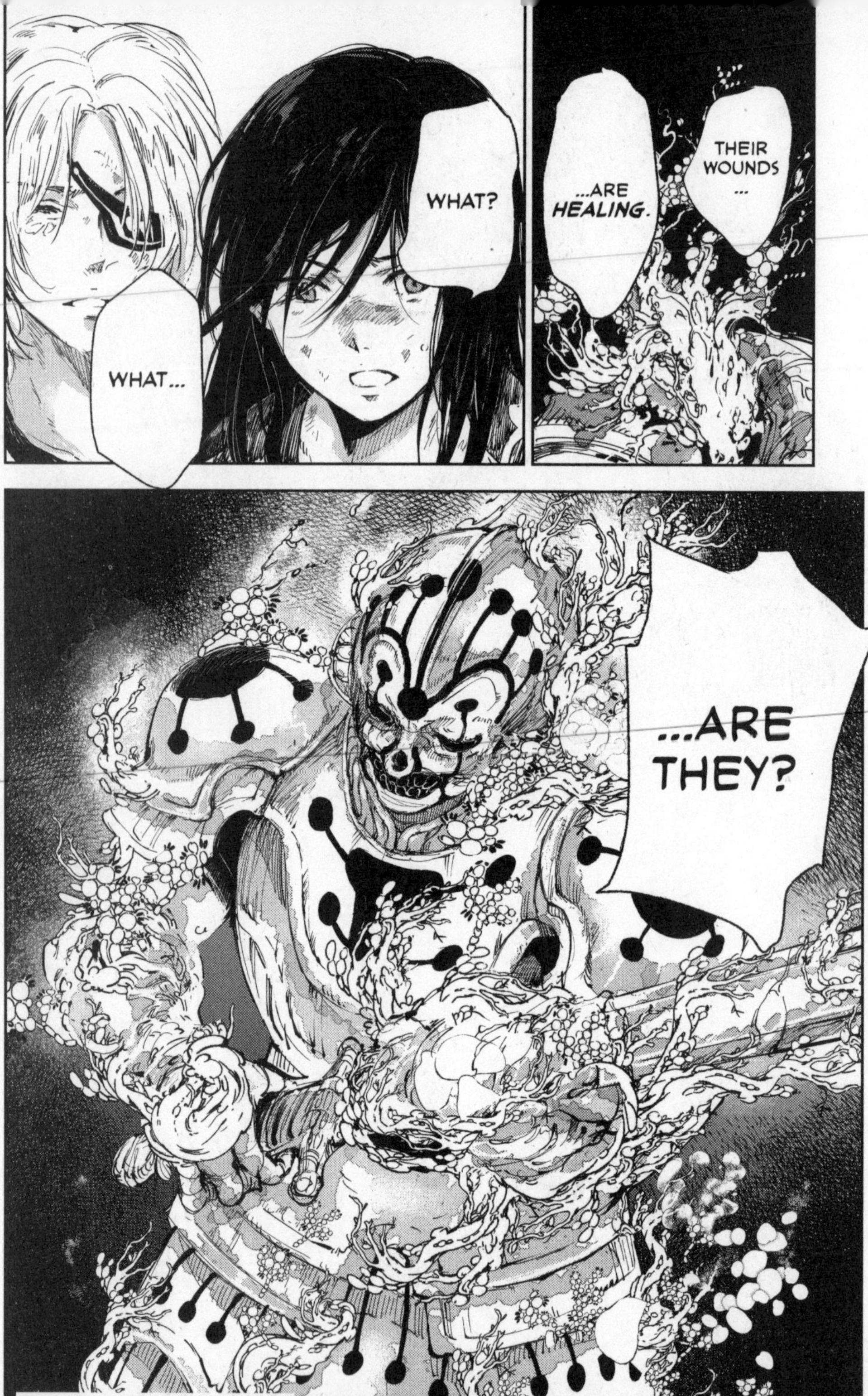
THEIR WOUNDS ...
...ARE HEALING.
WHAT?
WHAT...
...ARE THEY?

Evil Star on the Sand - The End-

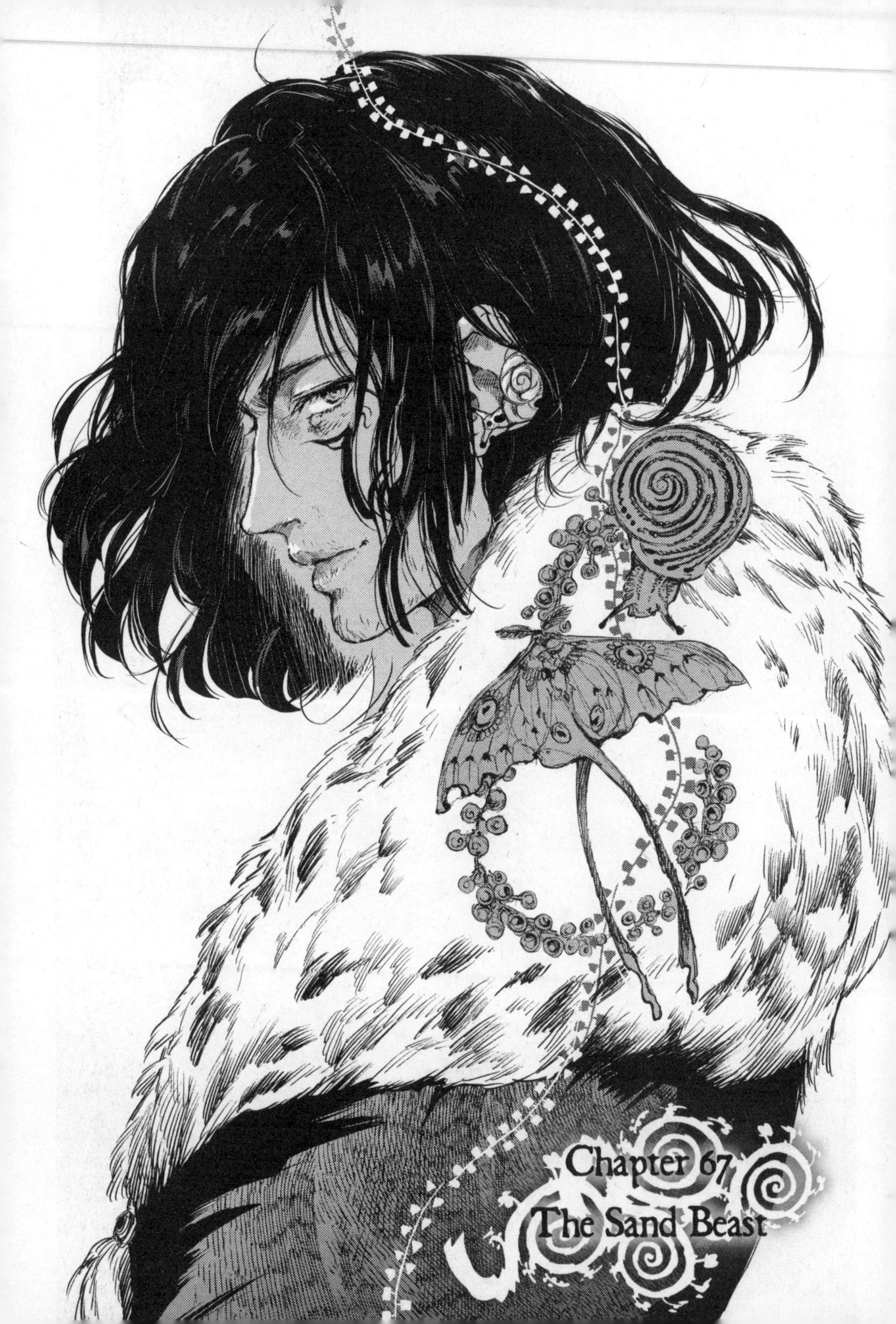
Chapter 67
The Sand Beast

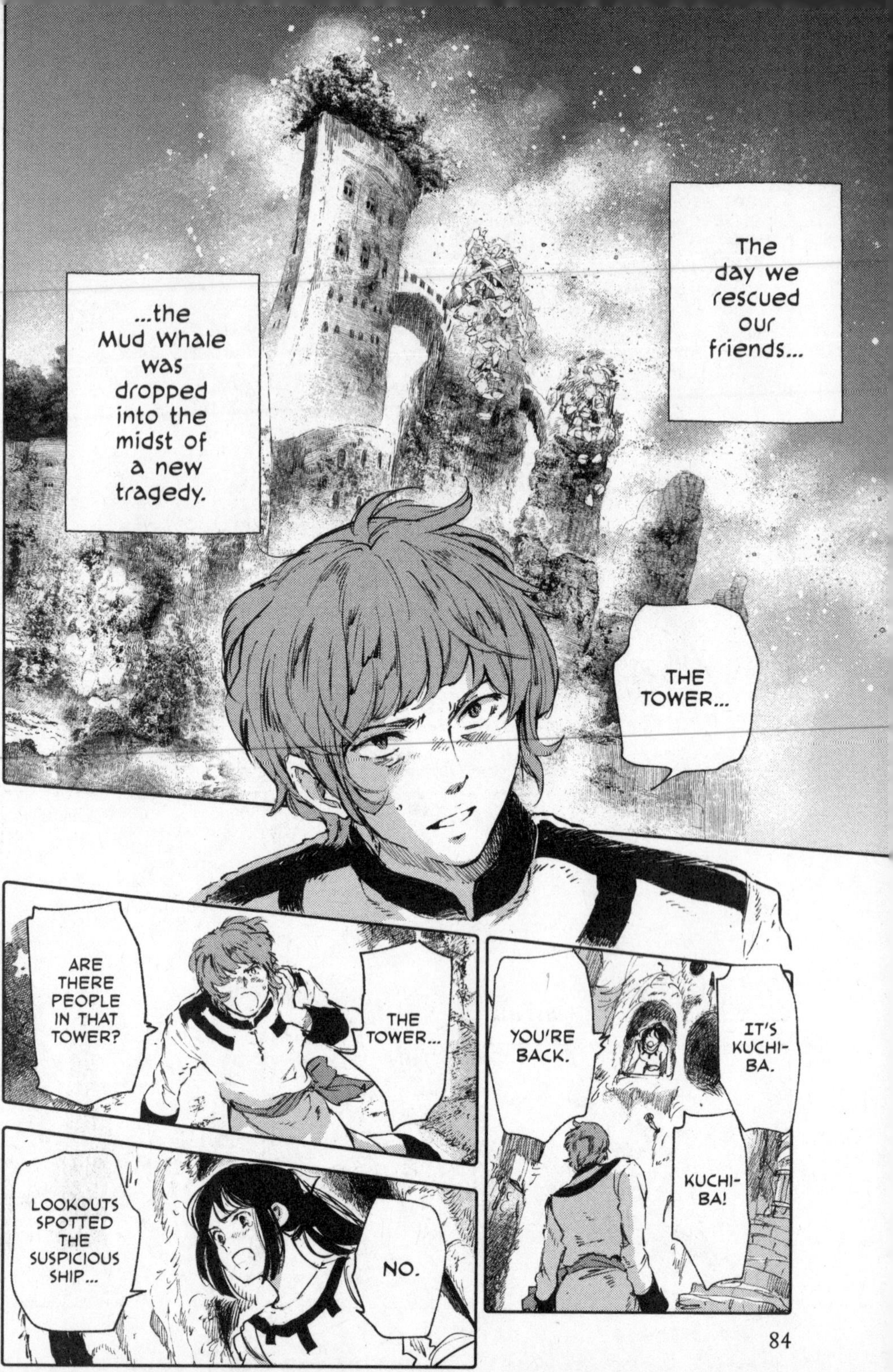
The day we rescued our friends...
...the Mud Whale was dropped into the midst of a new tragedy.
THE TOWER...
IT'S KUCHI-BA.
YOU'RE BACK.
KUCHI-BA!
THE TOWER...
ARE THERE PEOPLE IN THAT TOWER?
NO.
LOOKOUTS SPOTTED THE SUSPICIOUS SHIP...

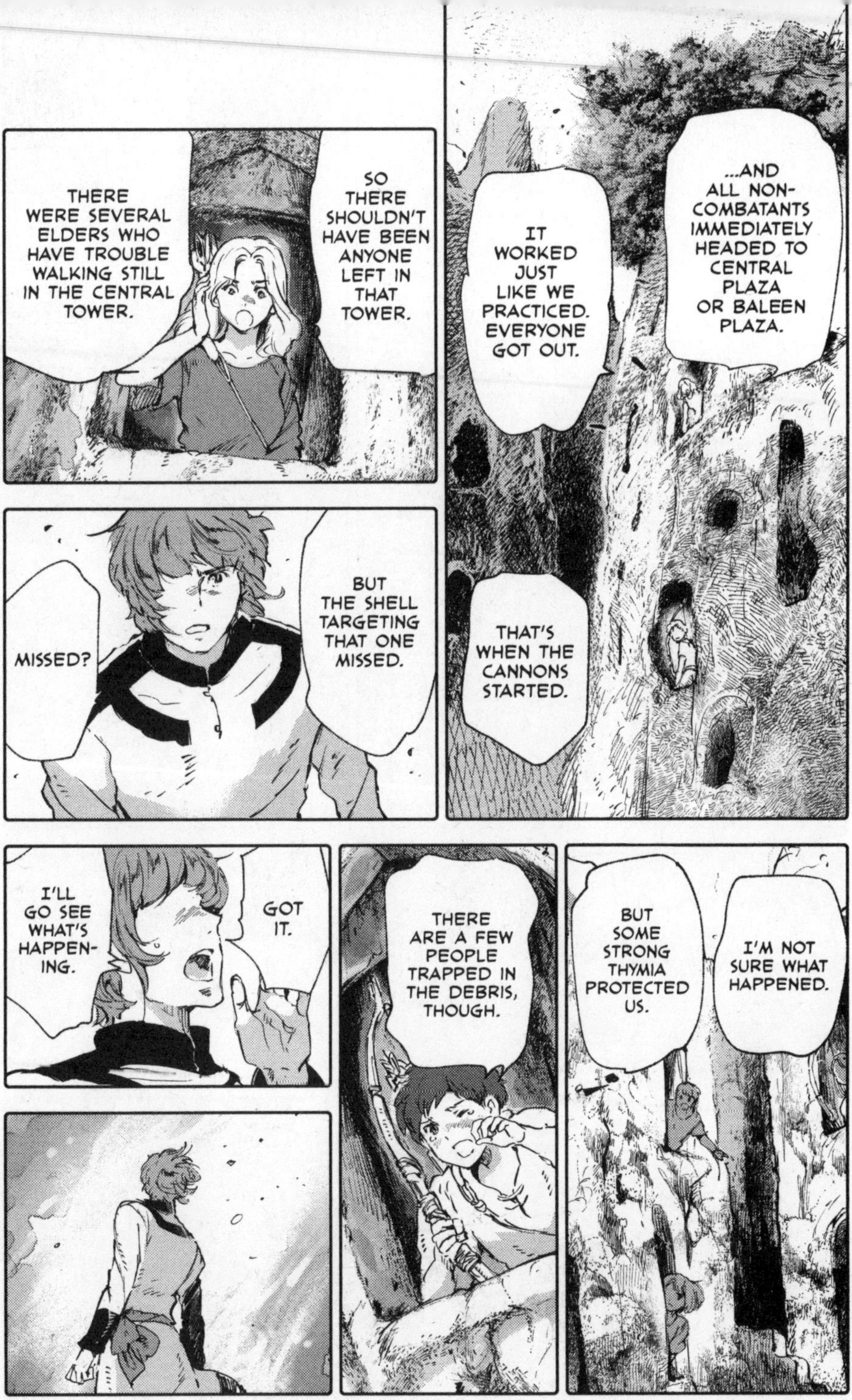
...AND ALL NON-COMBATANTS IMMEDIATELY HEADED TO CENTRAL PLAZA OR BALEEN PLAZA.
IT WORKED JUST LIKE WE PRACTICED. EVERYONE GOT OUT.
THAT'S WHEN THE CANNONS STARTED.
SO THERE SHOULDN'T HAVE BEEN ANYONE LEFT IN THAT TOWER.
THERE WERE SEVERAL ELDERS WHO HAVE TROUBLE WALKING STILL IN THE CENTRAL TOWER.
BUT THE SHELL TARGETING THAT ONE MISSED.
MISSED?
I'M NOT SURE WHAT HAPPENED.
BUT SOME STRONG THYMIA PROTECTED US.
THERE ARE A FEW PEOPLE TRAPPED IN THE DEBRIS, THOUGH.
GOT IT.
I'LL GO SEE WHAT'S HAPPEN-ING.

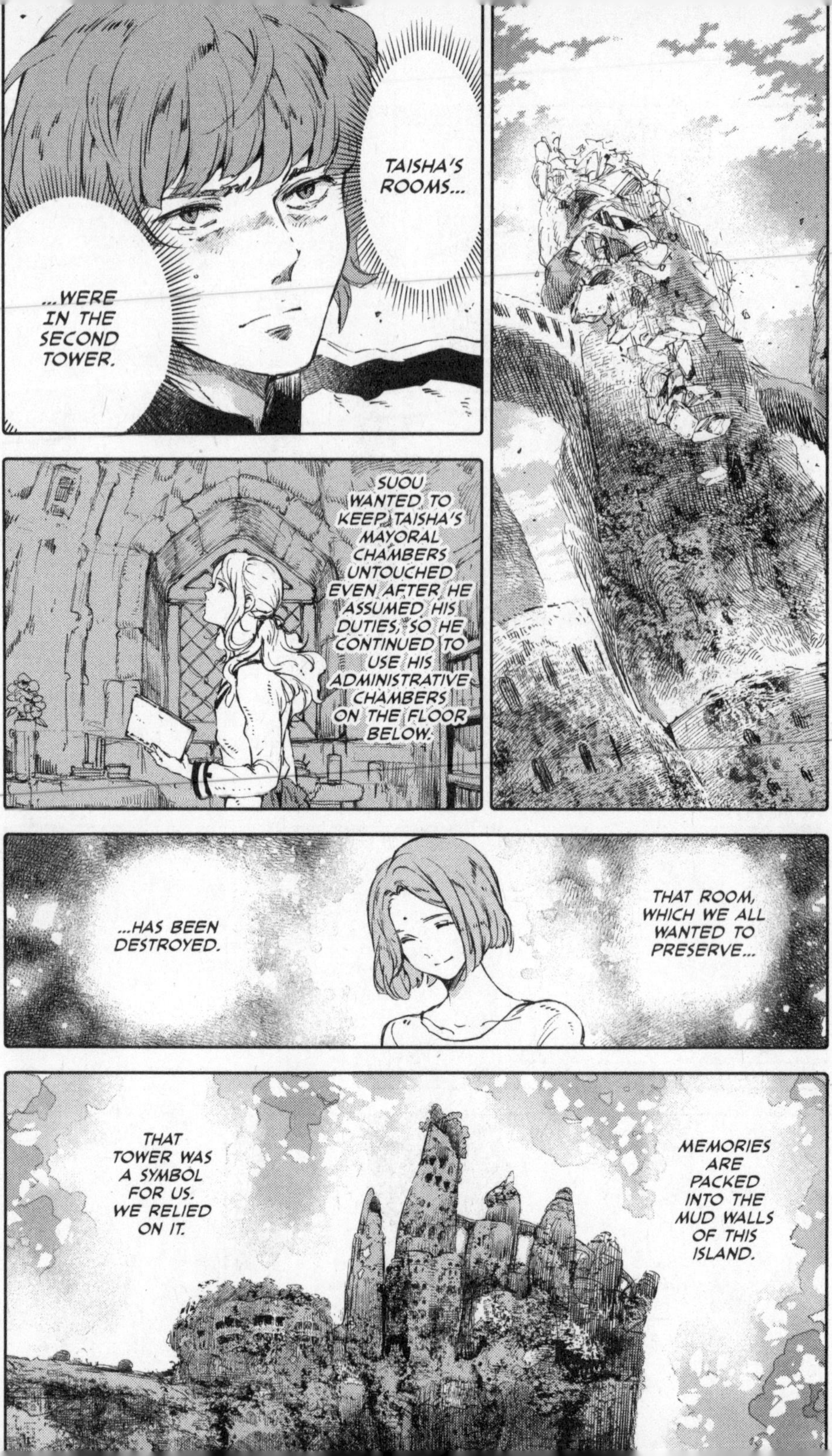
TAISHA'S ROOMS...
...WERE IN THE SECOND TOWER.
SUOU WANTED TO KEEP TAISHA'S MAYORAL CHAMBERS UNTOUCHED EVEN AFTER HE ASSUMED HIS DUTIES, SO HE CONTINUED TO USE HIS ADMINISTRATIVE CHAMBERS ON THE FLOOR BELOW.
THAT ROOM, WHICH WE ALL WANTED TO PRESERVE...
...HAS BEEN DESTROYED.
MEMORIES ARE PACKED INTO THE MUD WALLS OF THIS ISLAND.
THAT TOWER WAS A SYMBOL FOR US. WE RELIED ON IT.

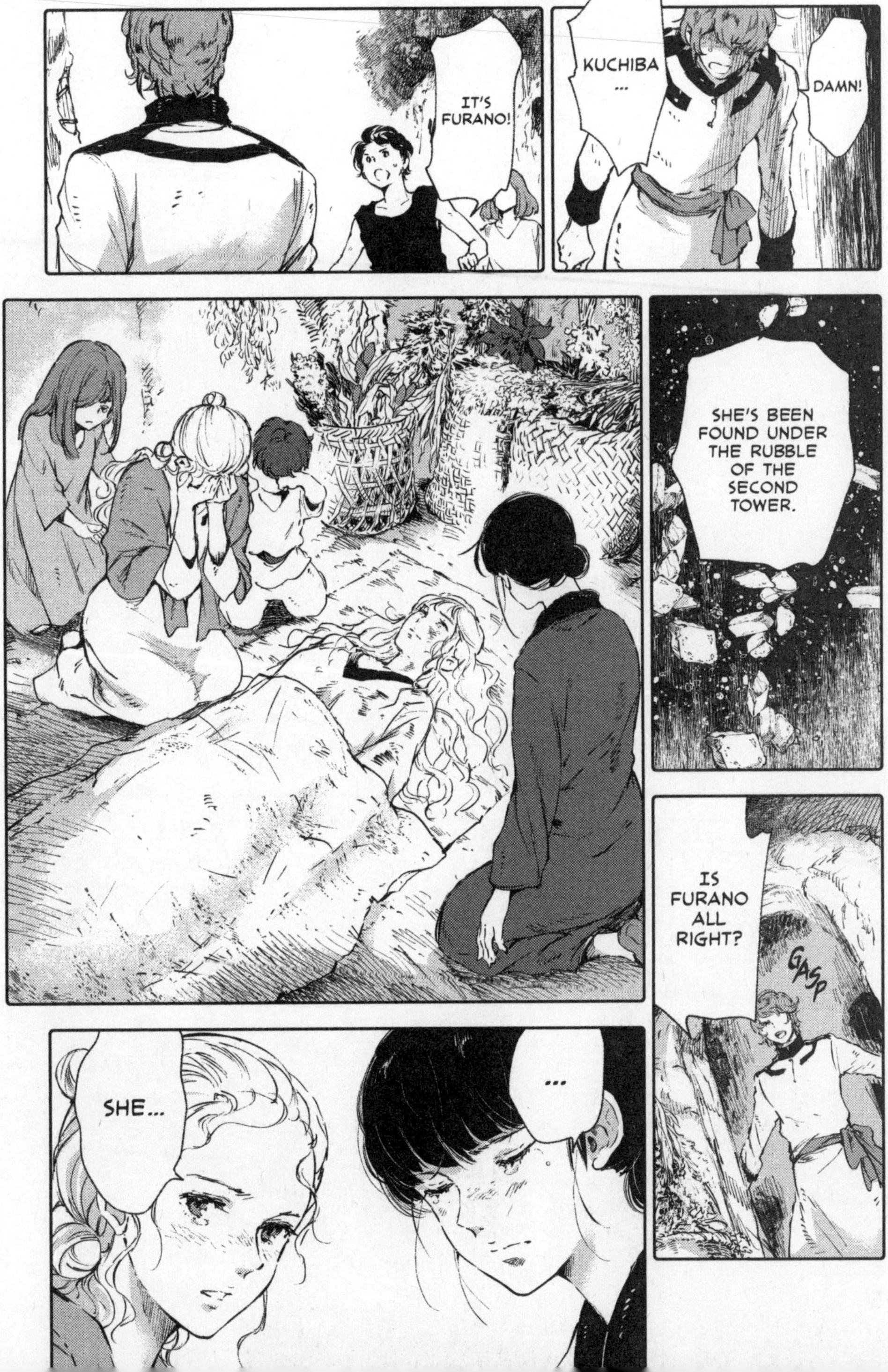
KUCHIBA ...
DAMN!
IT'S FURANO!
SHE'S BEEN FOUND UNDER THE RUBBLE OF THE SECOND TOWER.
IS FURANO ALL RIGHT?
GASP
...
SHE...

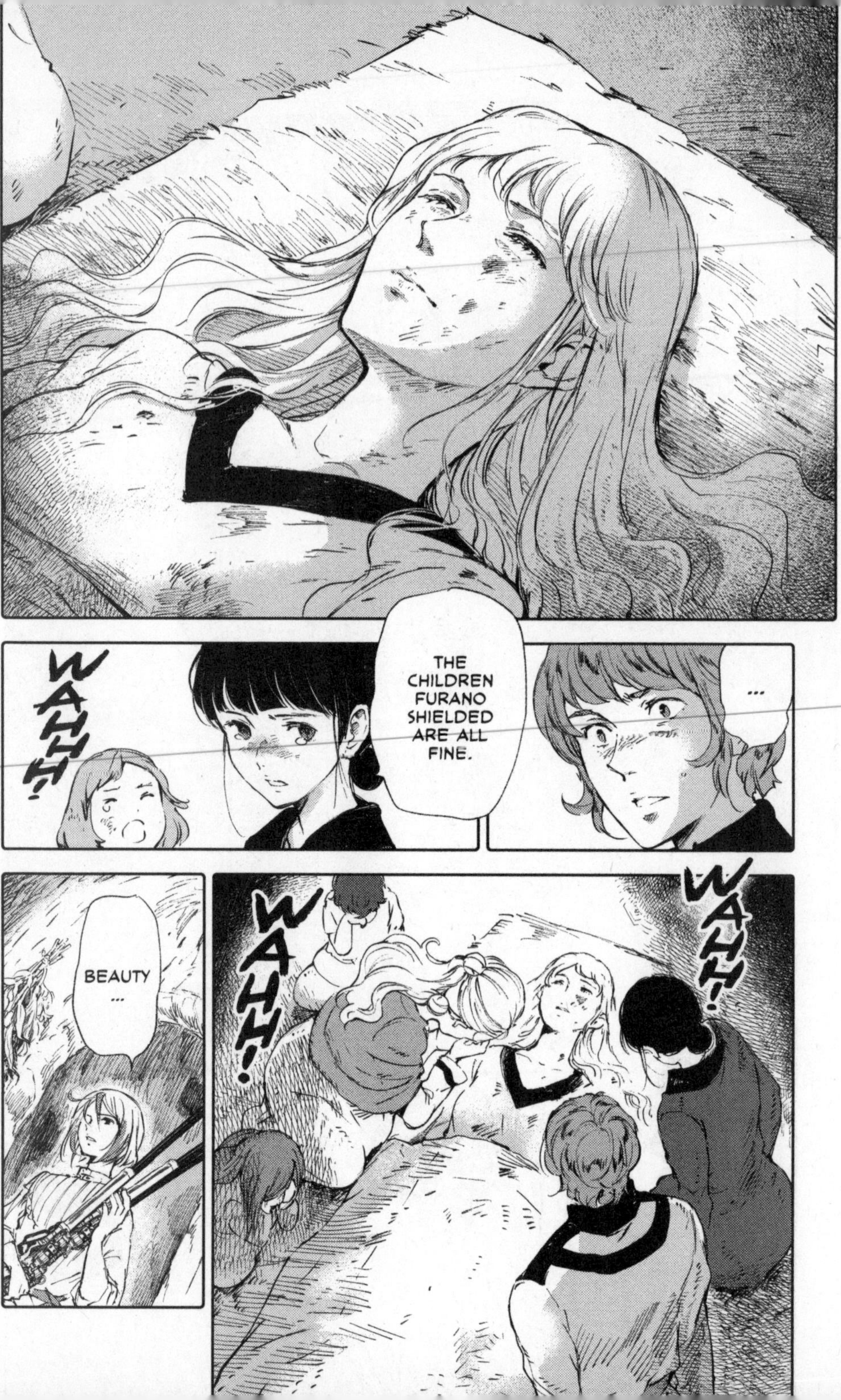
...
THE CHILDREN FURANO SHIELDED ARE ALL FINE.
WAHH!
WAHH!
WAHH!
BEAUTY ...

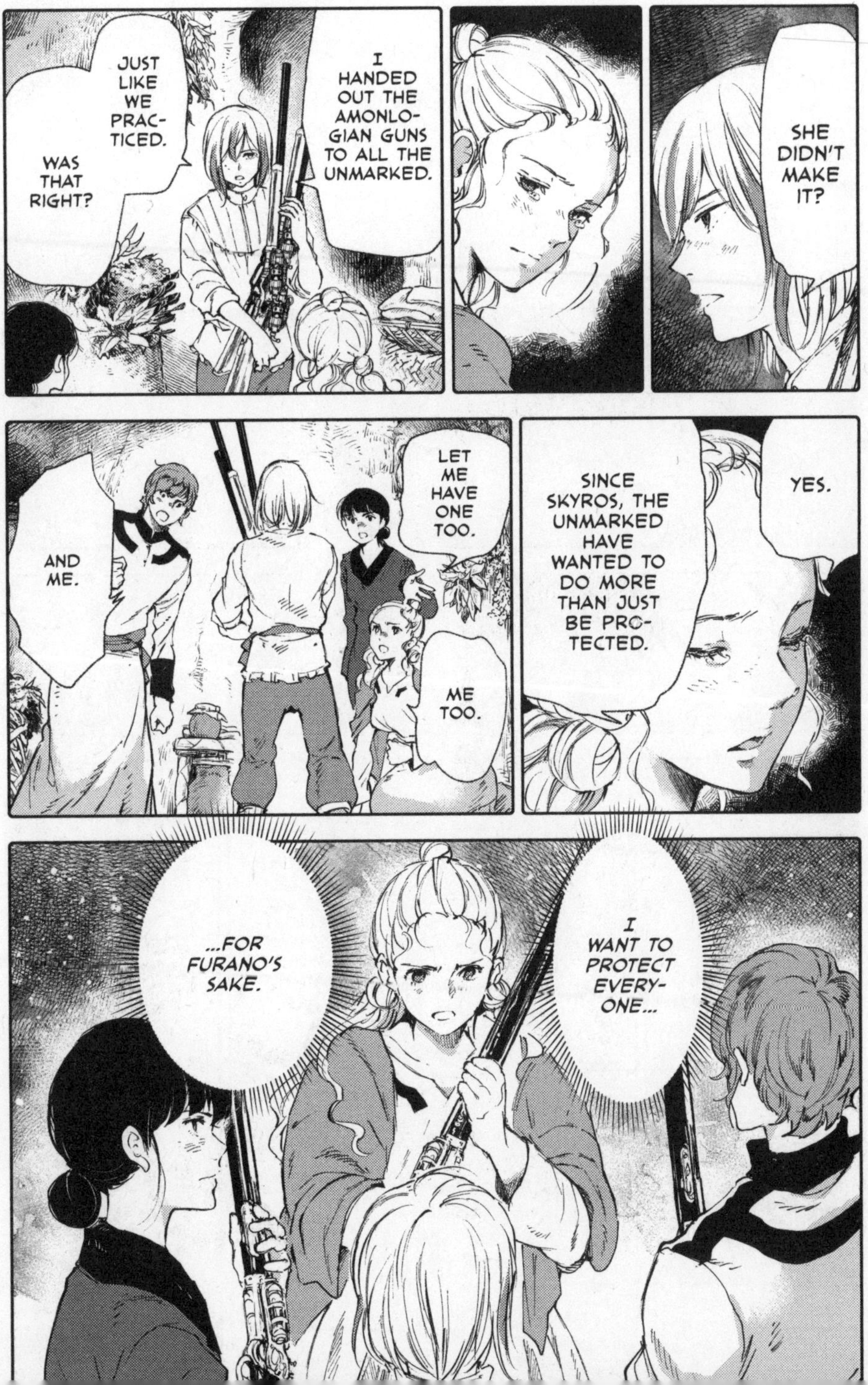
SHE DIDN'T MAKE IT?
I HANDED OUT THE AMONLOGIAN GUNS TO ALL THE UNMARKED.
JUST LIKE WE PRACTICED.
WAS THAT RIGHT?
YES.
SINCE SKYROS, THE UNMARKED HAVE WANTED TO DO MORE THAN JUST BE PROTECTED.
LET ME HAVE ONE TOO.
AND ME.
ME TOO.
I WANT TO PROTECT EVERYONE...
...FOR FURANO'S SAKE.

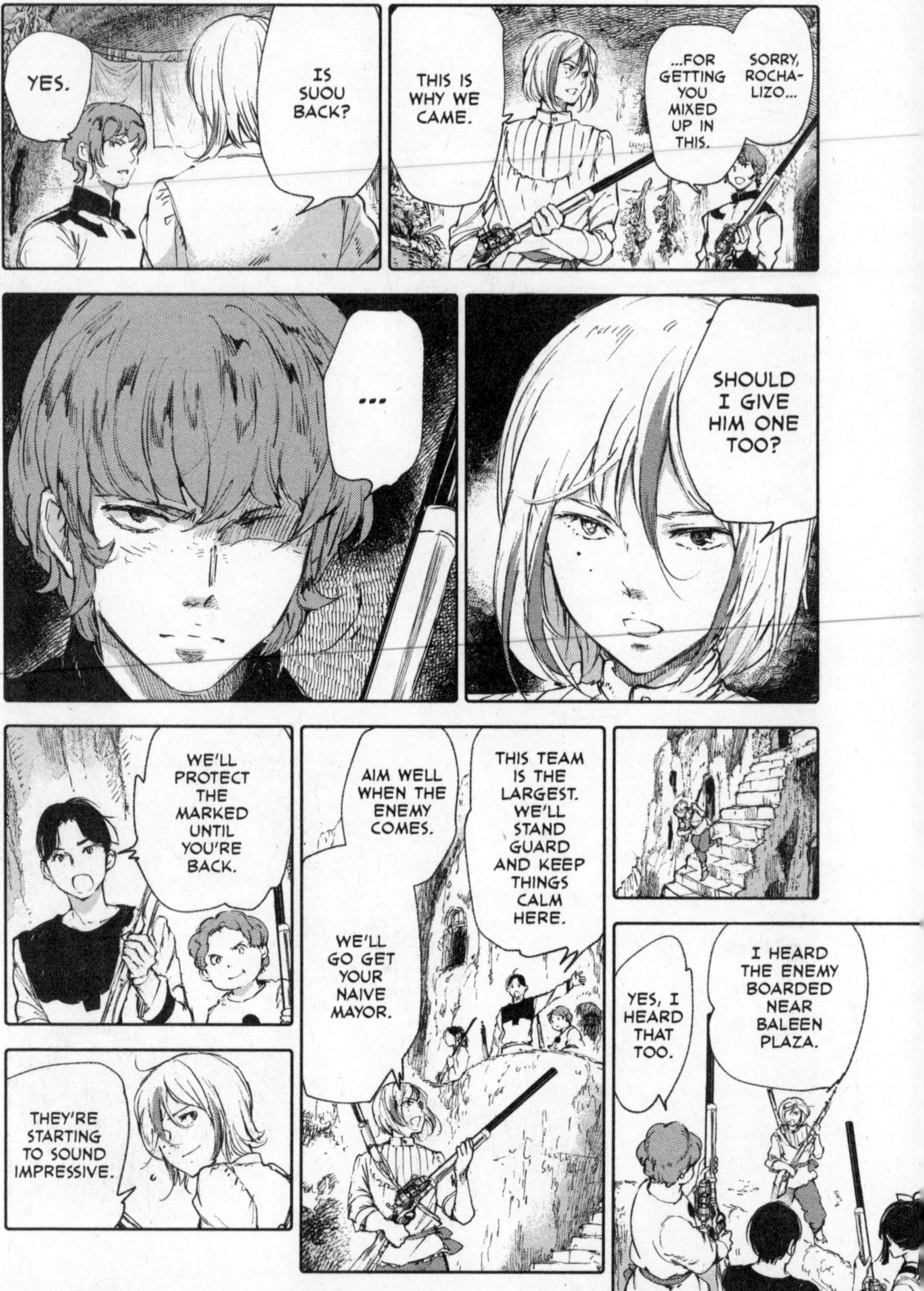
SORRY, ROCHALIZO...
...FOR GETTING YOU MIXED UP IN THIS.
THIS IS WHY WE CAME.
IS SUOU BACK?
YES.
SHOULD I GIVE HIM ONE TOO?
...
I HEARD THE ENEMY BOARDED NEAR BALEEN PLAZA.
YES, I HEARD THAT TOO.
THIS TEAM IS THE LARGEST. WE'LL STAND GUARD AND KEEP THINGS CALM HERE.
AIM WELL WHEN THE ENEMY COMES.
WE'LL GO GET YOUR NAIVE MAYOR.
WE'LL PROTECT THE MARKED UNTIL YOU'RE BACK.
THEY'RE STARTING TO SOUND IMPRESSIVE.

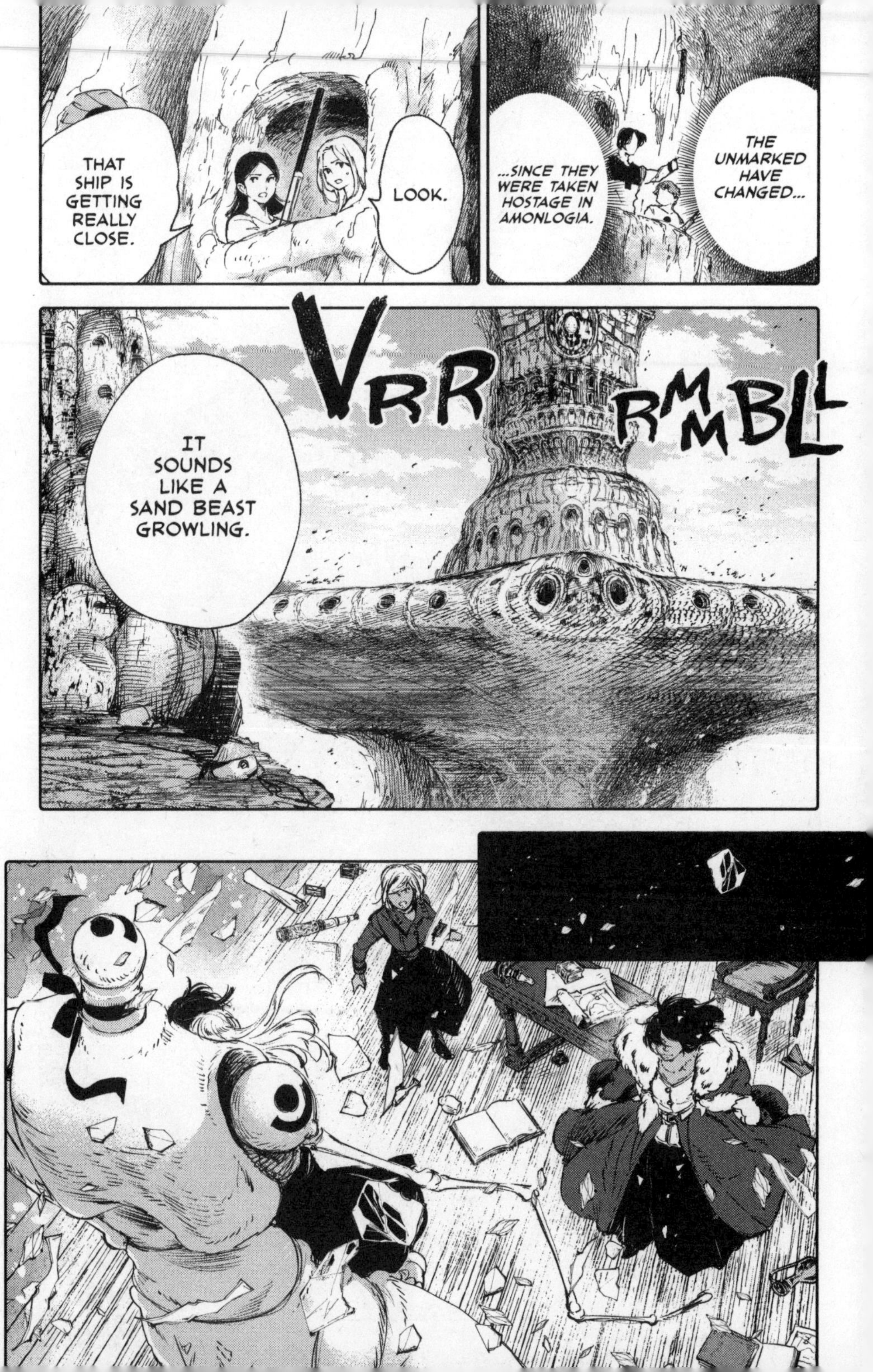
THE UNMARKED HAVE CHANGED...
...SINCE THEY WERE TAKEN HOSTAGE IN AMONLOGIA.
LOOK.
THAT SHIP IS GETTING REALLY CLOSE.
VRR
RMMBLL
IT SOUNDS LIKE A SAND BEAST GROWLING.

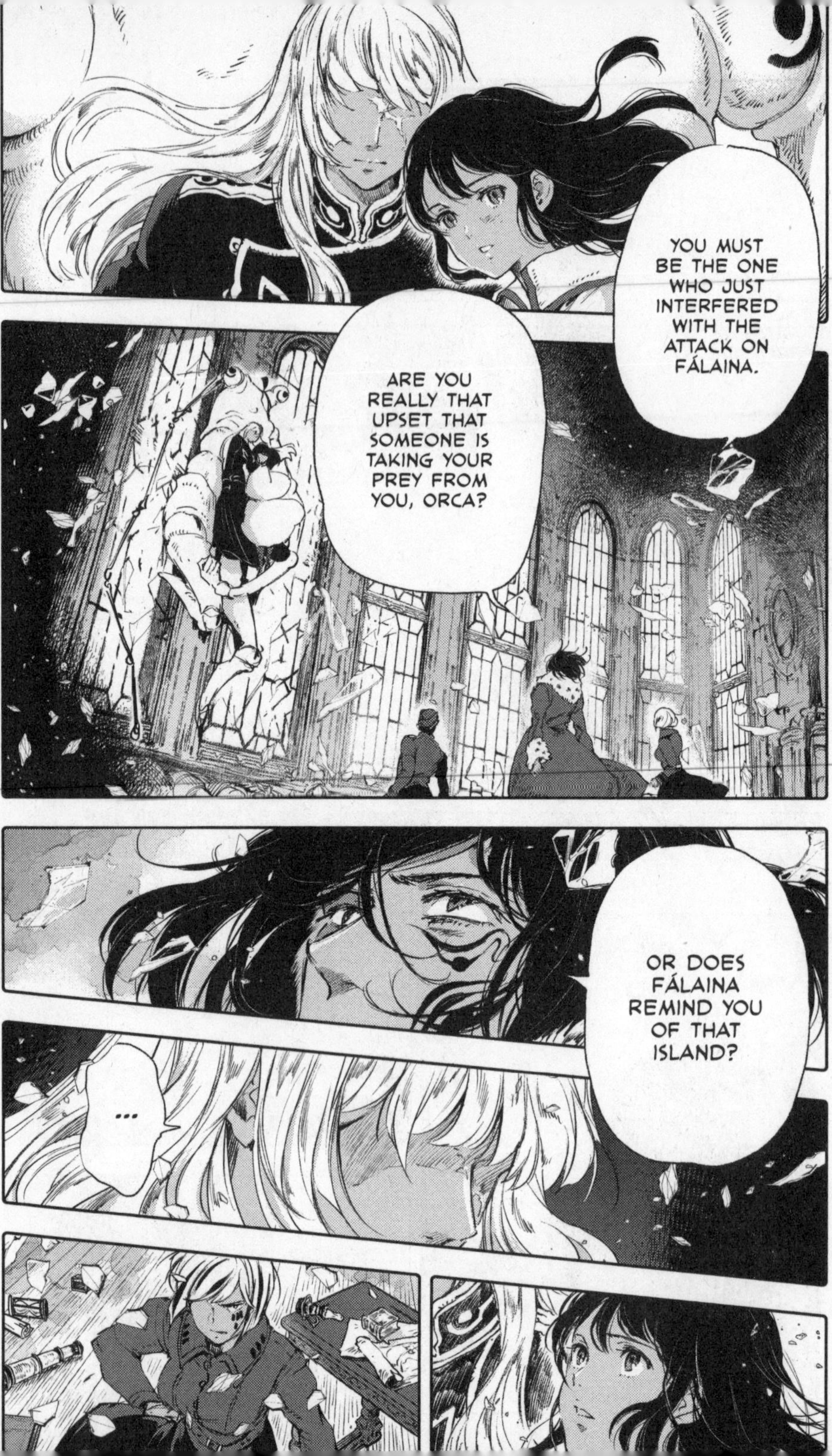
YOU MUST BE THE ONE WHO JUST INTERFERED WITH THE ATTACK ON FÁLAINA.
ARE YOU REALLY THAT UPSET THAT SOMEONE IS TAKING YOUR PREY FROM YOU, ORCA?
OR DOES FÁLAINA REMIND YOU OF THAT ISLAND?
...

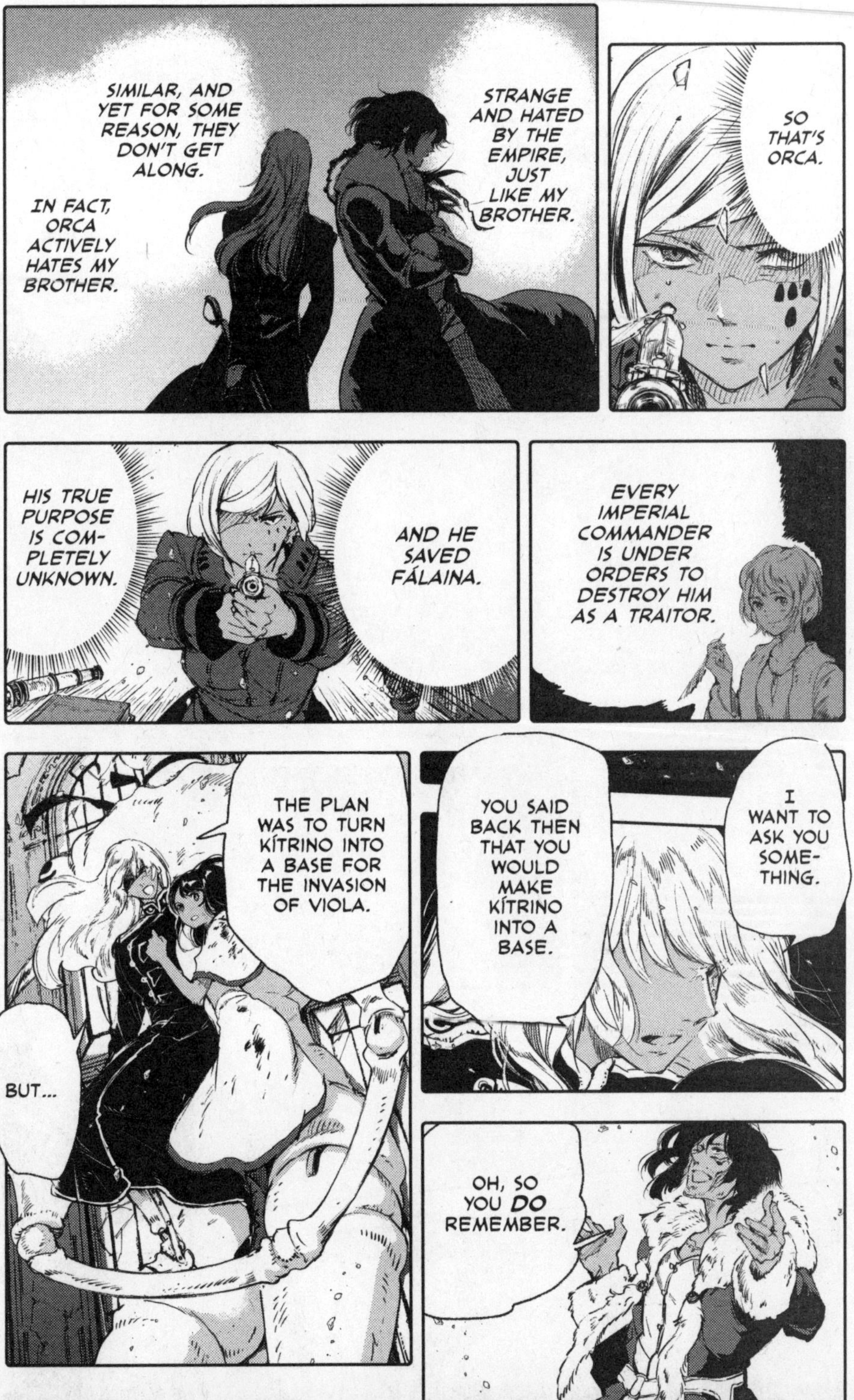
SO THAT'S ORCA.
STRANGE AND HATED BY THE EMPIRE, JUST LIKE MY BROTHER.
SIMILAR, AND YET FOR SOME REASON, THEY DON'T GET ALONG.
IN FACT, ORCA ACTIVELY HATES MY BROTHER.
EVERY IMPERIAL COMMANDER IS UNDER ORDERS TO DESTROY HIM AS A TRAITOR.
AND HE SAVED FÁLAINA.
HIS TRUE PURPOSE IS COM-PLETELY UNKNOWN.
I WANT TO ASK YOU SOME-THING.
YOU SAID BACK THEN THAT YOU WOULD MAKE KÍTRINO INTO A BASE.
OH, SO YOU DO REMEMBER.
THE PLAN WAS TO TURN KÍTRINO INTO A BASE FOR THE INVASION OF VIOLA.
BUT...

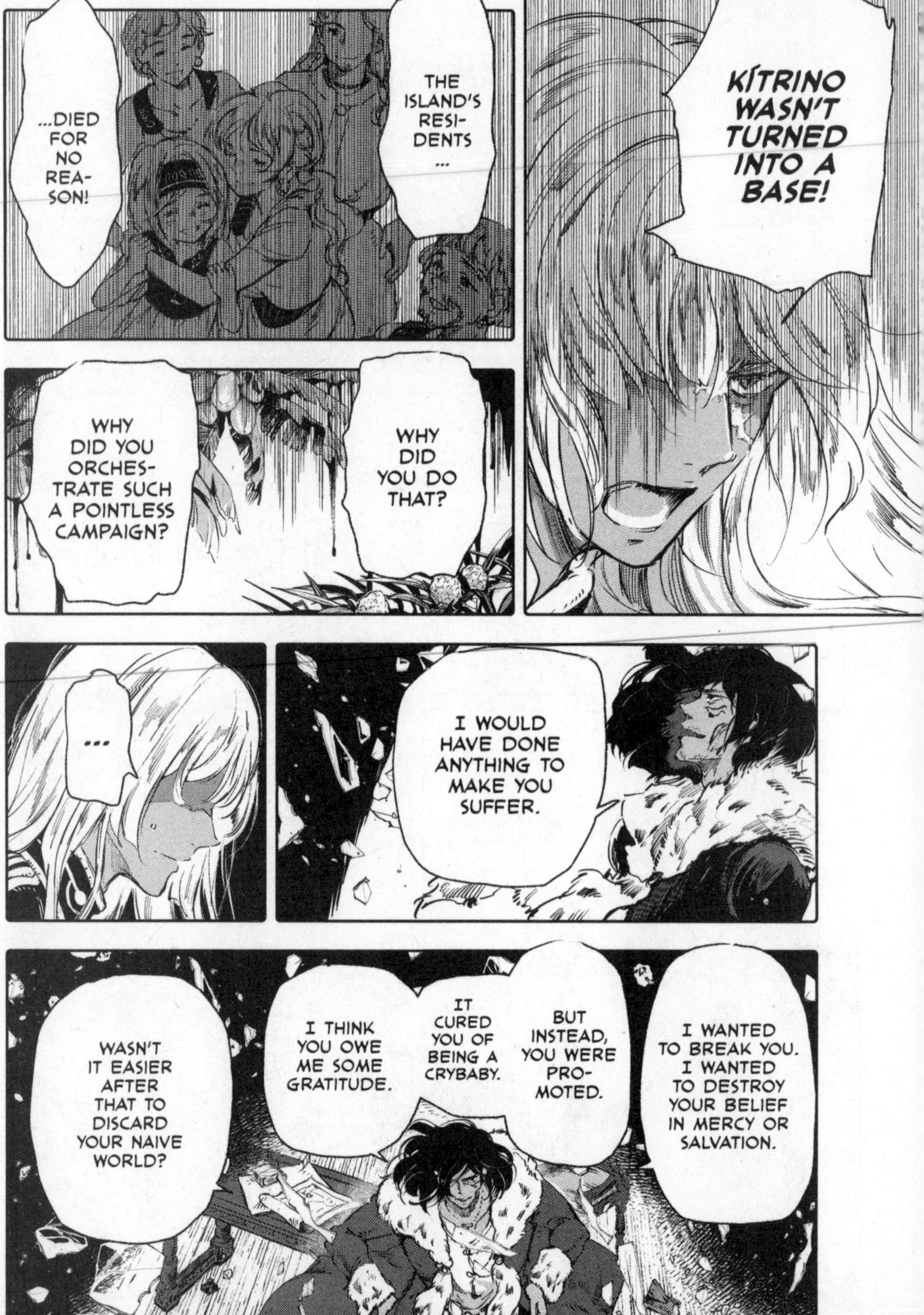
KÍTRINO WASN'T TURNED INTO A BASE!
THE ISLAND'S RESIDENTS ...
...DIED FOR NO REASON!
WHY DID YOU DO THAT?
WHY DID YOU ORCHESTRATE SUCH A POINTLESS CAMPAIGN?
I WOULD HAVE DONE ANYTHING TO MAKE YOU SUFFER.
...
I WANTED TO BREAK YOU. I WANTED TO DESTROY YOUR BELIEF IN MERCY OR SALVATION.
BUT INSTEAD, YOU WERE PROMOTED.
IT CURED YOU OF BEING A CRYBABY.
I THINK YOU OWE ME SOME GRATITUDE.
WASN'T IT EASIER AFTER THAT TO DISCARD YOUR NAIVE WORLD?

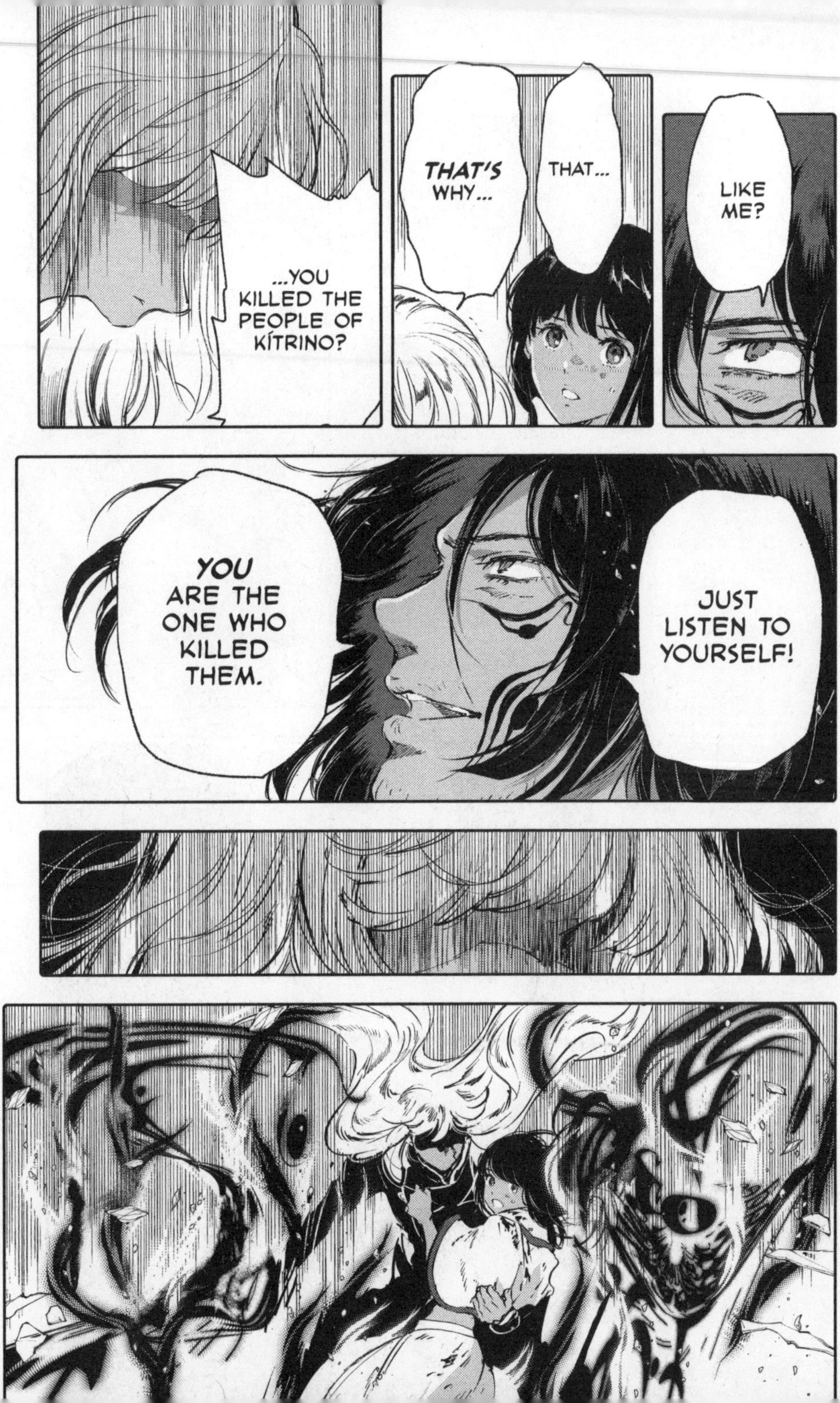
LIKE ME?
THAT...
THAT'S WHY...
...YOU KILLED THE PEOPLE OF KÍTRINO?
JUST LISTEN TO YOURSELF!
YOU ARE THE ONE WHO KILLED THEM.

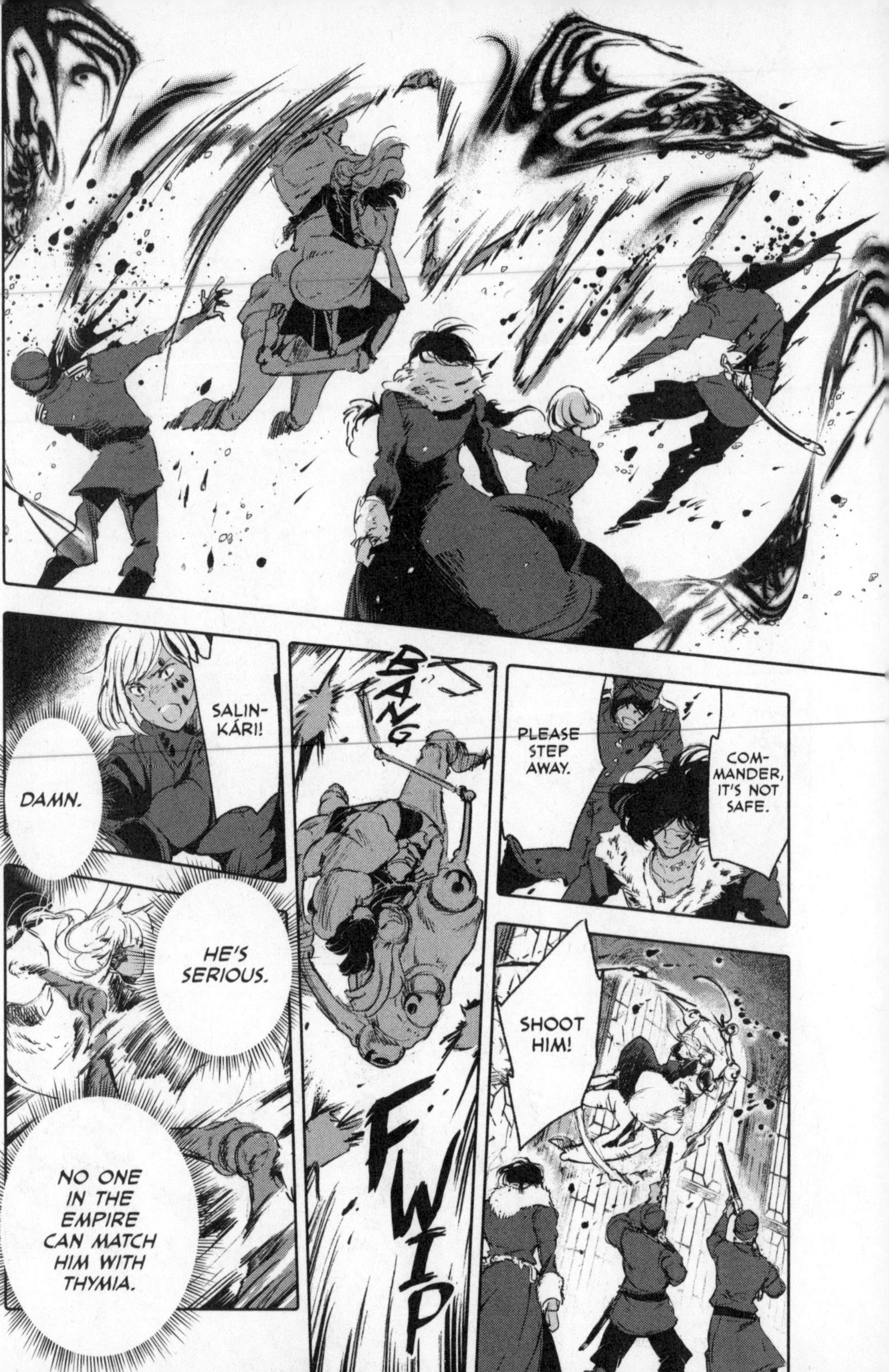
COMMANDER, IT'S NOT SAFE.
PLEASE STEP AWAY.
SHOOT HIM!
BANG
FWIP
SALIN-KÁRI!
DAMN.
HE'S SERIOUS.
NO ONE IN THE EMPIRE CAN MATCH HIM WITH THYMIA.

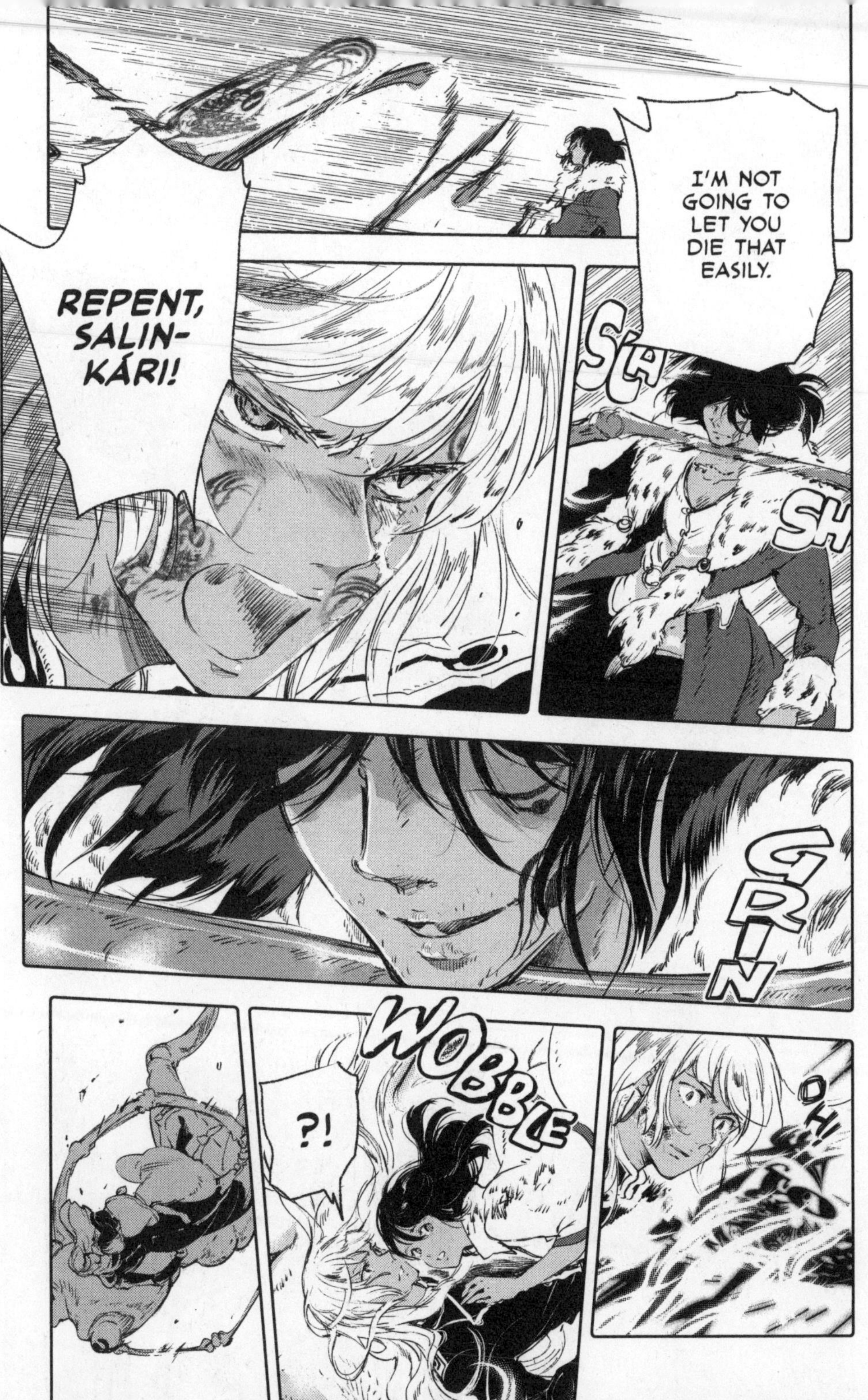
I'M NOT GOING TO LET YOU DIE THAT EASILY.
SH
REPENT, SALIN-KÁRI!
GRIN
OH!!
WOBBLE
?!

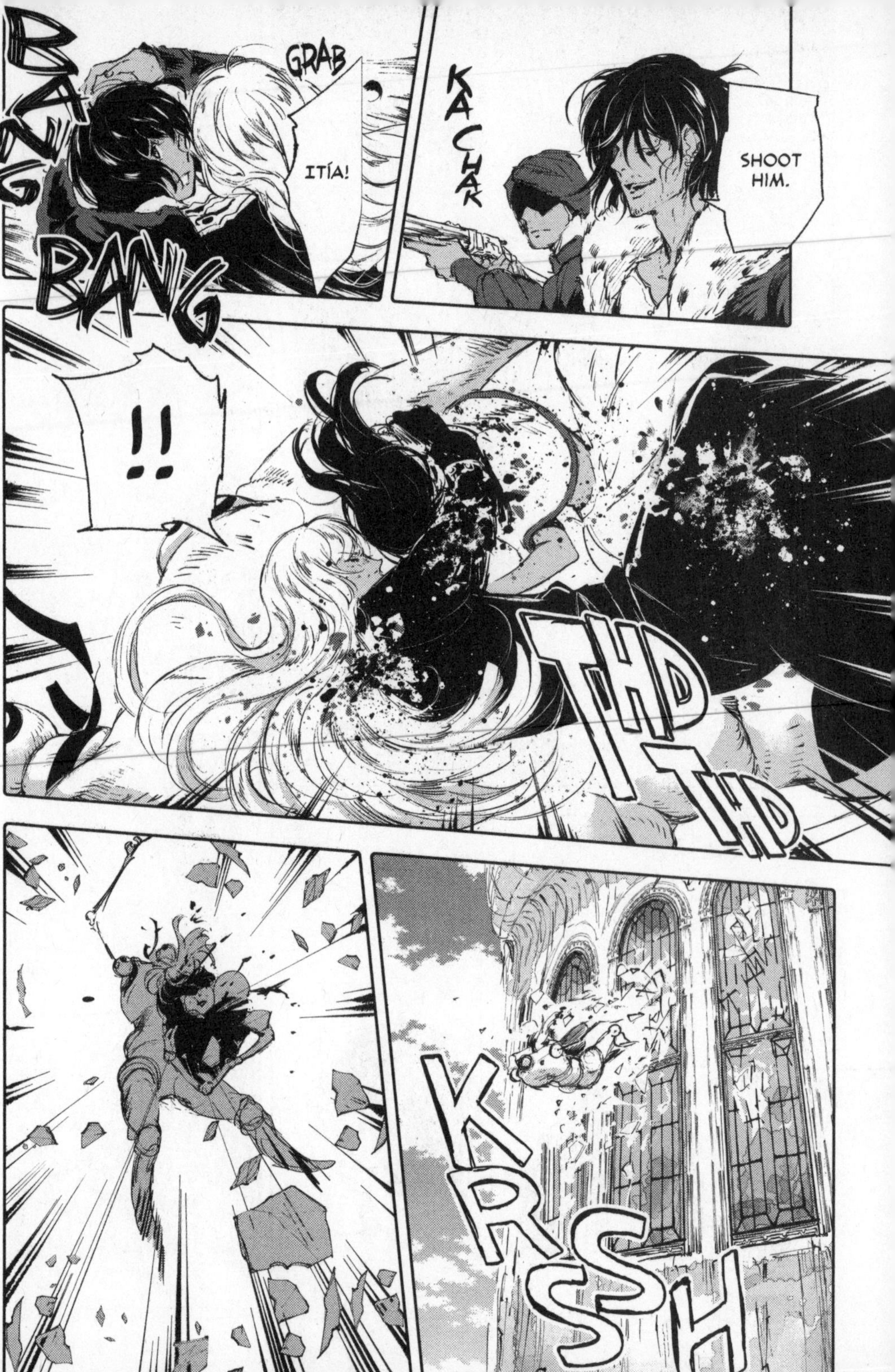
KACHAK
SHOOT HIM.
GRAB
ITÍA!
BANG
BANG
!!
THD
THD
KRSSH

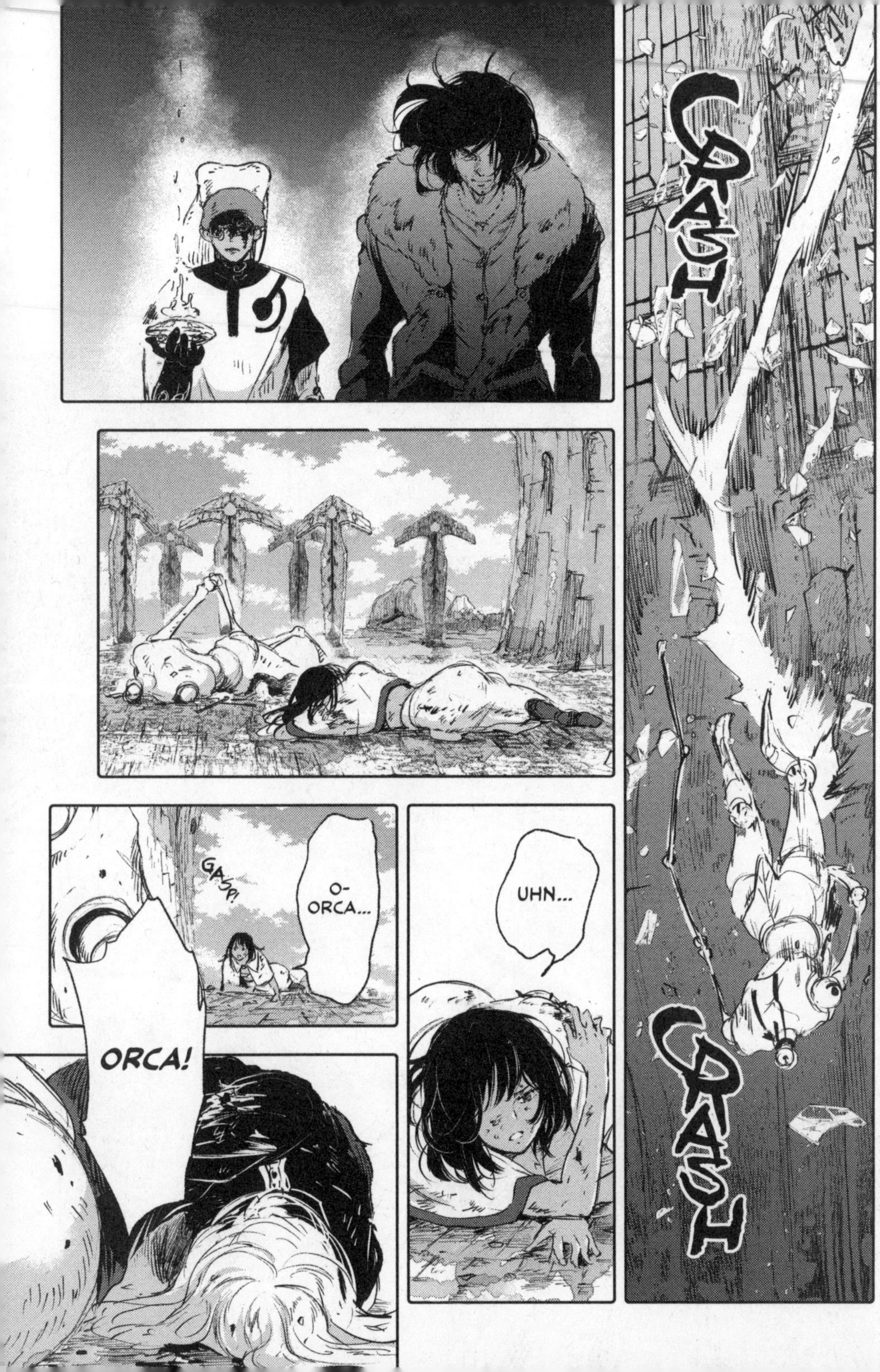
CRASH
CRASH
UHN...
O-ORCA...
GASP!
ORCA!

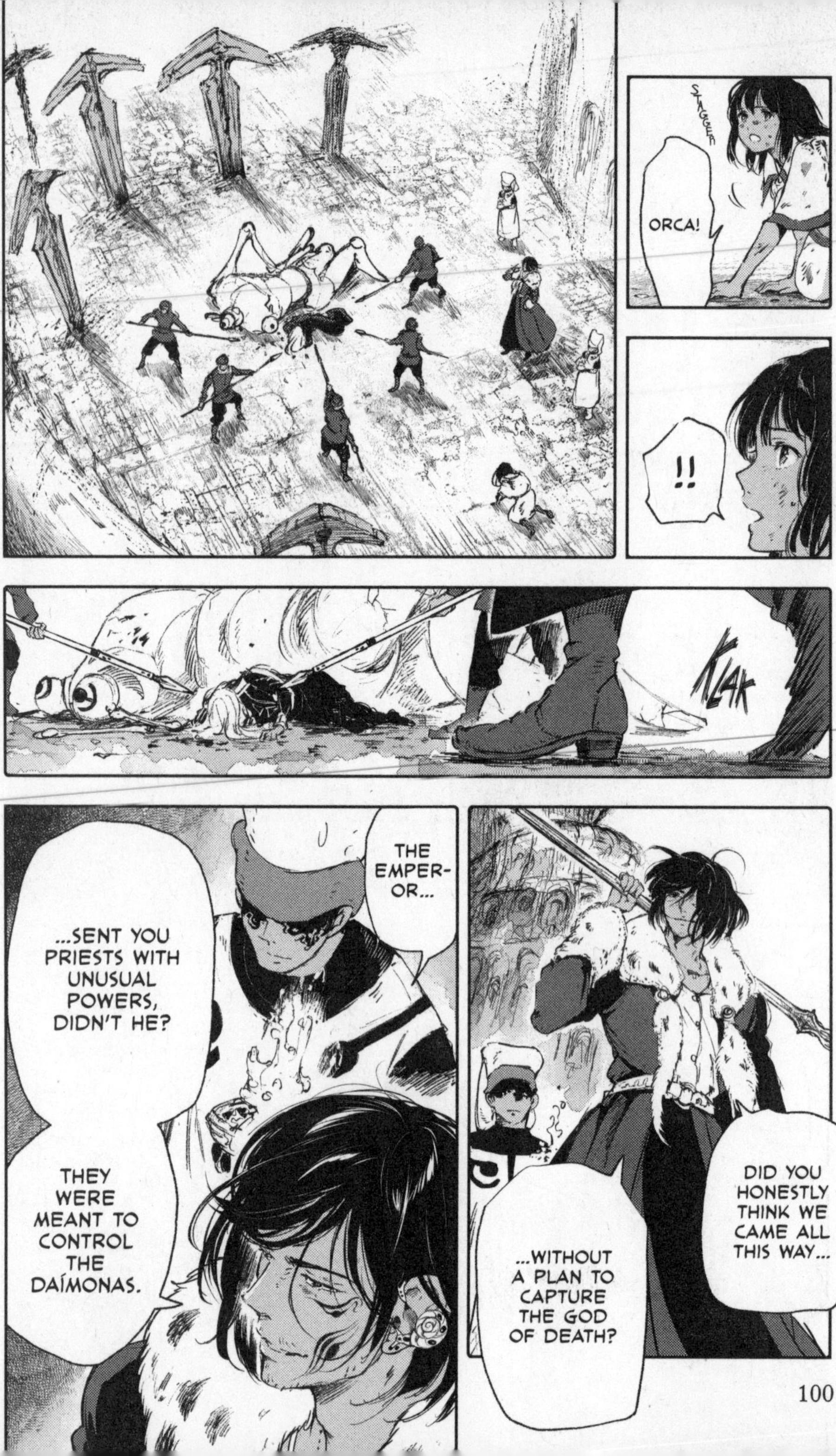
STAGGER
ORCA!
!!
KLAK
DID YOU HONESTLY THINK WE CAME ALL THIS WAY...
...WITHOUT A PLAN TO CAPTURE THE GOD OF DEATH?
THE EMPEROR...
...SENT YOU PRIESTS WITH UNUSUAL POWERS, DIDN'T HE?
THEY WERE MEANT TO CONTROL THE DAÍMONAS.

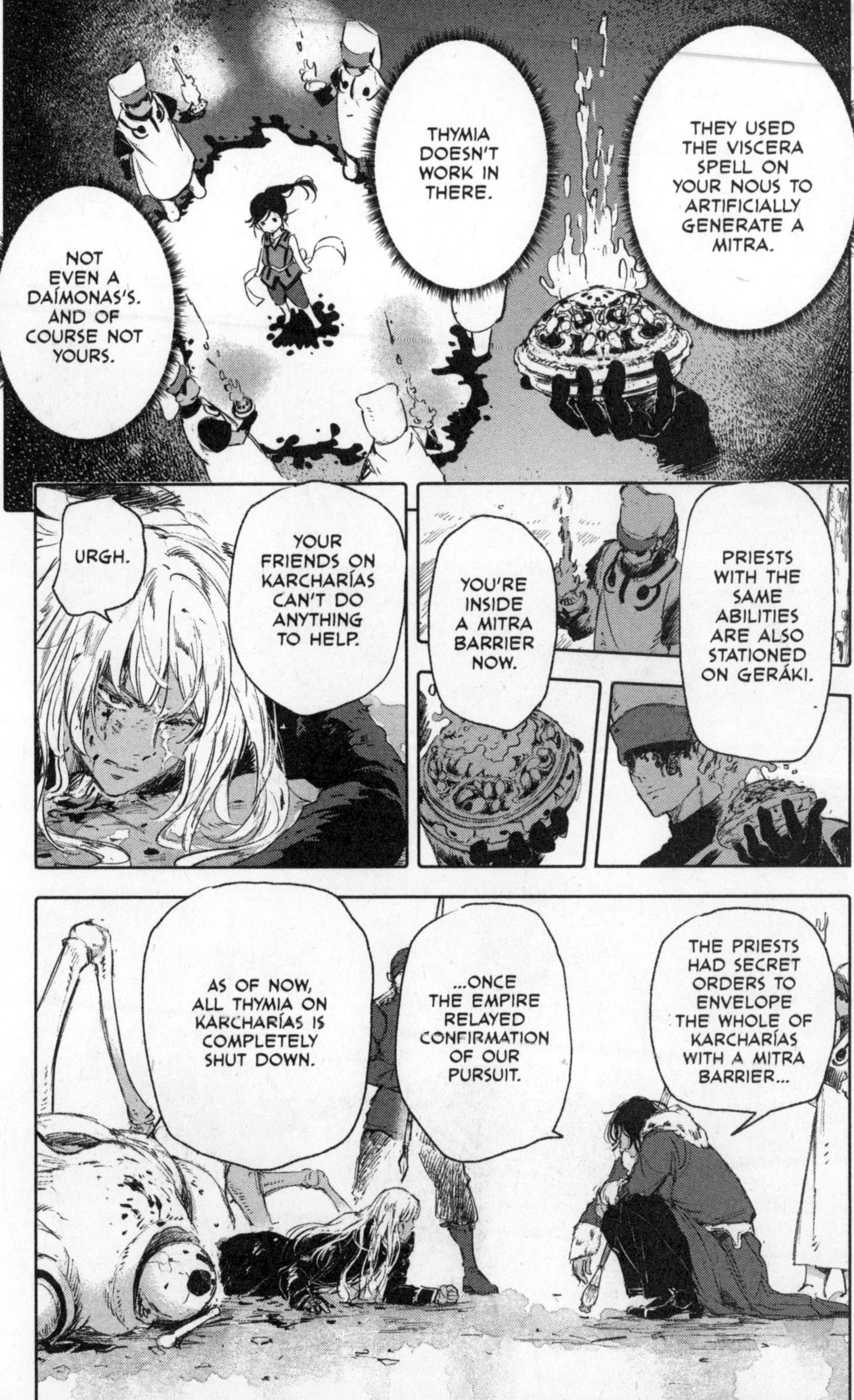
THEY USED THE VISCERA SPELL ON YOUR NOUS TO ARTIFICIALLY GENERATE A MITRA.
THYMIA DOESN'T WORK IN THERE.
NOT EVEN A DAÍMONAS'S. AND OF COURSE NOT YOURS.
PRIESTS WITH THE SAME ABILITIES ARE ALSO STATIONED ON GERÁKI.
YOU'RE INSIDE A MITRA BARRIER NOW.
YOUR FRIENDS ON KARCHARÍAS CAN'T DO ANYTHING TO HELP.
URGH.
THE PRIESTS HAD SECRET ORDERS TO ENVELOPE THE WHOLE OF KARCHARÍAS WITH A MITRA BARRIER...
...ONCE THE EMPIRE RELAYED CONFIRMATION OF OUR PURSUIT.
AS OF NOW, ALL THYMIA ON KARCHARÍAS IS COMPLETELY SHUT DOWN.

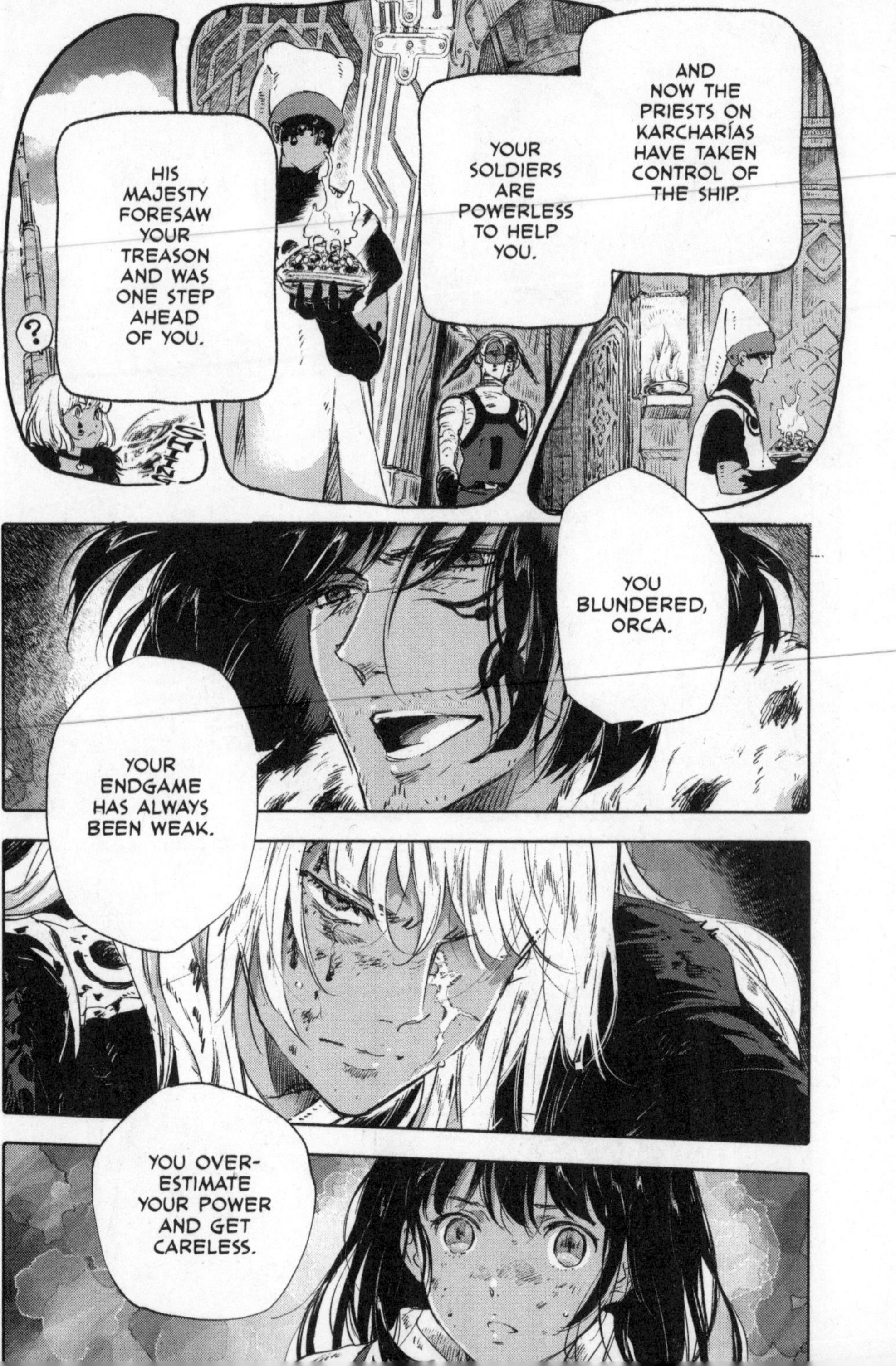
AND NOW THE PRIESTS ON KARCHARÍAS HAVE TAKEN CONTROL OF THE SHIP.
YOUR SOLDIERS ARE POWERLESS TO HELP YOU.
HIS MAJESTY FORESAW YOUR TREASON AND WAS ONE STEP AHEAD OF YOU.
?
SHIING
YOU BLUNDERED, ORCA.
YOUR ENDGAME HAS ALWAYS BEEN WEAK.
YOU OVER-ESTIMATE YOUR POWER AND GET CARELESS.

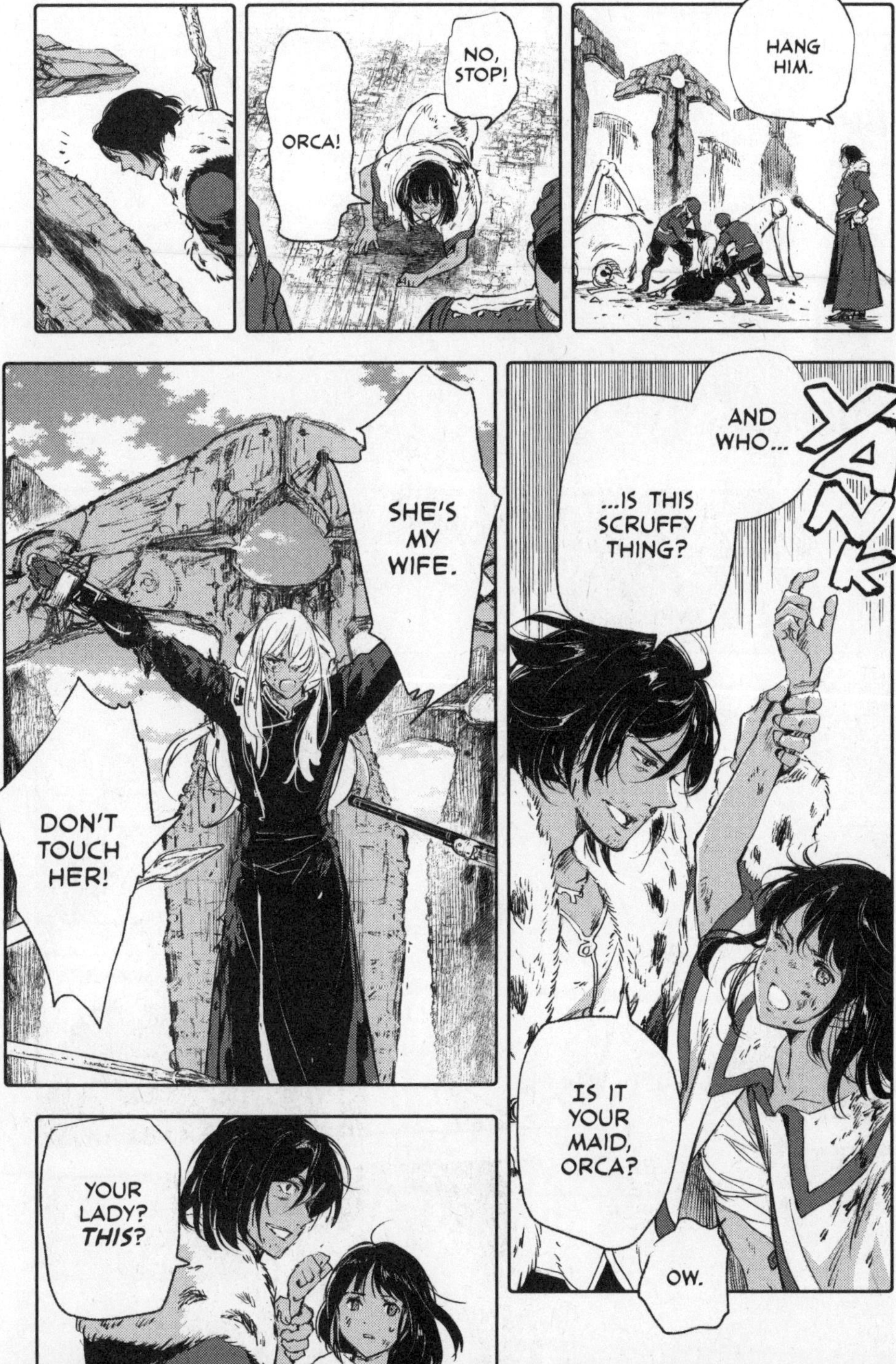
HANG HIM.
NO, STOP!
ORCA!
YANK
AND WHO...
...IS THIS SCRUFFY THING?
IS IT YOUR MAID, ORCA?
OW.
SHE'S MY WIFE.
DON'T TOUCH HER!
YOUR LADY? *THIS*?

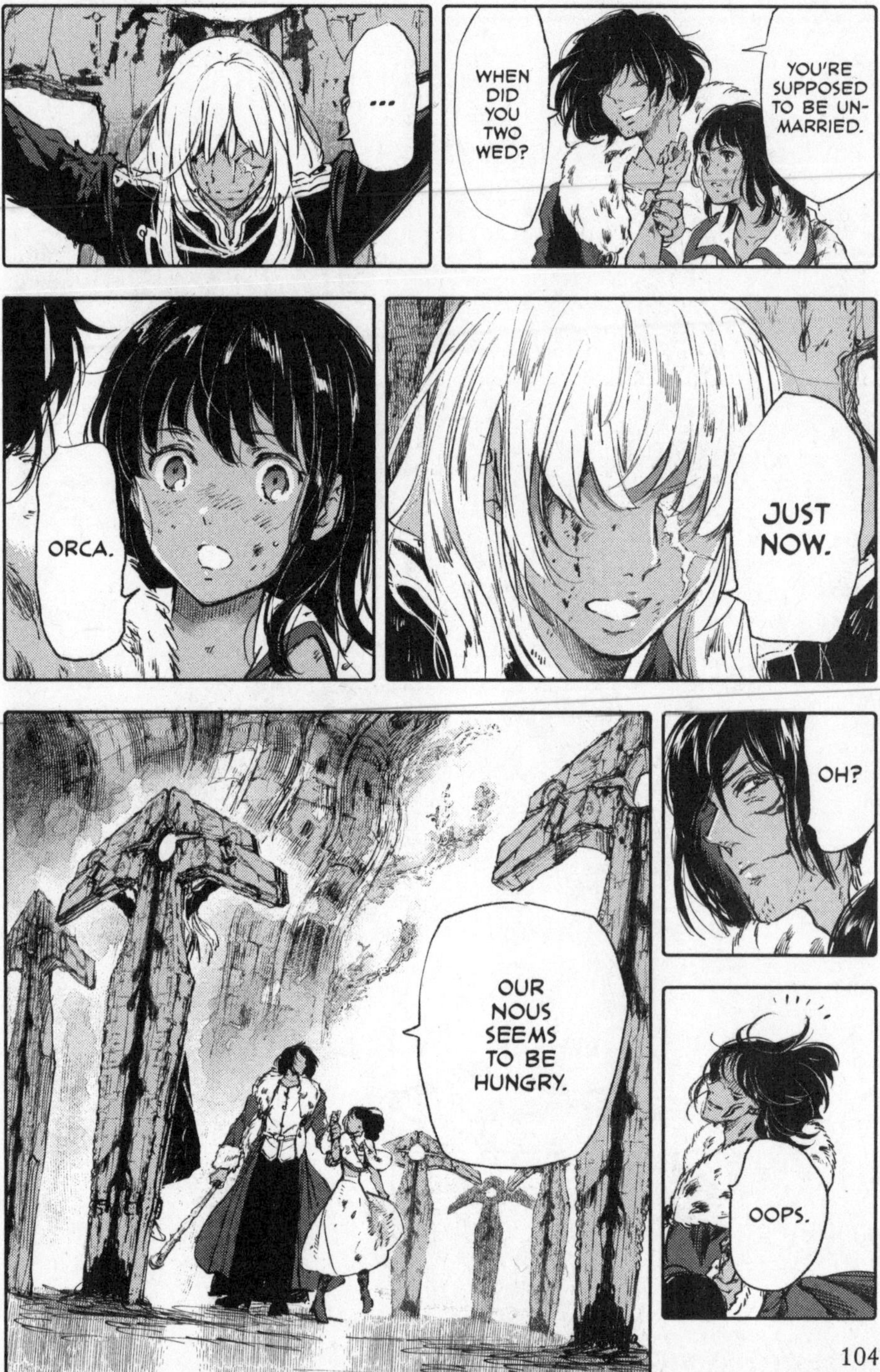
YOU'RE SUPPOSED TO BE UN-MARRIED.
WHEN DID YOU TWO WED?
...
JUST NOW.
ORCA.
OH?
OOPS.
OUR NOUS SEEMS TO BE HUNGRY.

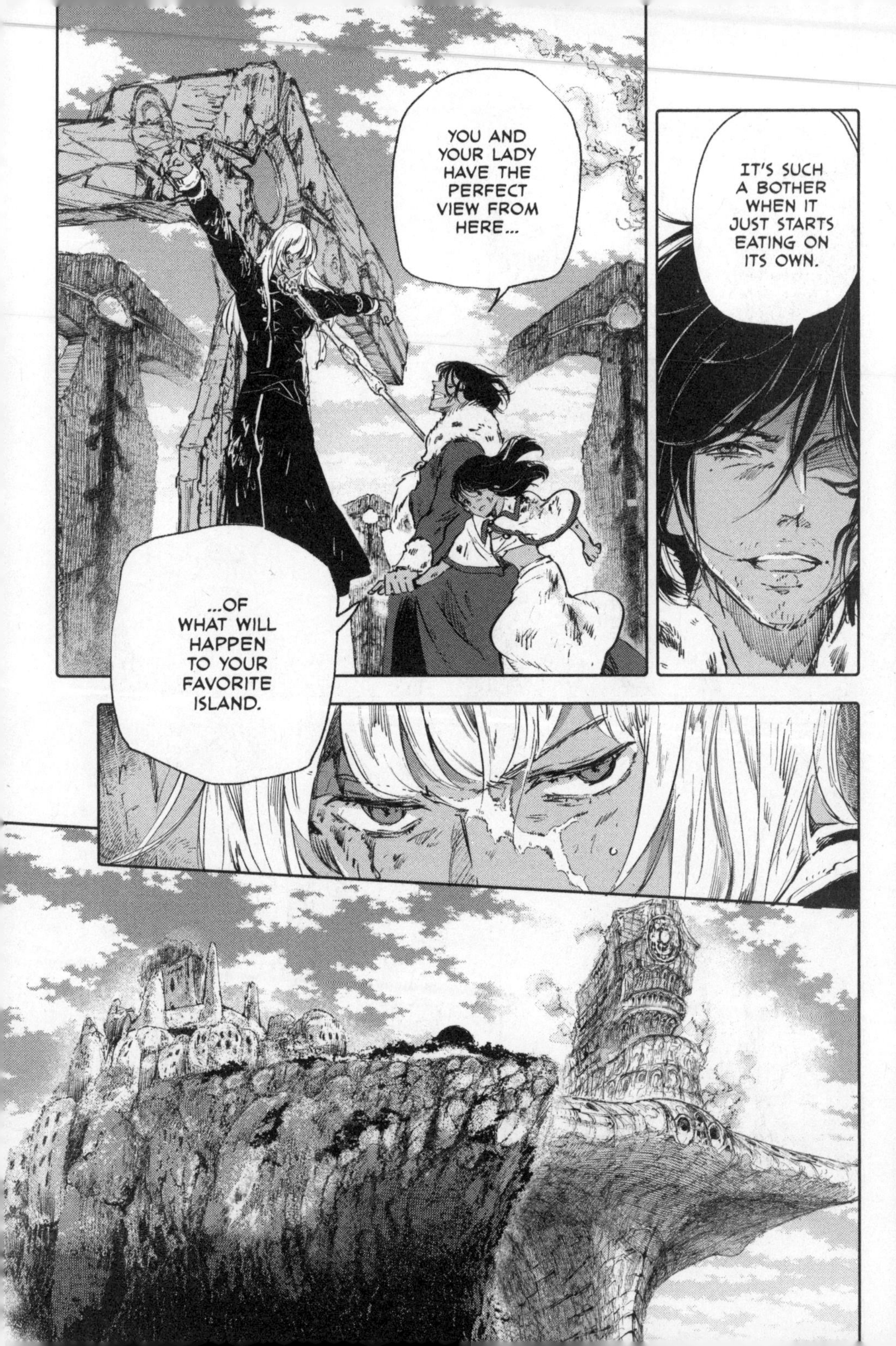
IT'S SUCH A BOTHER WHEN IT JUST STARTS EATING ON ITS OWN.
YOU AND YOUR LADY HAVE THE PERFECT VIEW FROM HERE...
...OF WHAT WILL HAPPEN TO YOUR FAVORITE ISLAND.

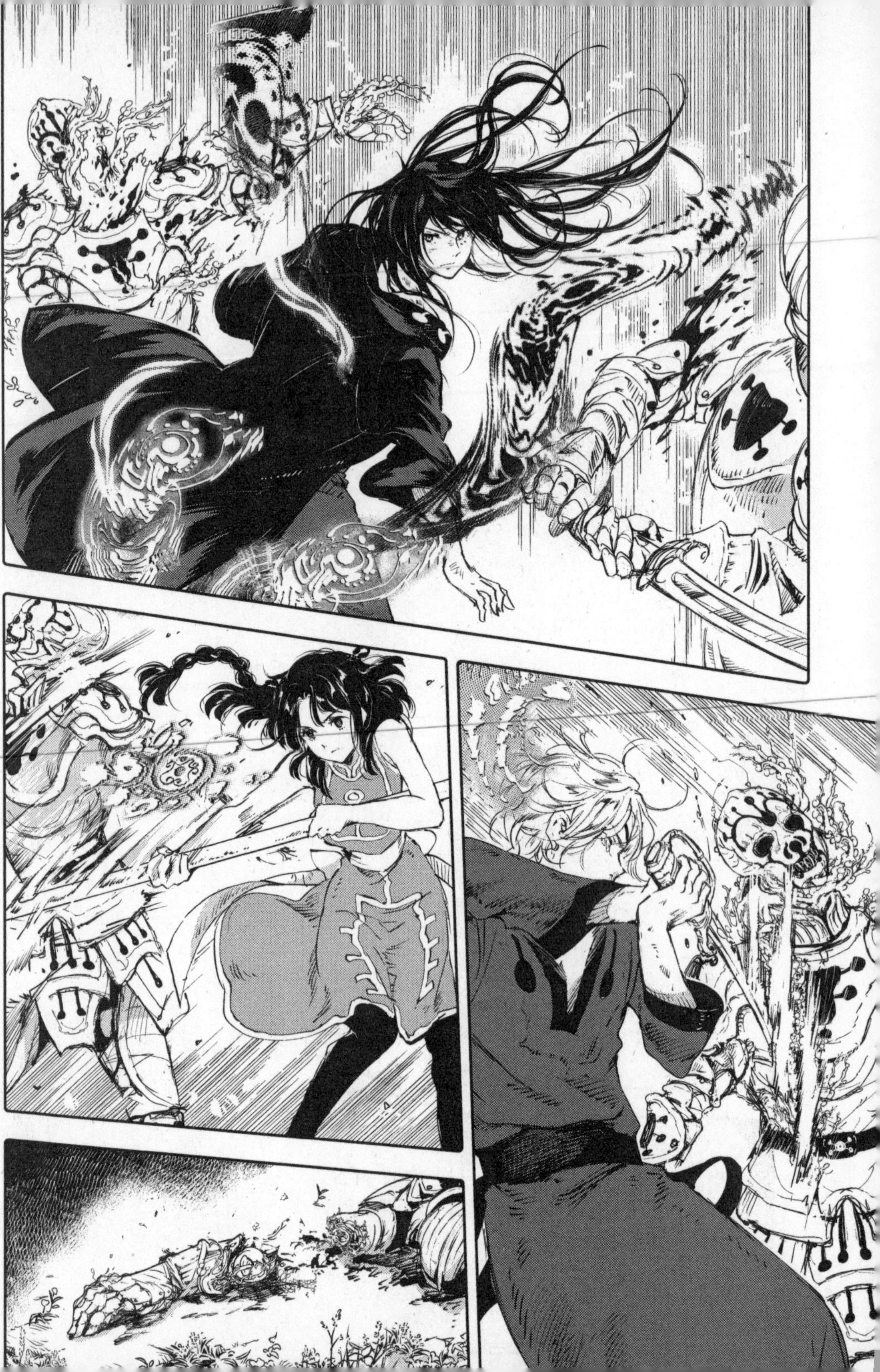

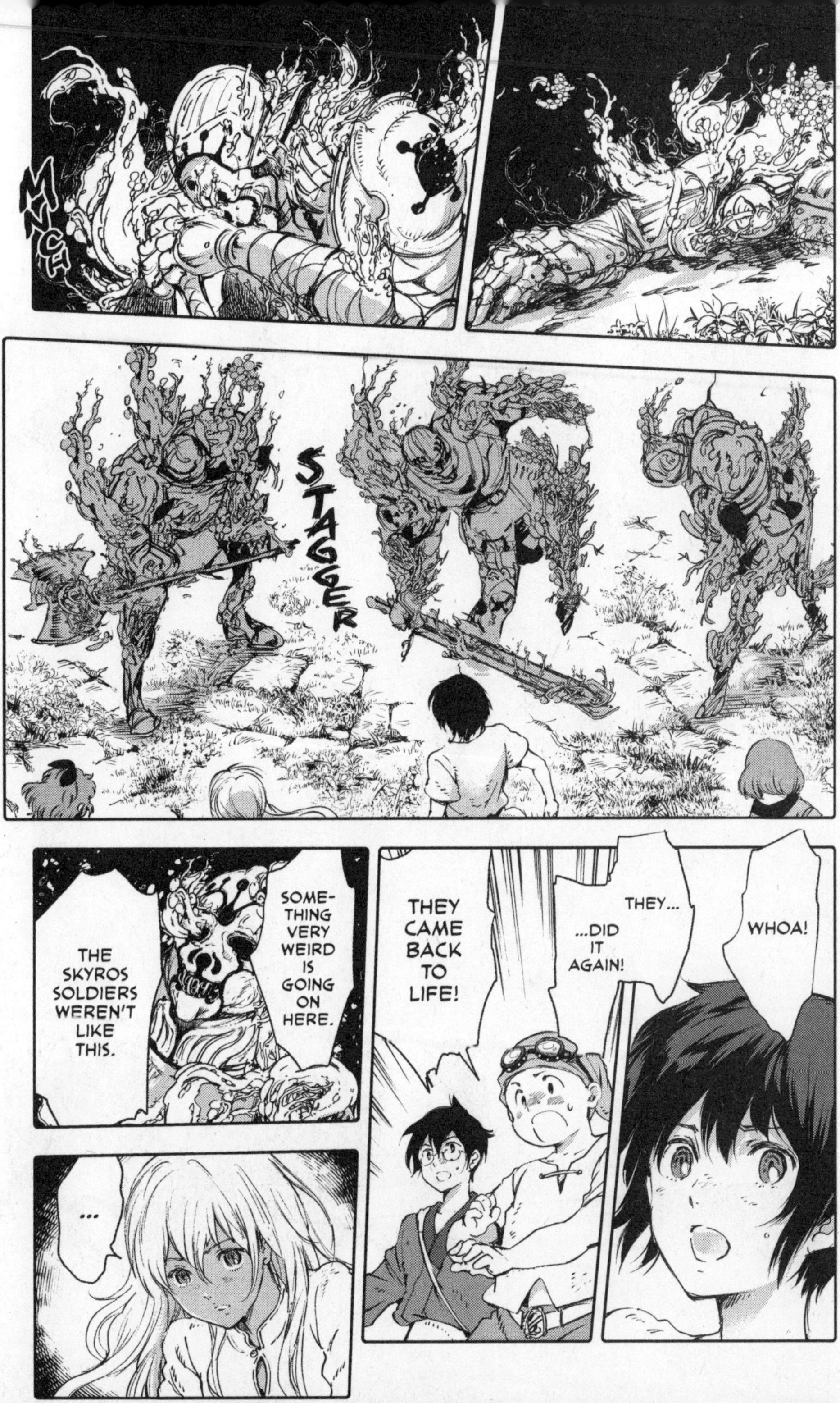
MUNCH
STAGGER
WHOA!
THEY...
...DID IT AGAIN!
THEY CAME BACK TO LIFE!
SOME-THING VERY WEIRD IS GOING ON HERE.
THE SKYROS SOLDIERS WEREN'T LIKE THIS.
...

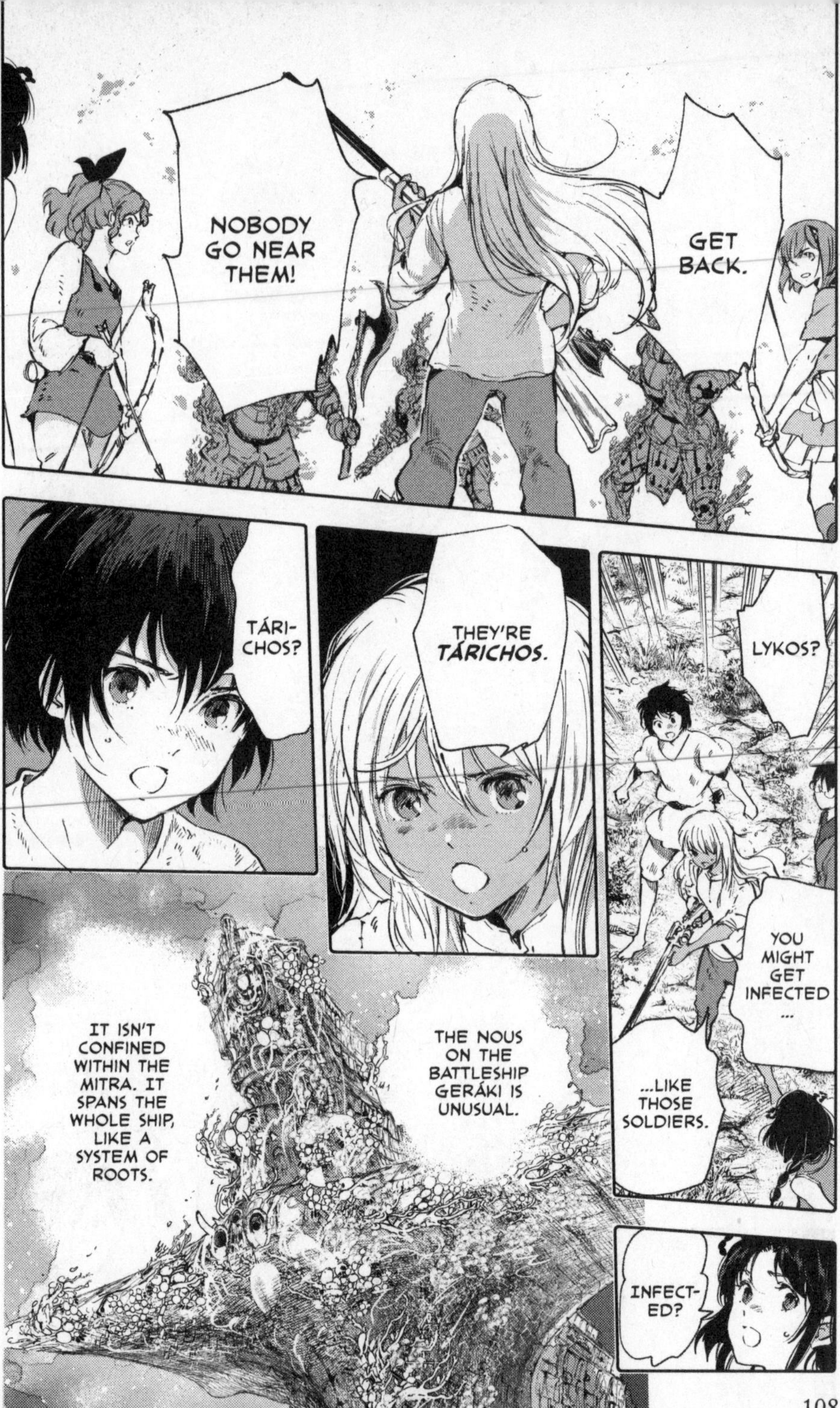
GET BACK.
NOBODY GO NEAR THEM!
LYKOS?
YOU MIGHT GET INFECTED ...
...LIKE THOSE SOLDIERS.
INFECT-ED?
THEY'RE *TÁRICHOS*.
TÁRI-CHOS?
THE NOUS ON THE BATTLESHIP GERÁKI IS UNUSUAL.
IT ISN'T CONFINED WITHIN THE MITRA. IT SPANS THE WHOLE SHIP, LIKE A SYSTEM OF ROOTS.

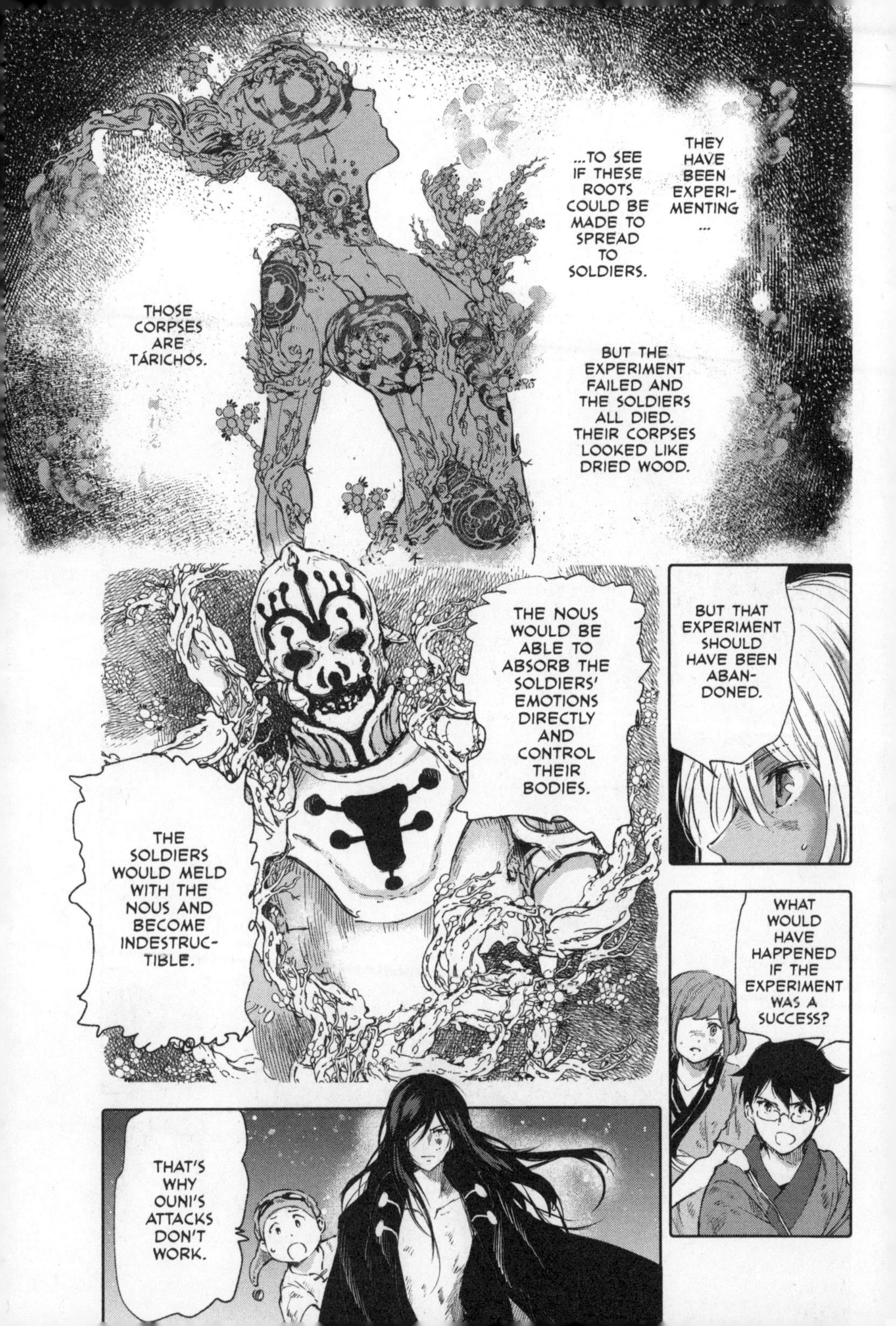
THEY HAVE BEEN EXPERIMENTING ...
...TO SEE IF THESE ROOTS COULD BE MADE TO SPREAD TO SOLDIERS.
BUT THE EXPERIMENT FAILED AND THE SOLDIERS ALL DIED. THEIR CORPSES LOOKED LIKE DRIED WOOD.
THOSE CORPSES ARE TÁRICHOS.
BUT THAT EXPERIMENT SHOULD HAVE BEEN ABANDONED.
WHAT WOULD HAVE HAPPENED IF THE EXPERIMENT WAS A SUCCESS?
THE NOUS WOULD BE ABLE TO ABSORB THE SOLDIERS' EMOTIONS DIRECTLY AND CONTROL THEIR BODIES.
THE SOLDIERS WOULD MELD WITH THE NOUS AND BECOME INDESTRUCTIBLE.
THAT'S WHY OUNI'S ATTACKS DON'T WORK.

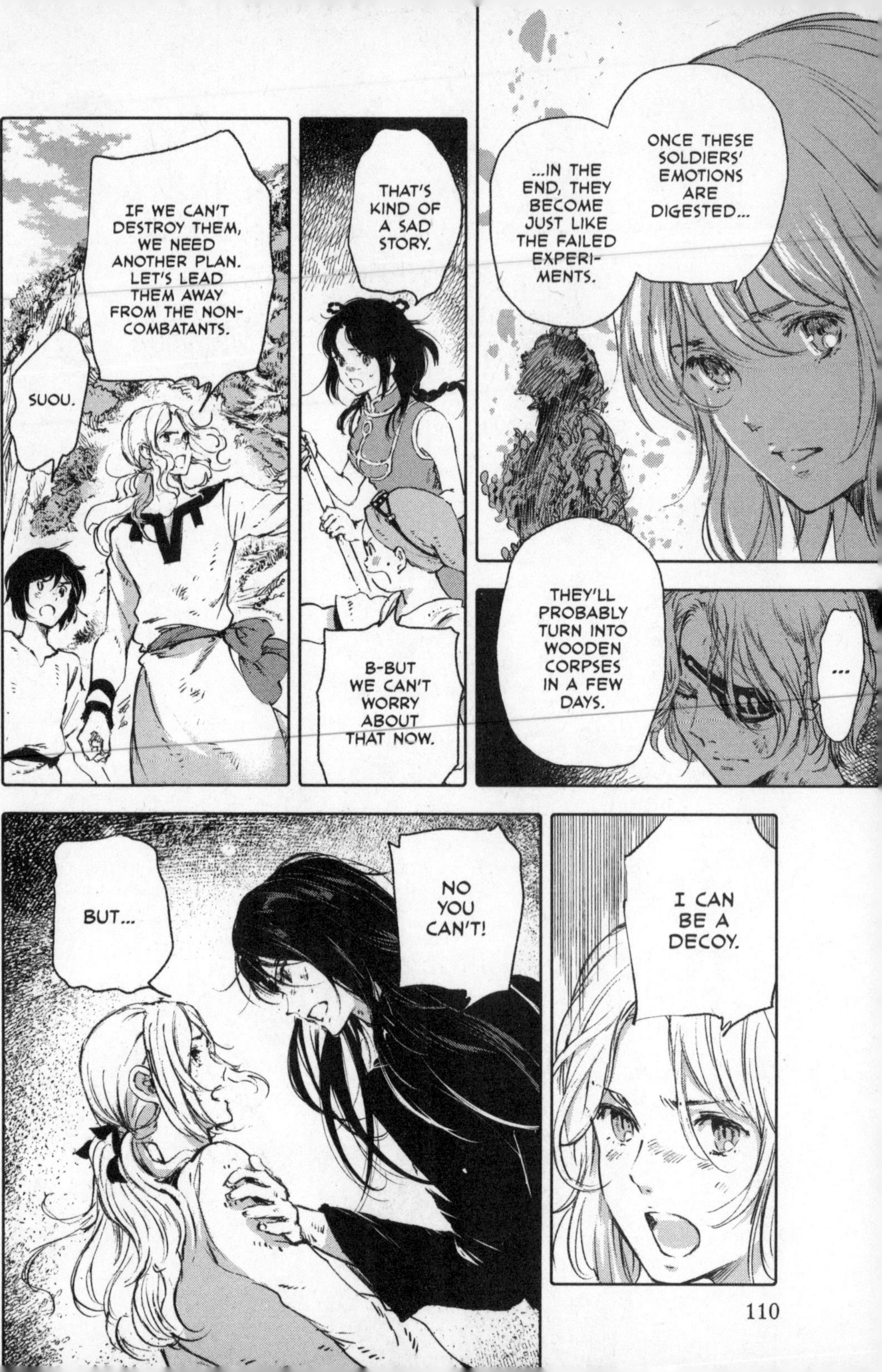
ONCE THESE SOLDIERS' EMOTIONS ARE DIGESTED...
...IN THE END, THEY BECOME JUST LIKE THE FAILED EXPERIMENTS.
THEY'LL PROBABLY TURN INTO WOODEN CORPSES IN A FEW DAYS.
...
THAT'S KIND OF A SAD STORY.
B-BUT WE CAN'T WORRY ABOUT THAT NOW.
IF WE CAN'T DESTROY THEM, WE NEED ANOTHER PLAN. LET'S LEAD THEM AWAY FROM THE NON-COMBATANTS.
SUOU.
I CAN BE A DECOY.
NO YOU CAN'T!
BUT...

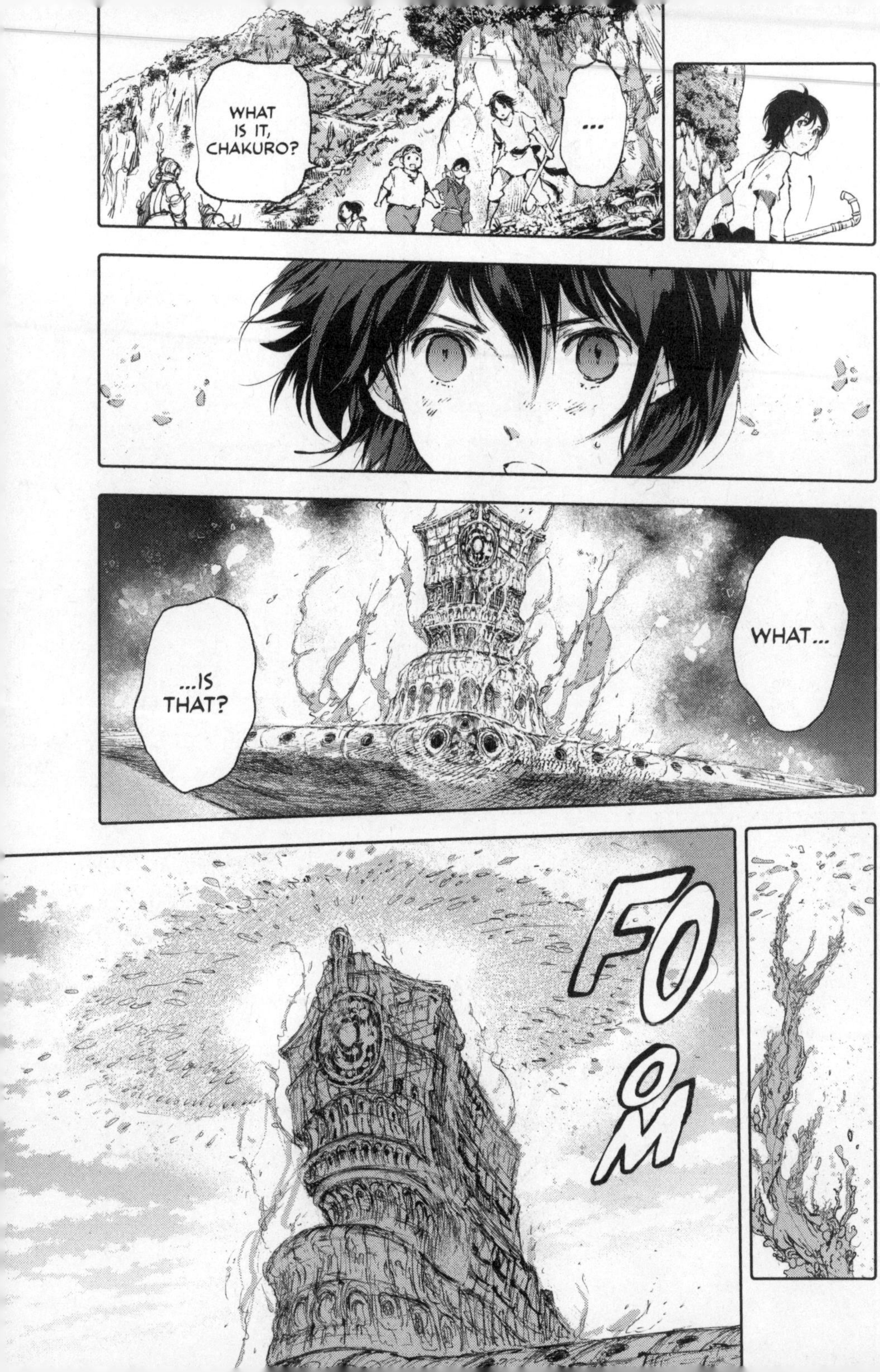
...
WHAT IS IT, CHAKURO?
WHAT...
...IS THAT?
FOOM

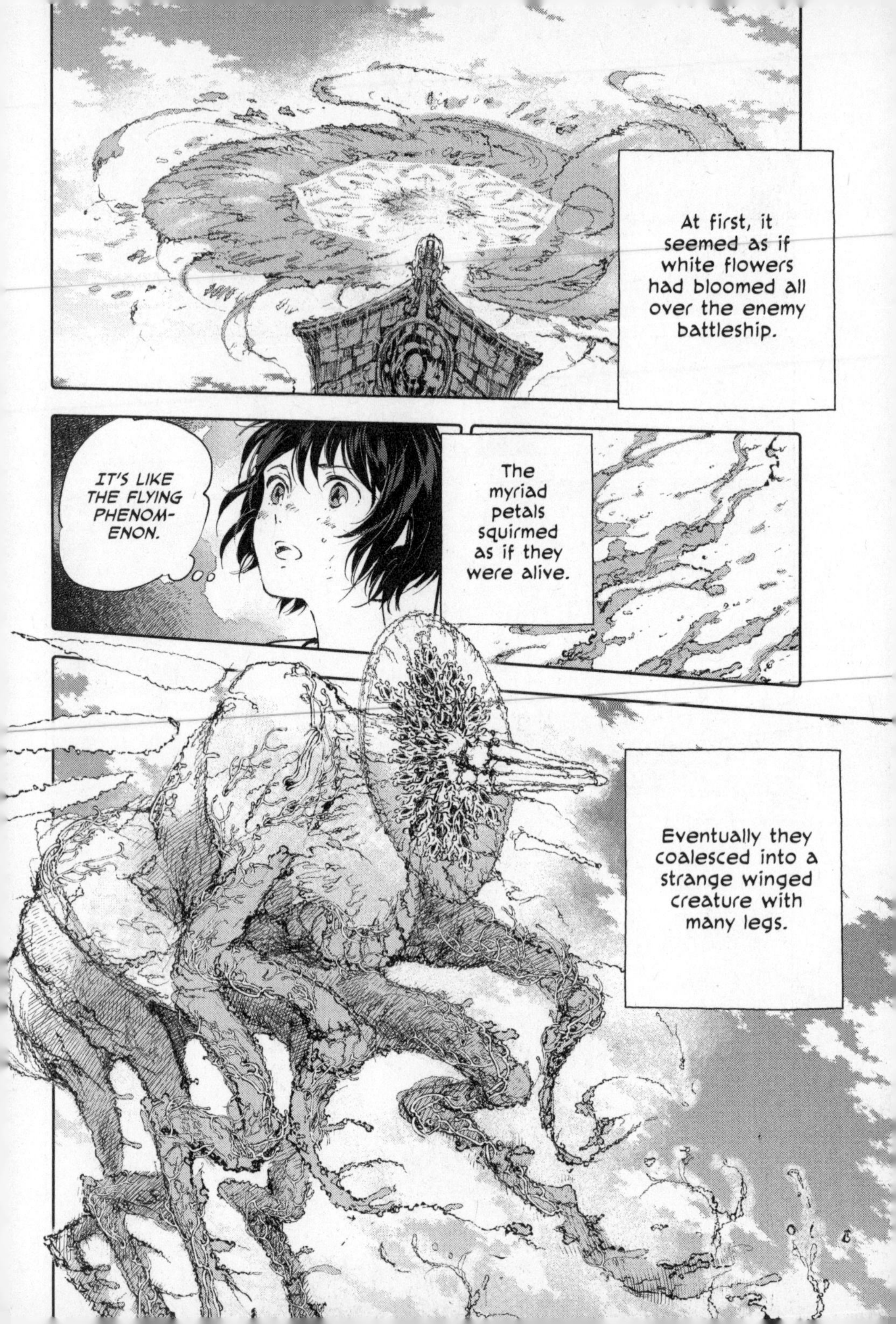
At first, it seemed as if white flowers had bloomed all over the enemy battleship.
The myriad petals squirmed as if they were alive.
IT'S LIKE THE FLYING PHENOM-ENON.
Eventually they coalesced into a strange winged creature with many legs.

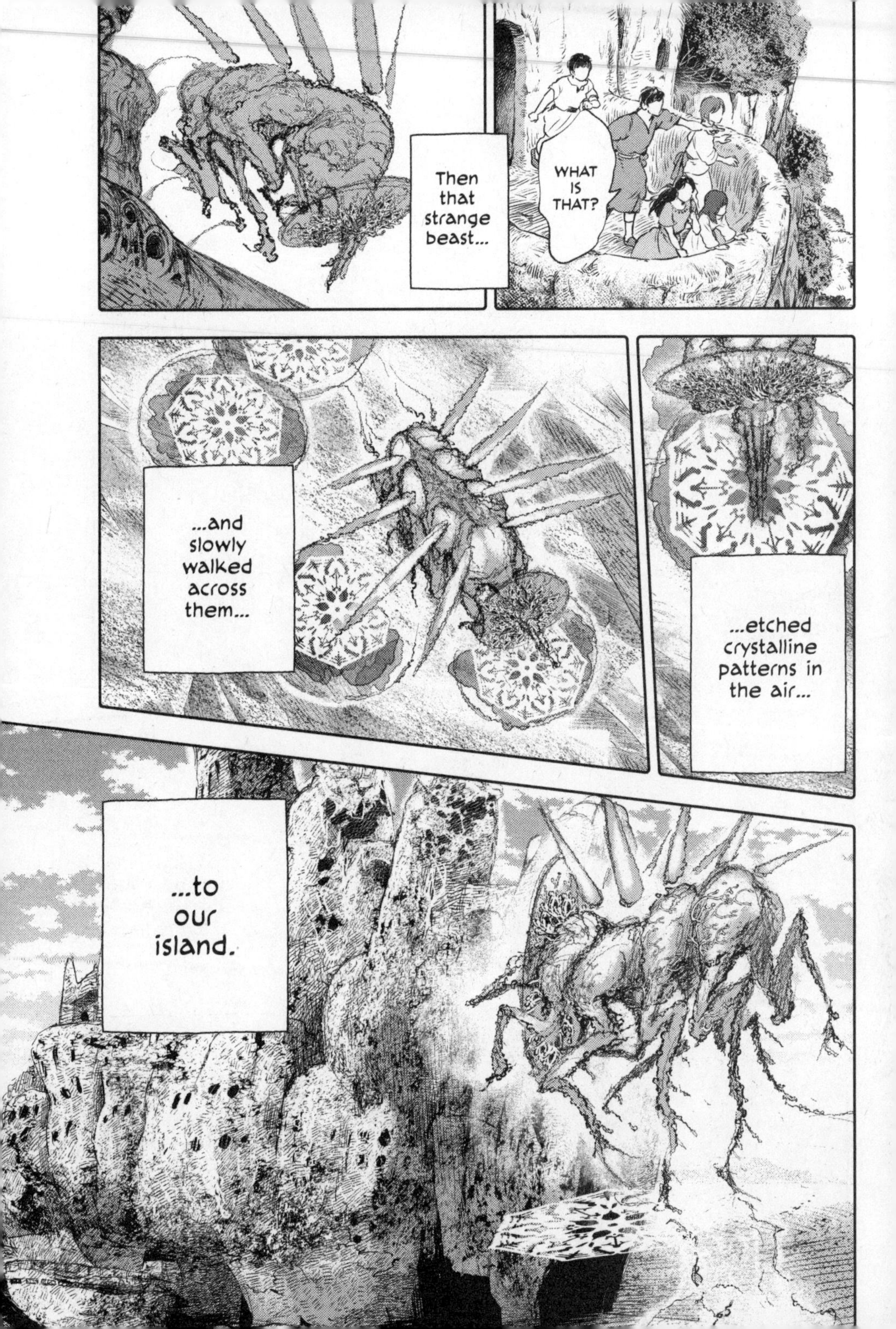
WHAT IS THAT?
Then that strange beast...
...etched crystalline patterns in the air...
...and slowly walked across them...
...to our island.

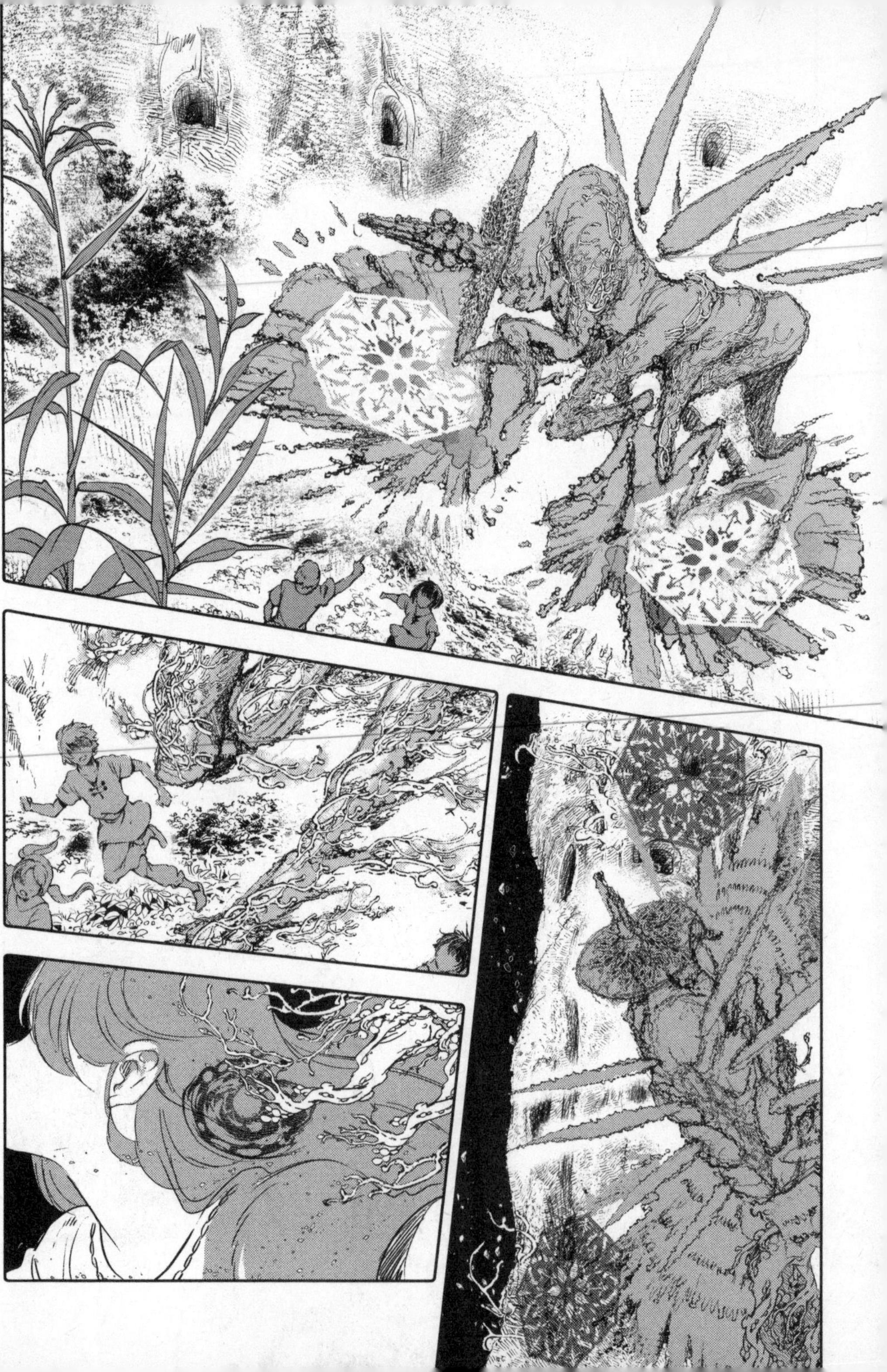

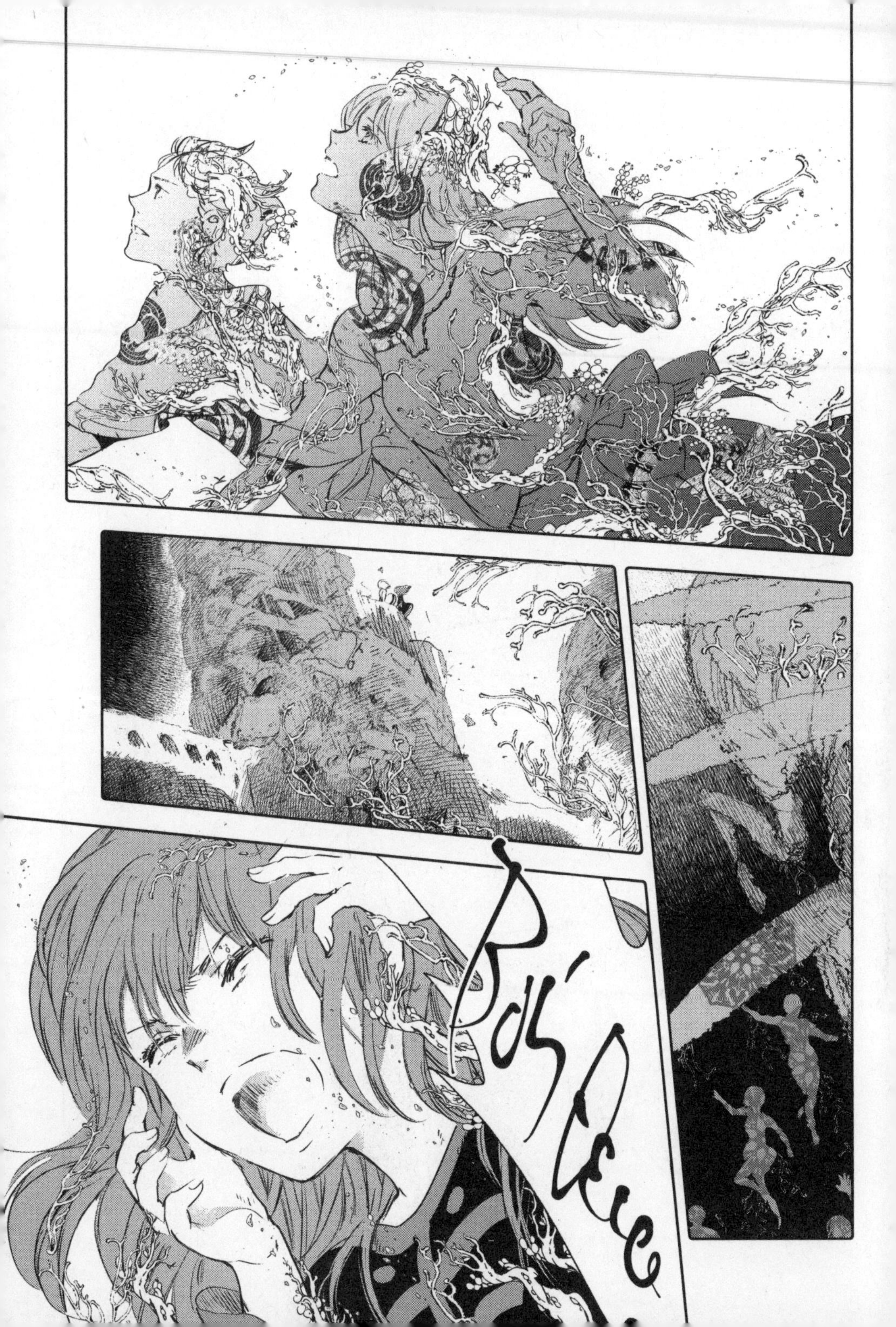

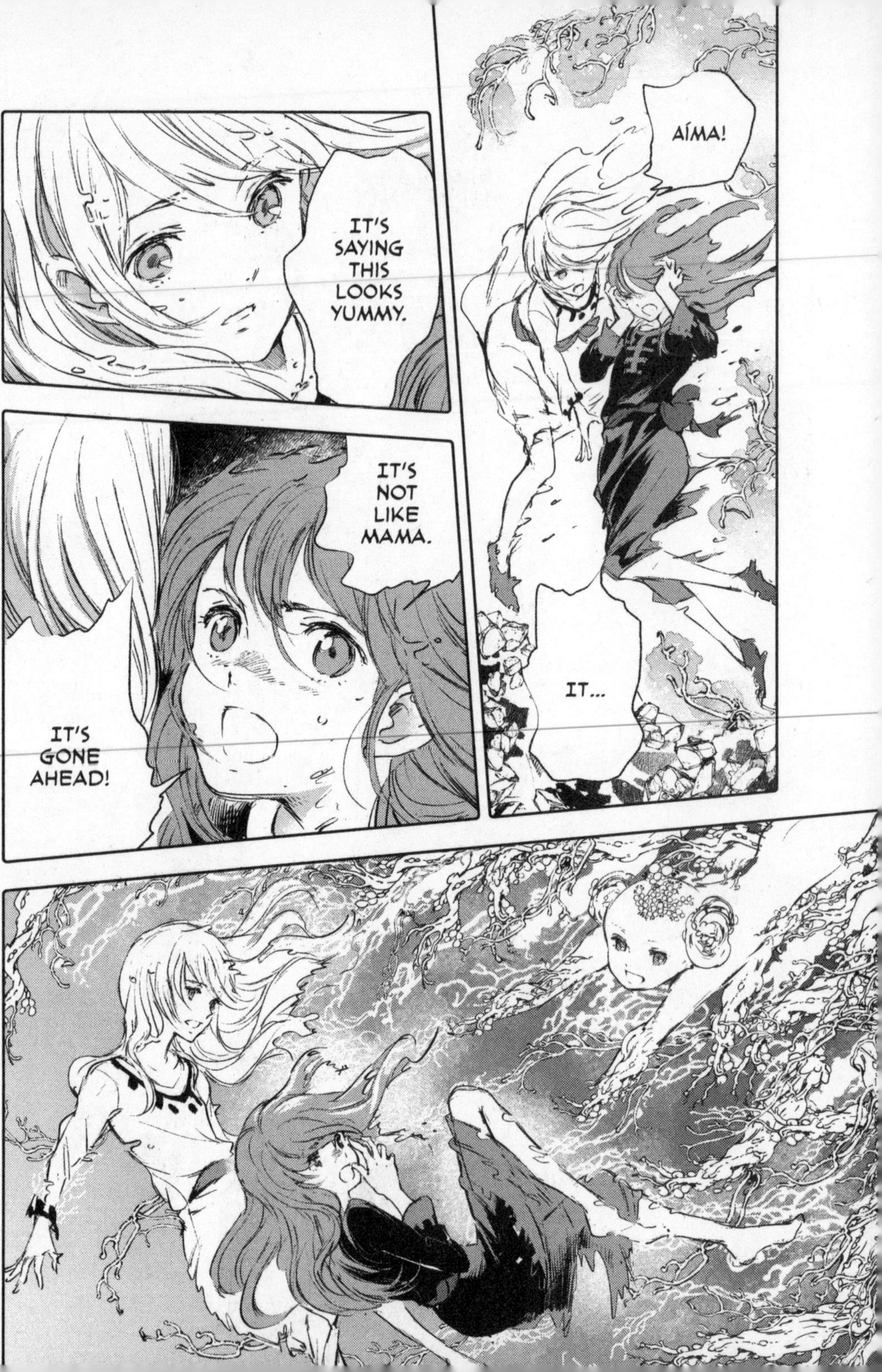
AÍMA!
IT...
IT'S SAYING THIS LOOKS YUMMY.
IT'S NOT LIKE MAMA.
IT'S GONE AHEAD!

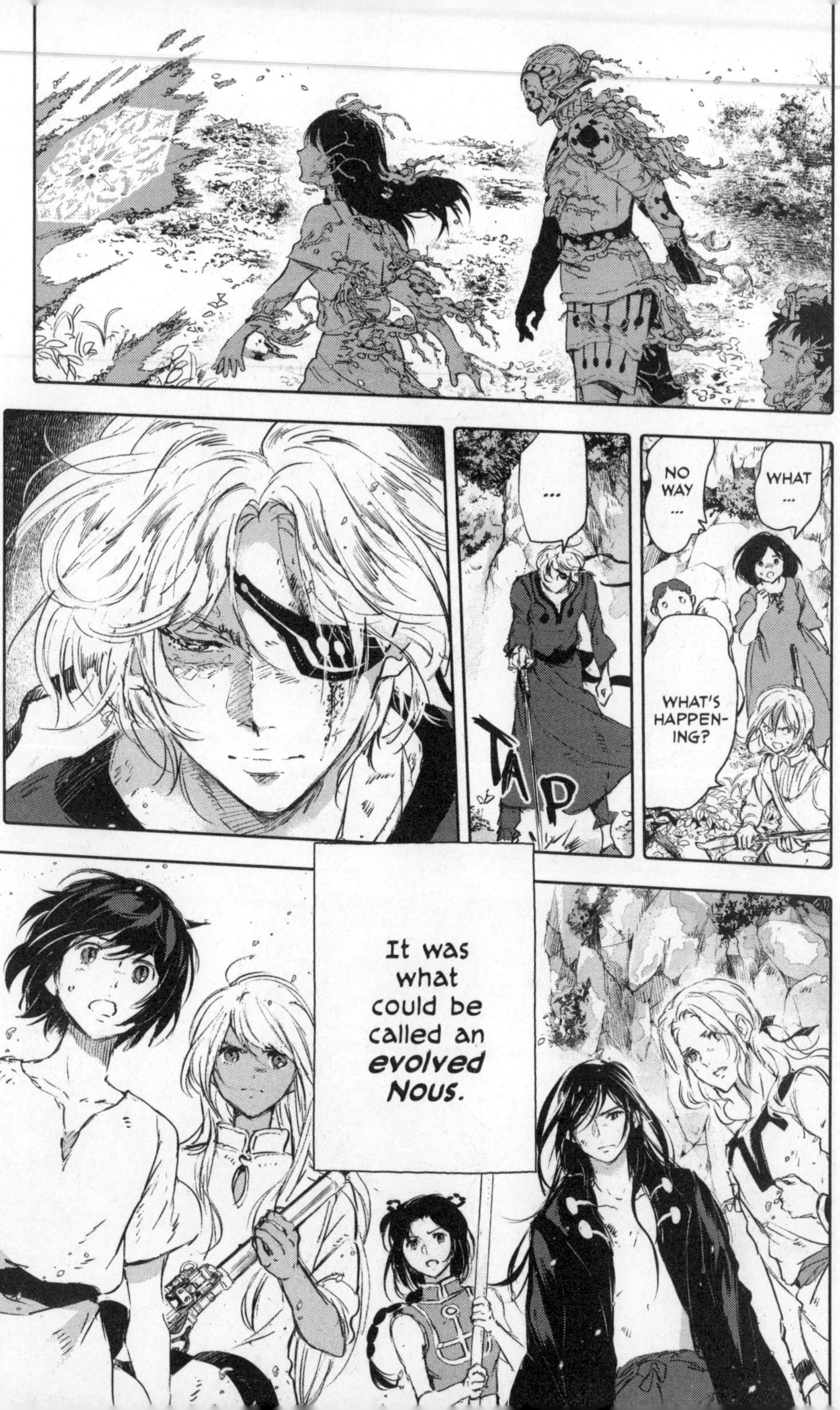
WHAT ...
NO WAY ...
WHAT'S HAPPEN-ING?
...
TAP
It was what could be called an *evolved Nous*.

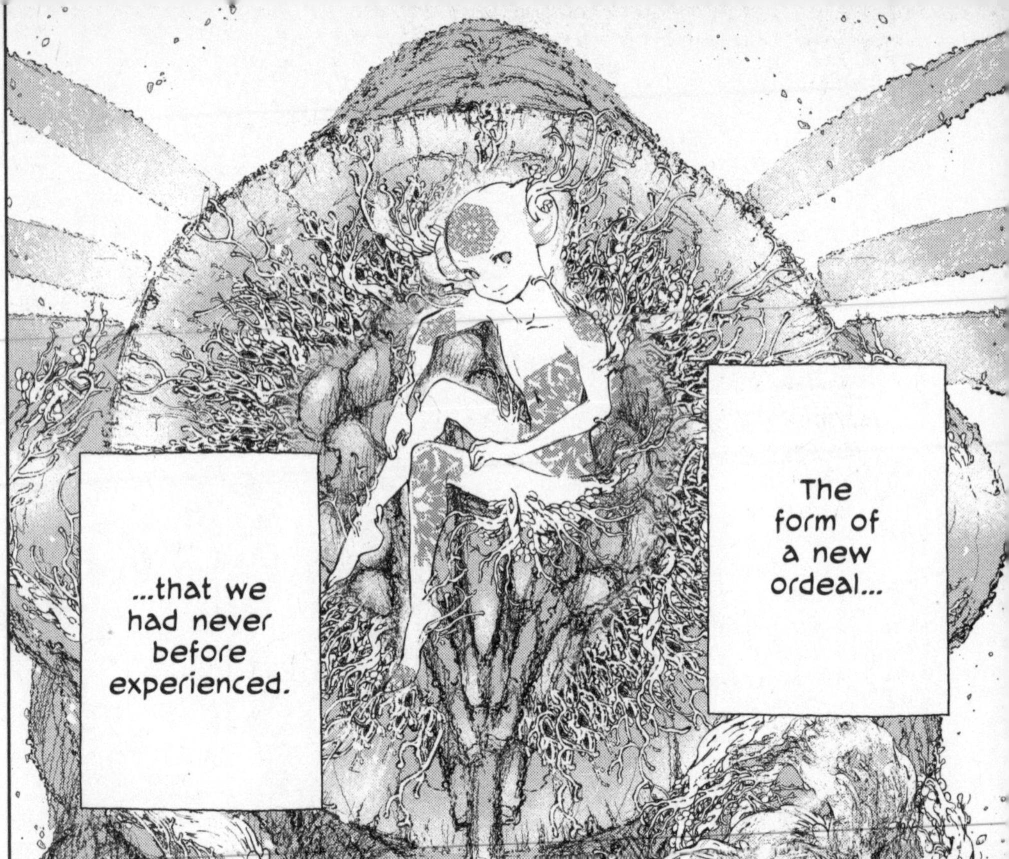
The form of a new ordeal...
...that we had never before experienced.
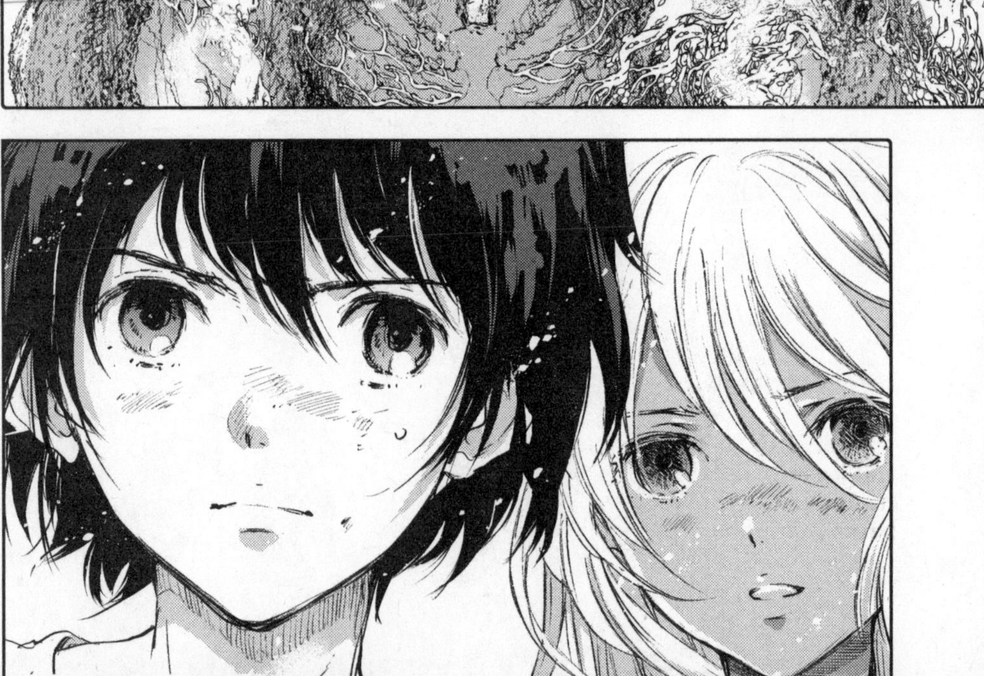

The Sand Beast - The End-

Chaos is coming.
O, chaos is coming.
The vanished morning star has spread his hands in loneliness.
Plip plop... Clink clunk... It connects...
...and wanders through paradise...
...while the joy of redemption burns ever higher.

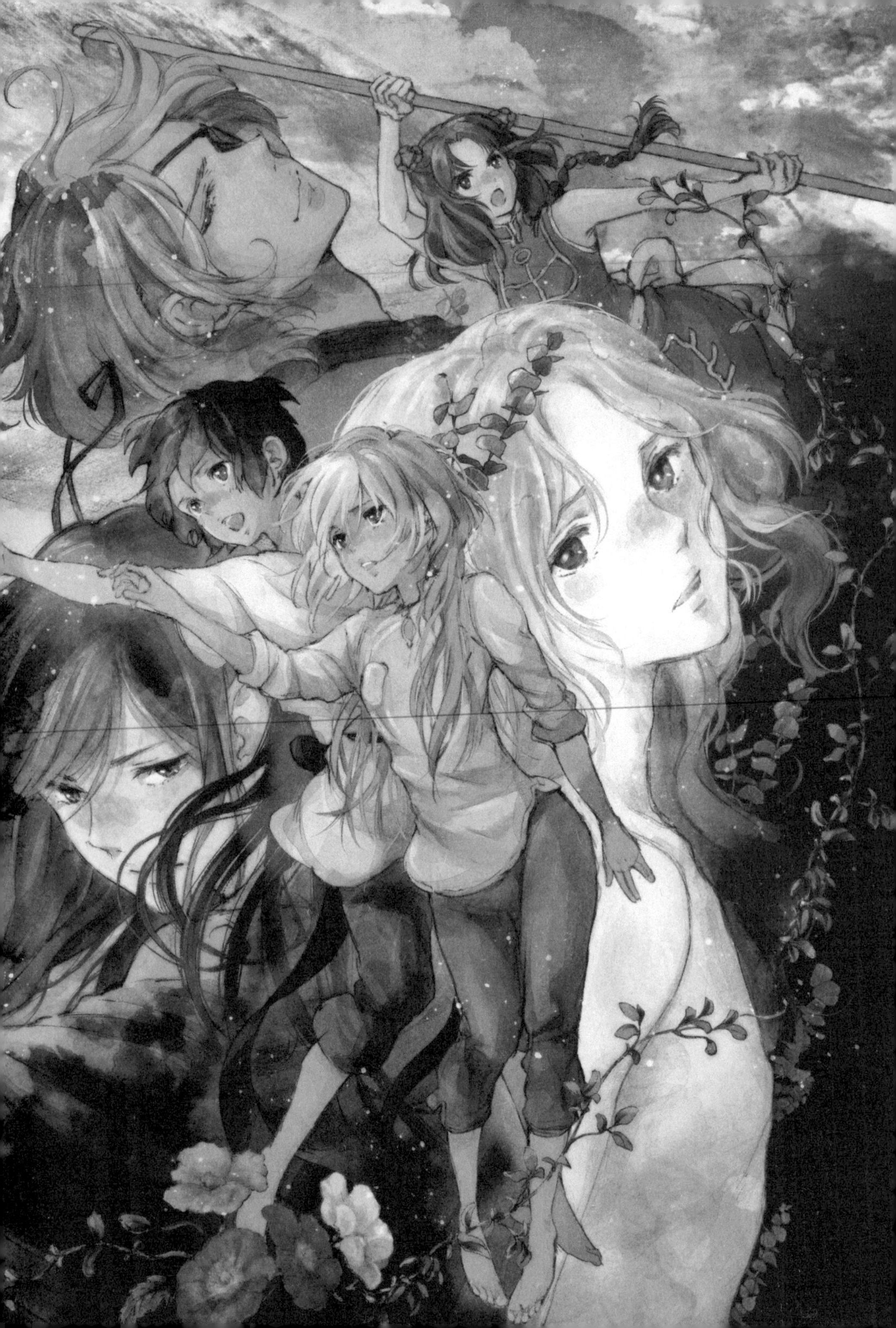

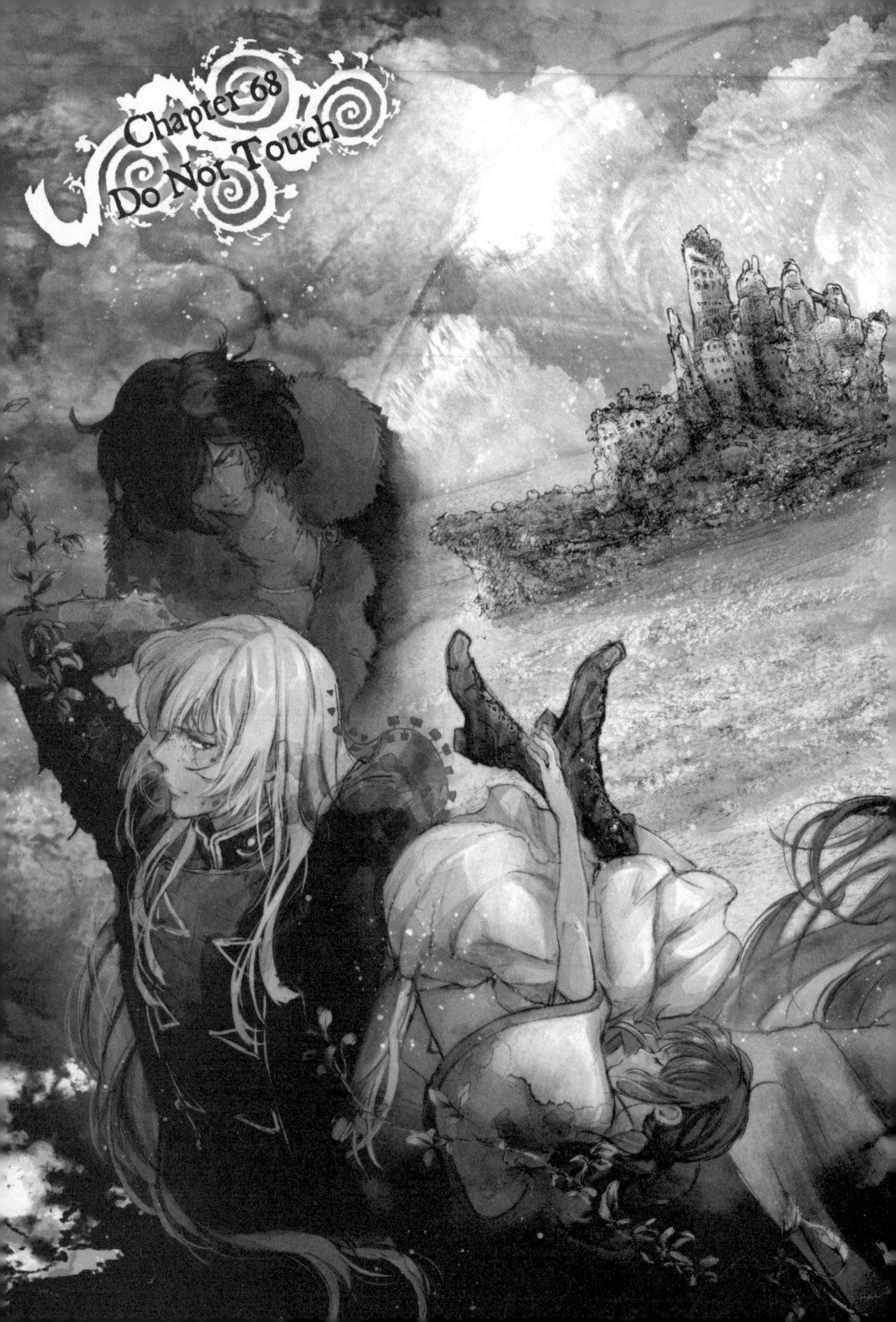
Chapter 68
Do Not Touch

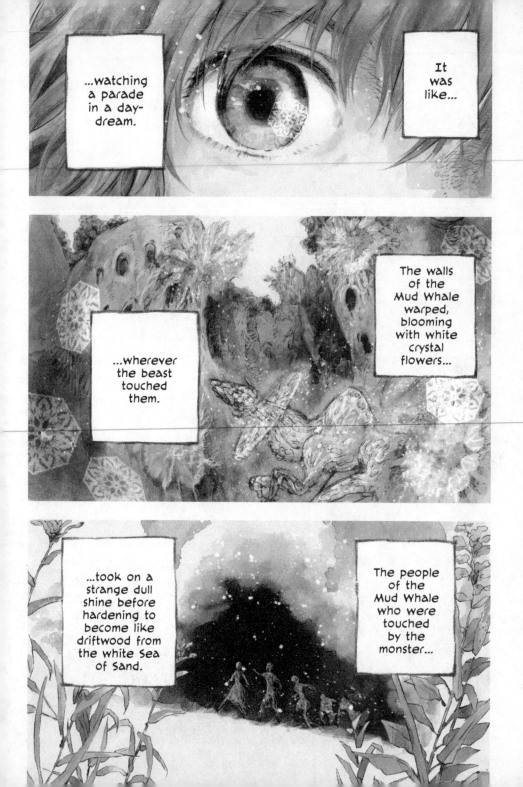

It was like...

...watching a parade in a day-dream.

The walls of the Mud Whale warped, blooming with white crystal flowers...

...wherever the beast touched them.

The people of the Mud Whale who were touched by the monster...

...took on a strange dull shine before hardening to become like driftwood from the white Sea of Sand.

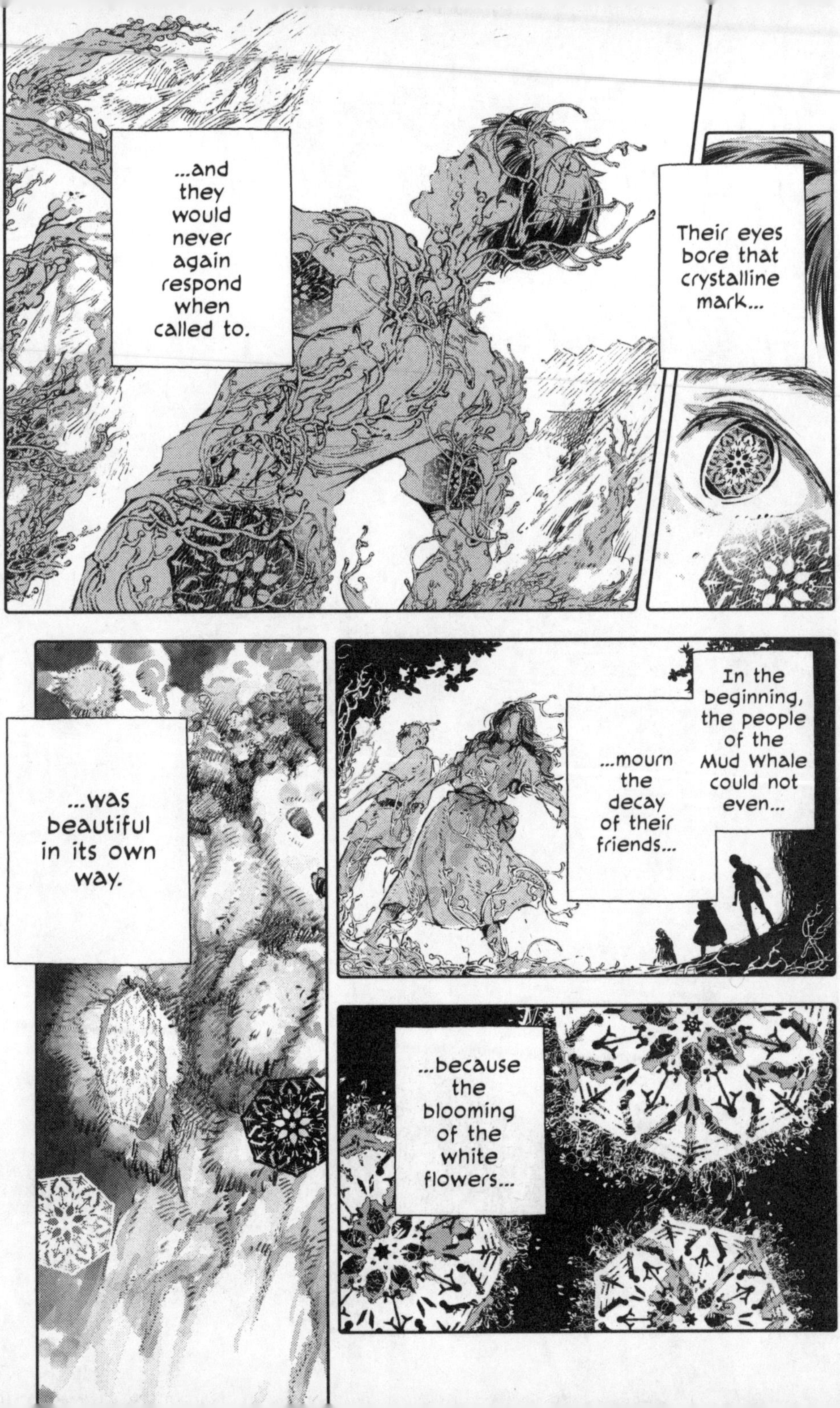
Their eyes bore that crystalline mark...
...and they would never again respond when called to.
In the beginning, the people of the Mud Whale could not even...
...mourn the decay of their friends...
...because the blooming of the white flowers...
...was beautiful in its own way.

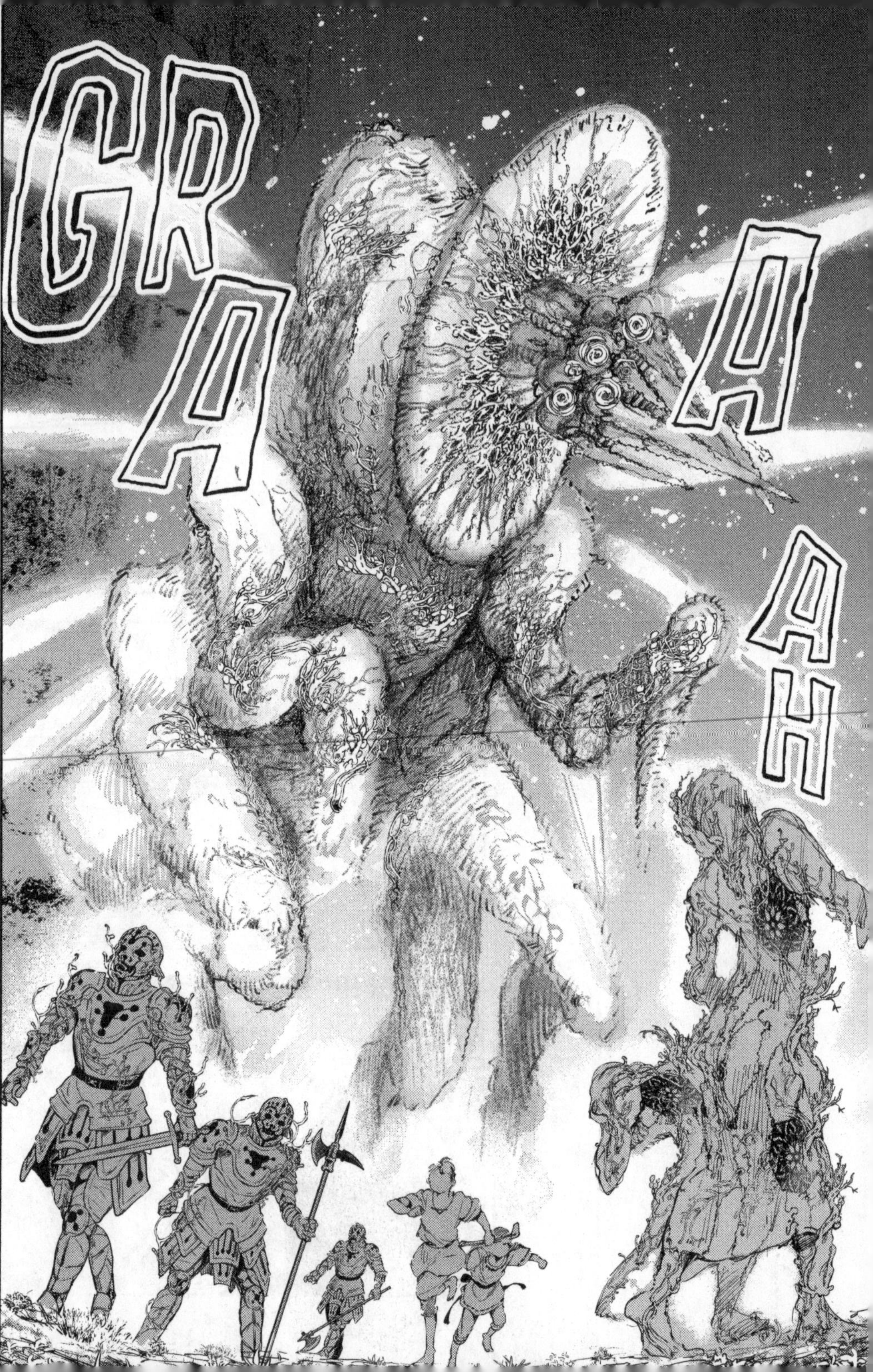
GRAAAAH

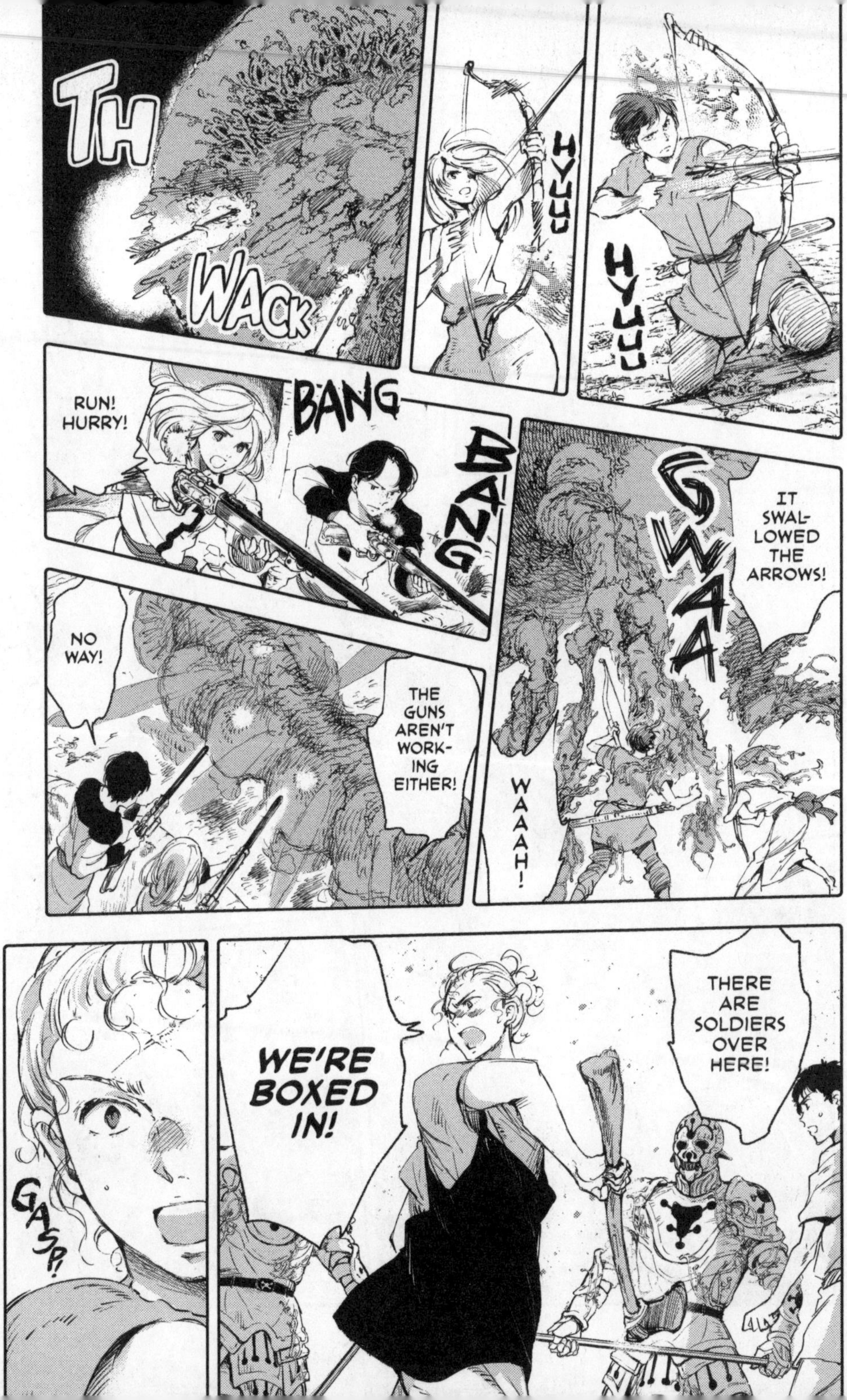
HYUUU
HYUUU
THWACK
GWAA
IT SWAL-LOWED THE ARROWS!
WAAAH!
RUN! HURRY!
BANG
BANG BANG
THE GUNS AREN'T WORKING EITHER!
NO WAY!
THERE ARE SOLDIERS OVER HERE!
WE'RE BOXED IN!
GASP!

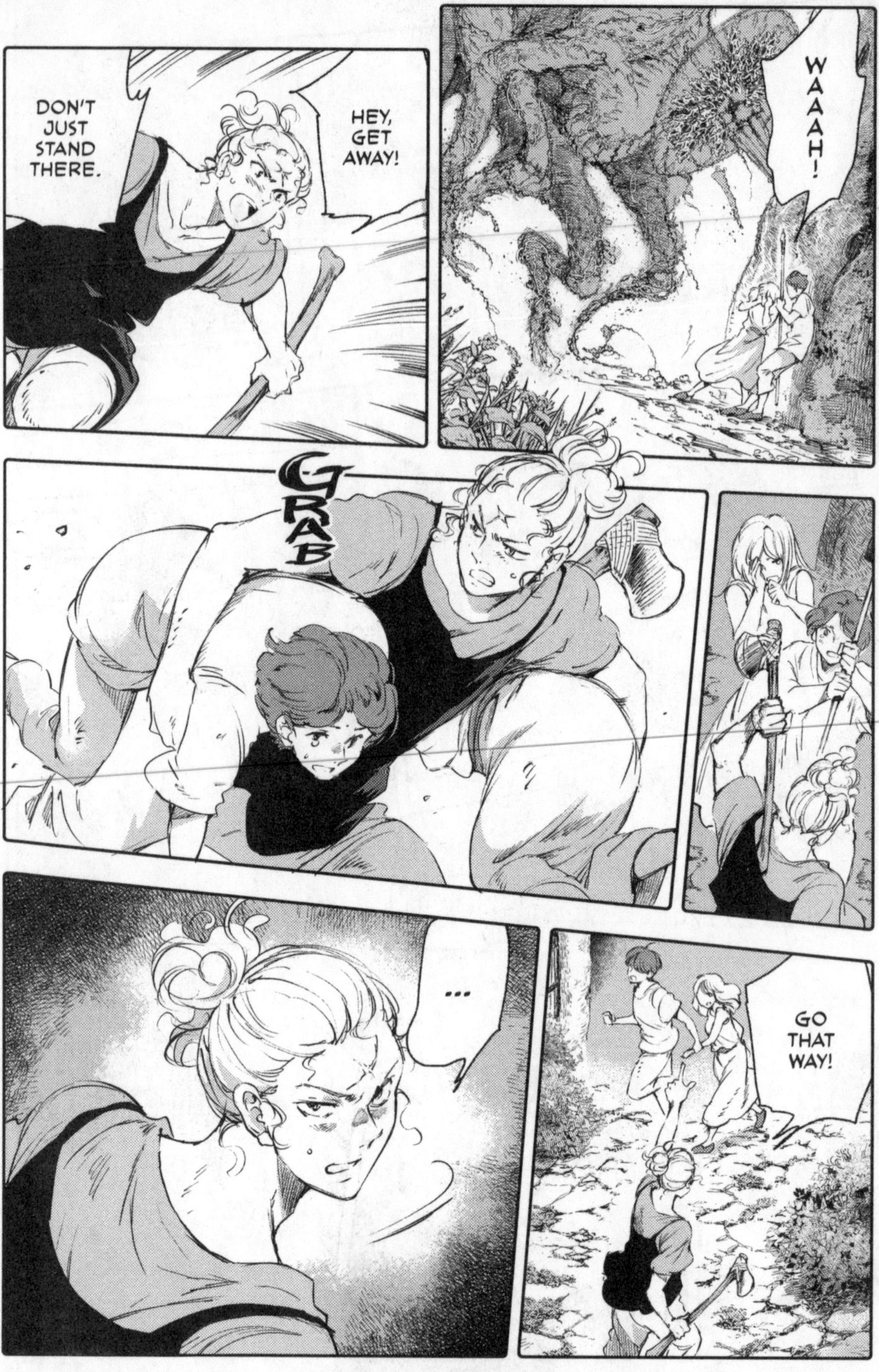
WAAAH!
HEY, GET AWAY!
DON'T JUST STAND THERE.
GRAB
GO THAT WAY!
...

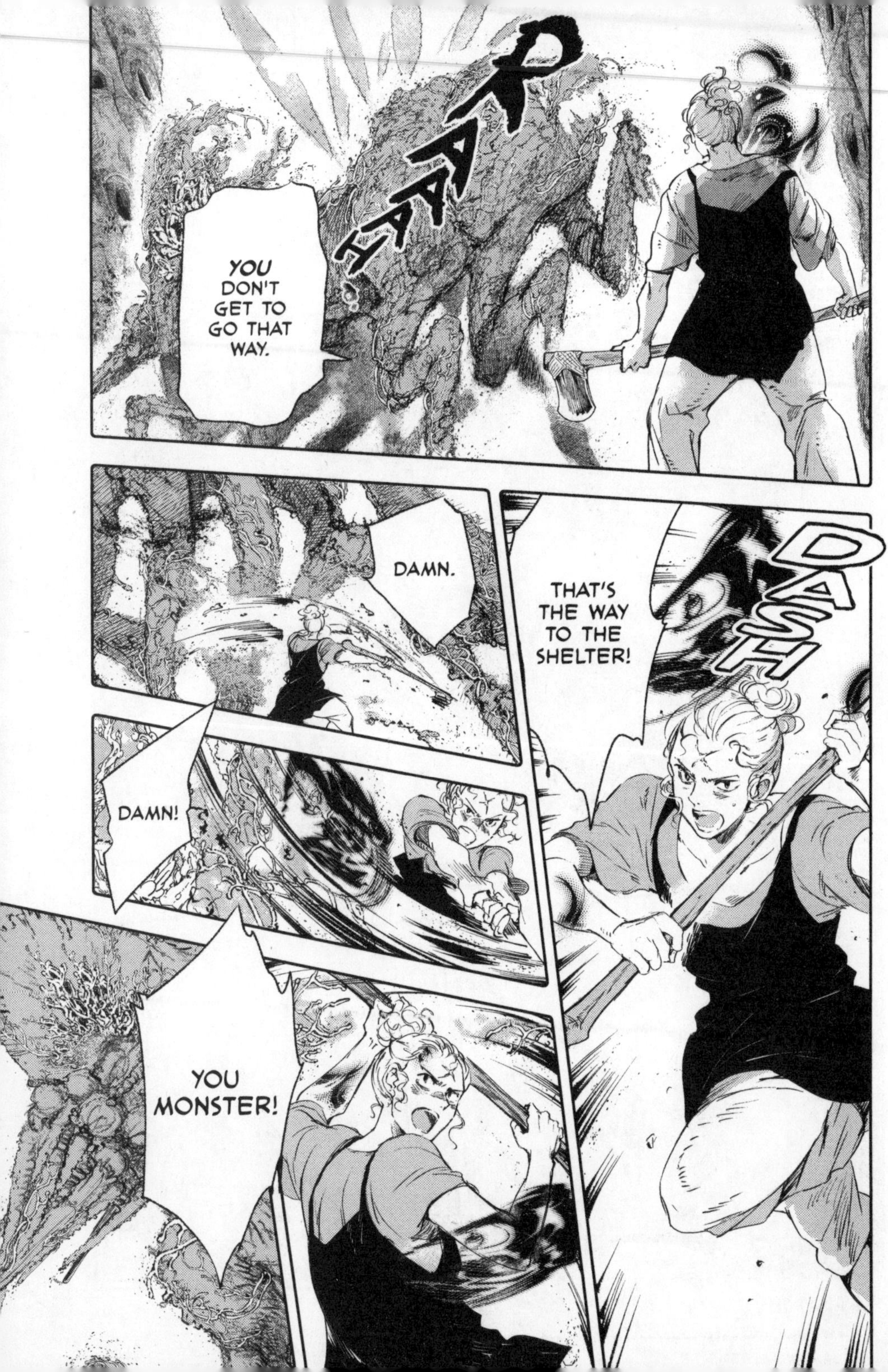
RAAAH
YOU DON'T GET TO GO THAT WAY.
DASH
THAT'S THE WAY TO THE SHELTER!
DAMN.
DAMN!
YOU MONSTER!

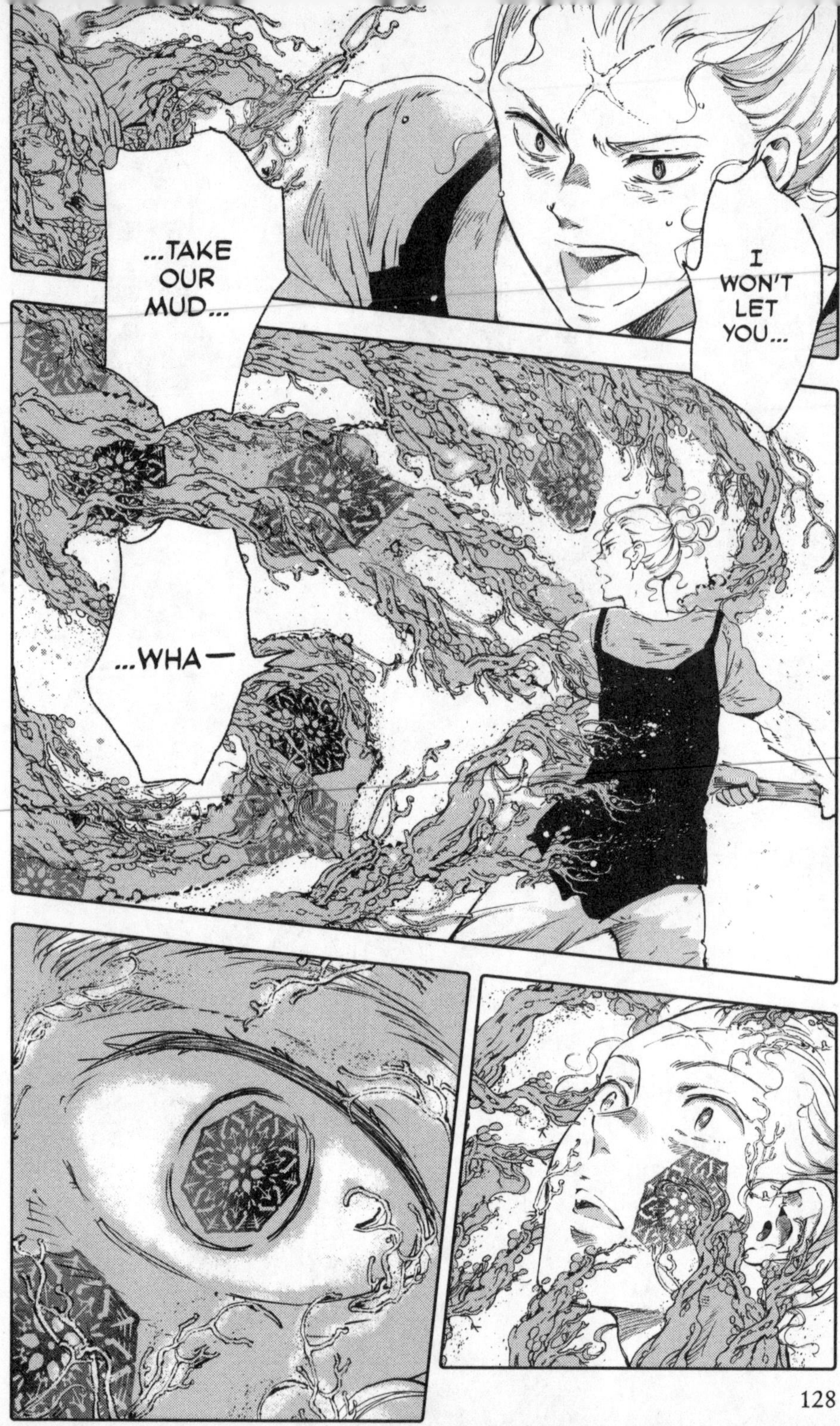
I WON'T LET YOU...
...TAKE OUR MUD...
...WHA—

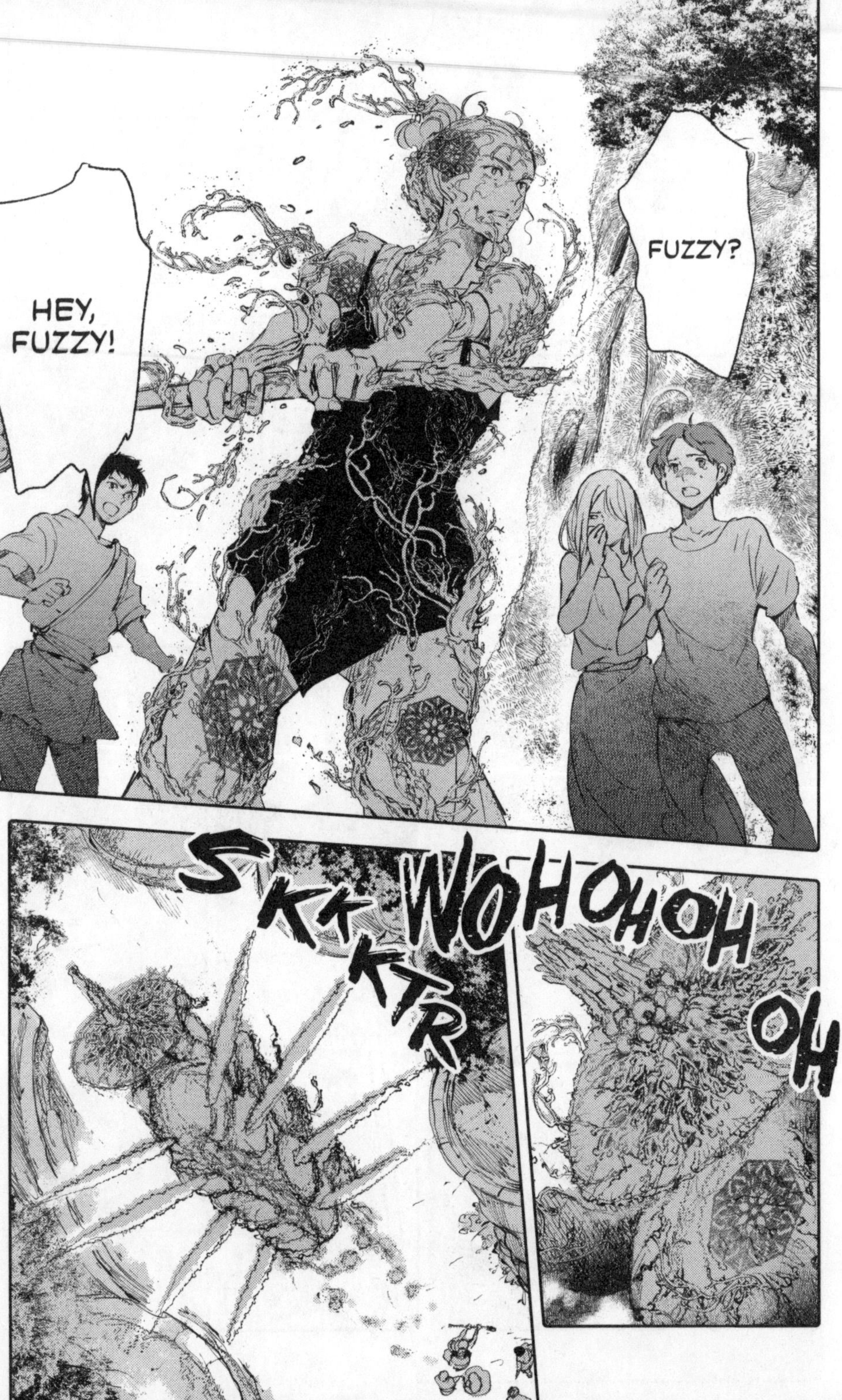
FUZZY?
HEY, FUZZY!
WOHOHOHOH OH
SKKKKTR

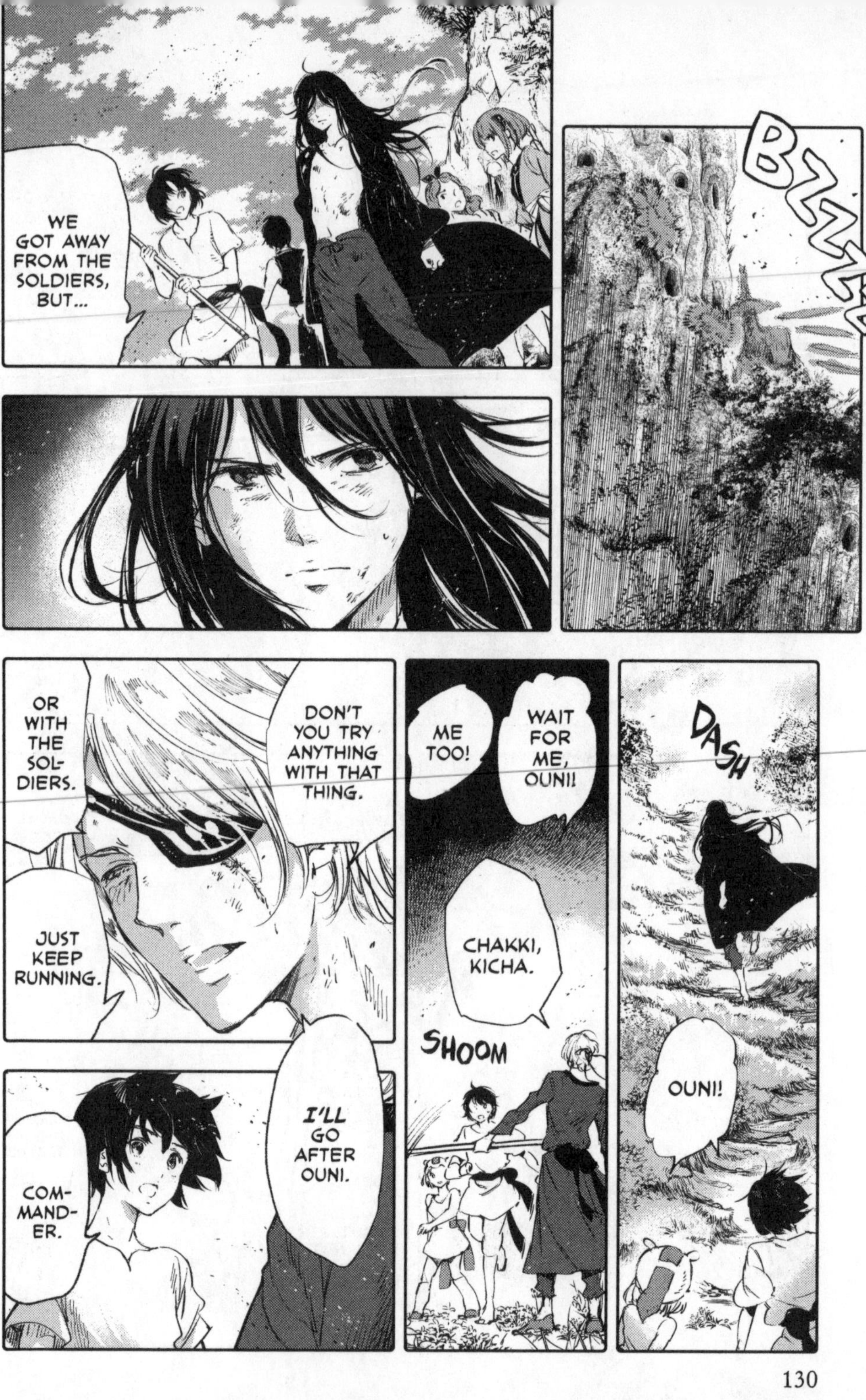
BZZZZZ
WE GOT AWAY FROM THE SOLDIERS, BUT...
DASH
OUNI!
WAIT FOR ME, OUNI!
ME TOO!
CHAKKI, KICHA.
SHOOM
DON'T YOU TRY ANYTHING WITH THAT THING.
OR WITH THE SOL-DIERS.
JUST KEEP RUNNING.
I'LL GO AFTER OUNI.
COM-MAND-ER.

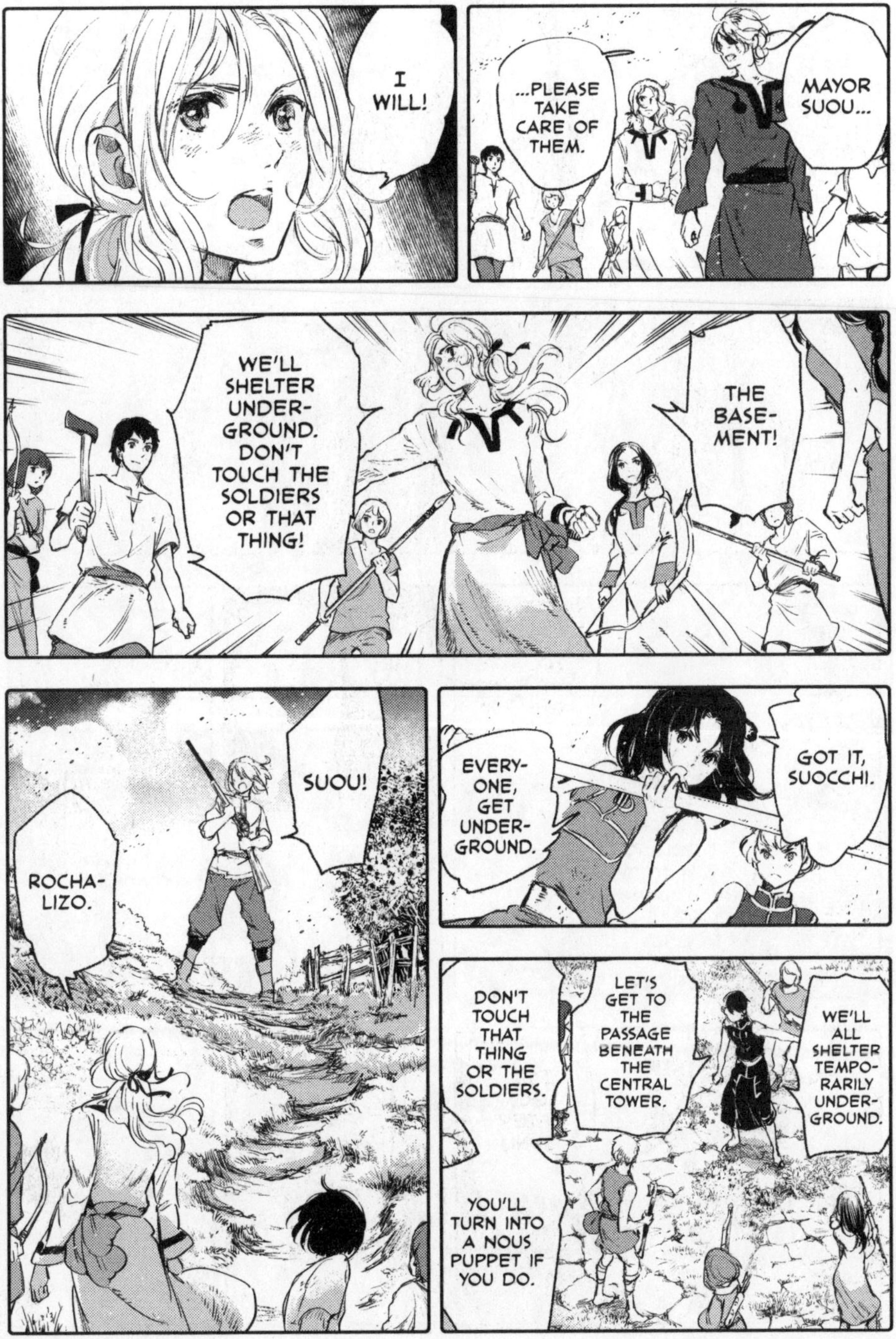
MAYOR SUOU...
...PLEASE TAKE CARE OF THEM.
I WILL!
THE BASEMENT!
WE'LL SHELTER UNDERGROUND. DON'T TOUCH THE SOLDIERS OR THAT THING!
GOT IT, SUOCCHI.
EVERYONE, GET UNDERGROUND.
WE'LL ALL SHELTER TEMPORARILY UNDERGROUND.
LET'S GET TO THE PASSAGE BENEATH THE CENTRAL TOWER.
DON'T TOUCH THAT THING OR THE SOLDIERS.
YOU'LL TURN INTO A NOUS PUPPET IF YOU DO.
SUOU!
ROCHALIZO.

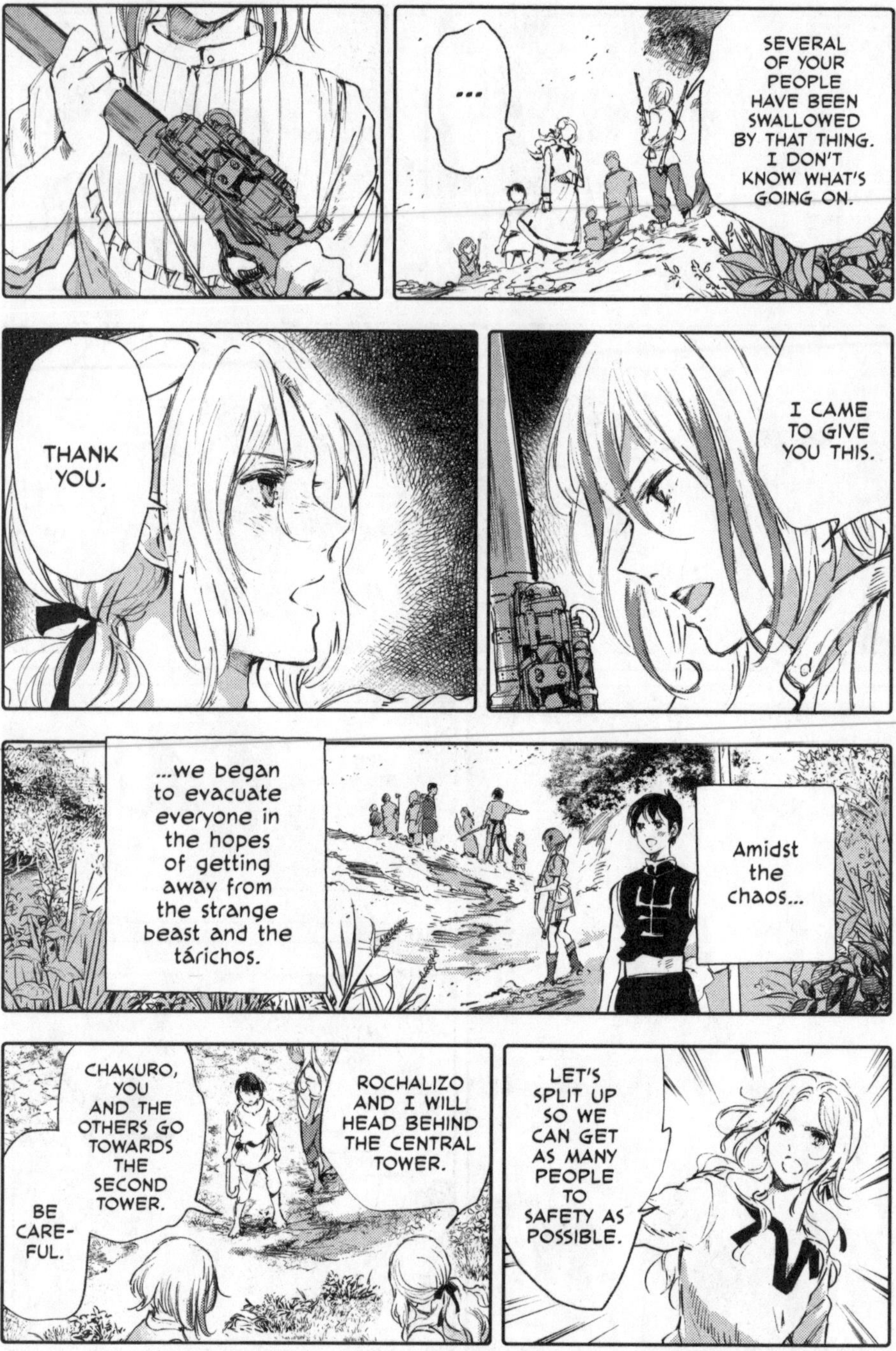
SEVERAL OF YOUR PEOPLE HAVE BEEN SWALLOWED BY THAT THING. I DON'T KNOW WHAT'S GOING ON.
...
I CAME TO GIVE YOU THIS.
THANK YOU.
Amidst the chaos...
...we began to evacuate everyone in the hopes of getting away from the strange beast and the tárichos.
LET'S SPLIT UP SO WE CAN GET AS MANY PEOPLE TO SAFETY AS POSSIBLE.
ROCHALIZO AND I WILL HEAD BEHIND THE CENTRAL TOWER.
CHAKURO, YOU AND THE OTHERS GO TOWARDS THE SECOND TOWER.
BE CARE-FUL.

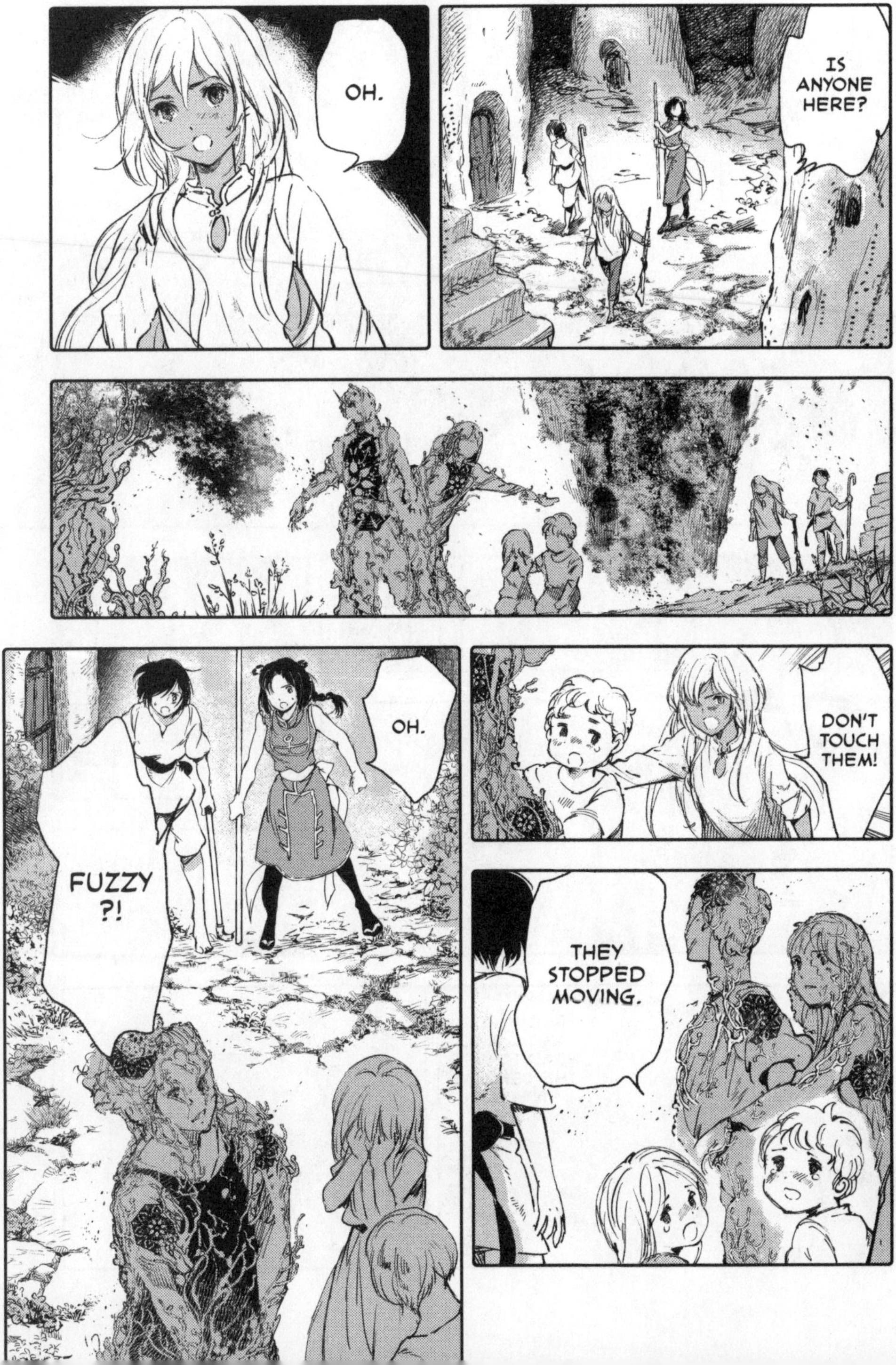
IS ANYONE HERE?
OH.
DON'T TOUCH THEM!
THEY STOPPED MOVING.
OH.
FUZZY ?!

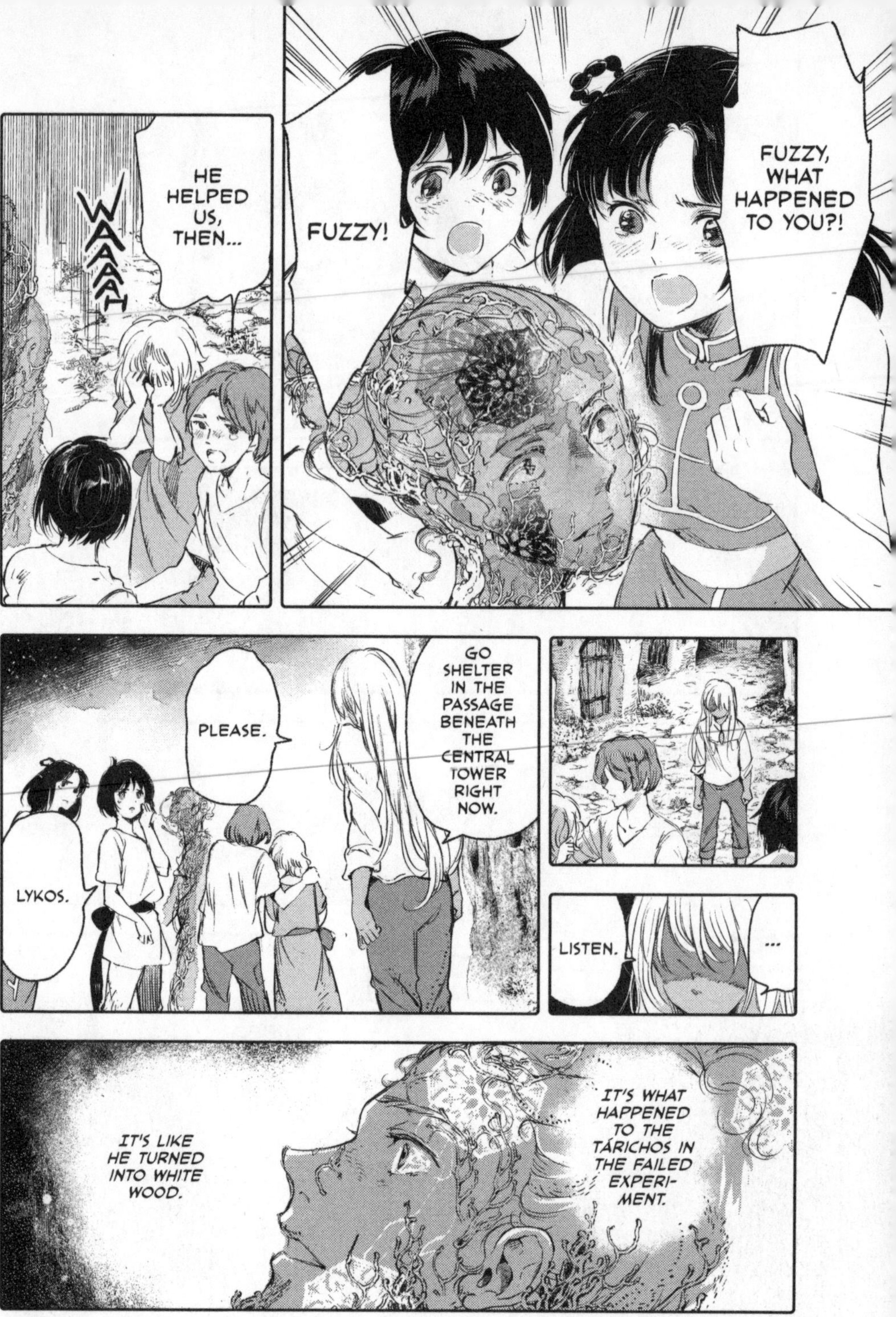
FUZZY, WHAT HAPPENED TO YOU?!
FUZZY!
HE HELPED US, THEN...
WAAAAH
...
LISTEN.
GO SHELTER IN THE PASSAGE BENEATH THE CENTRAL TOWER RIGHT NOW.
PLEASE.
LYKOS.
IT'S WHAT HAPPENED TO THE TÁRICHOS IN THE FAILED EXPERIMENT.
IT'S LIKE HE TURNED INTO WHITE WOOD.

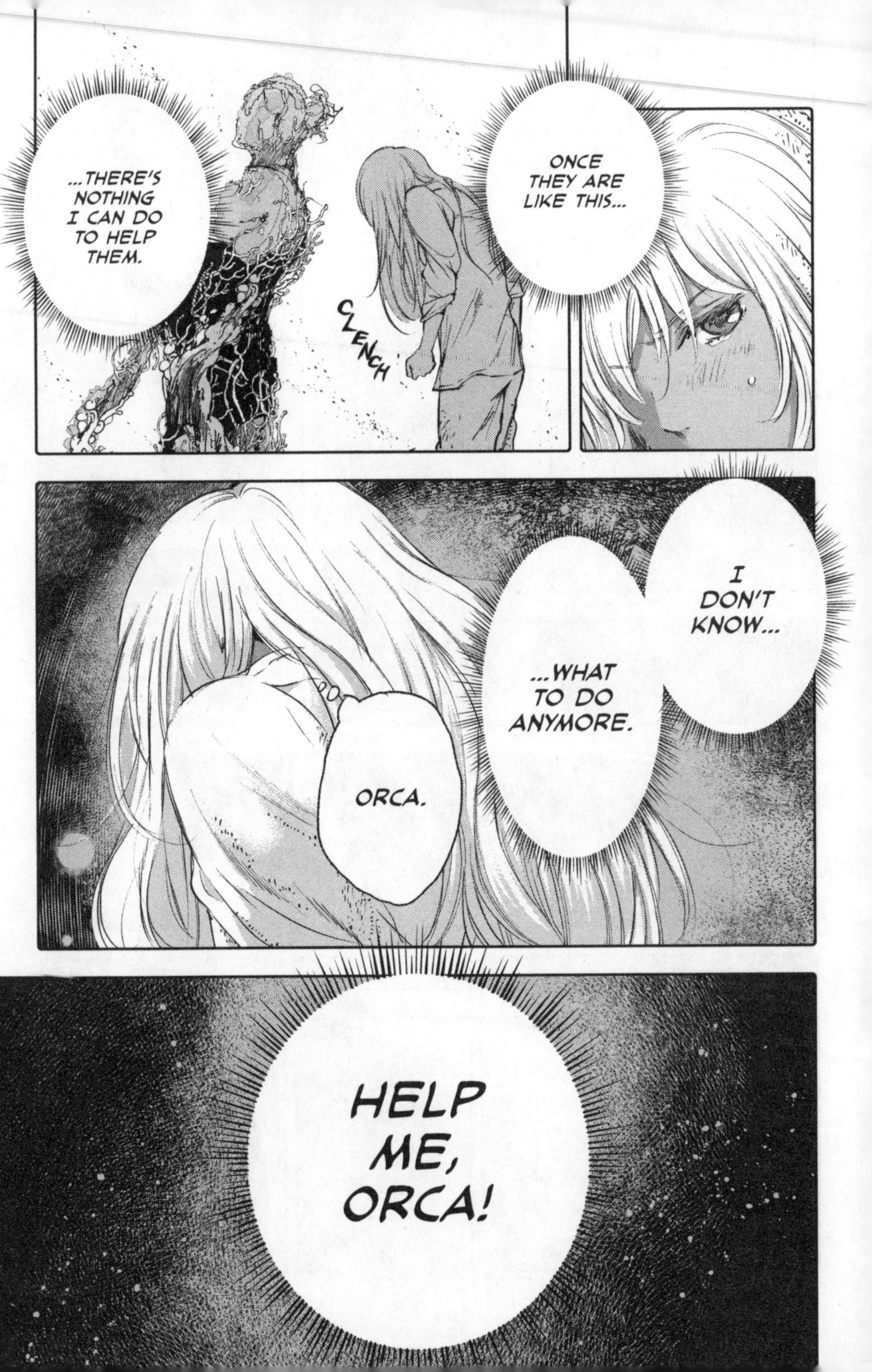
ONCE THEY ARE LIKE THIS...
...THERE'S NOTHING I CAN DO TO HELP THEM.
CLENCH
I DON'T KNOW...
...WHAT TO DO ANYMORE.
ORCA.
HELP ME, ORCA!

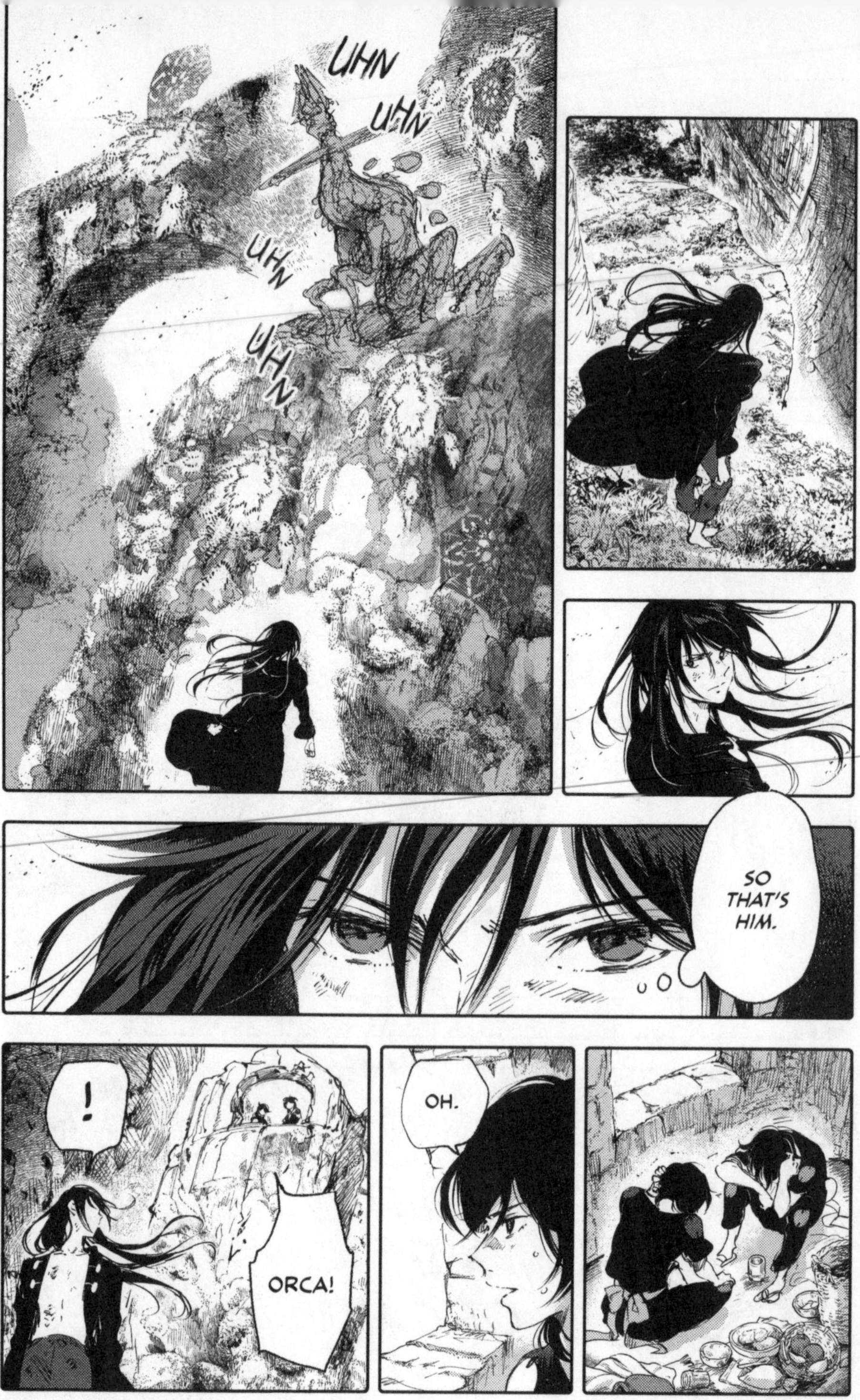
UHN
UHN
UHN
UHN
SO THAT'S HIM.
OH.
ORCA!
!

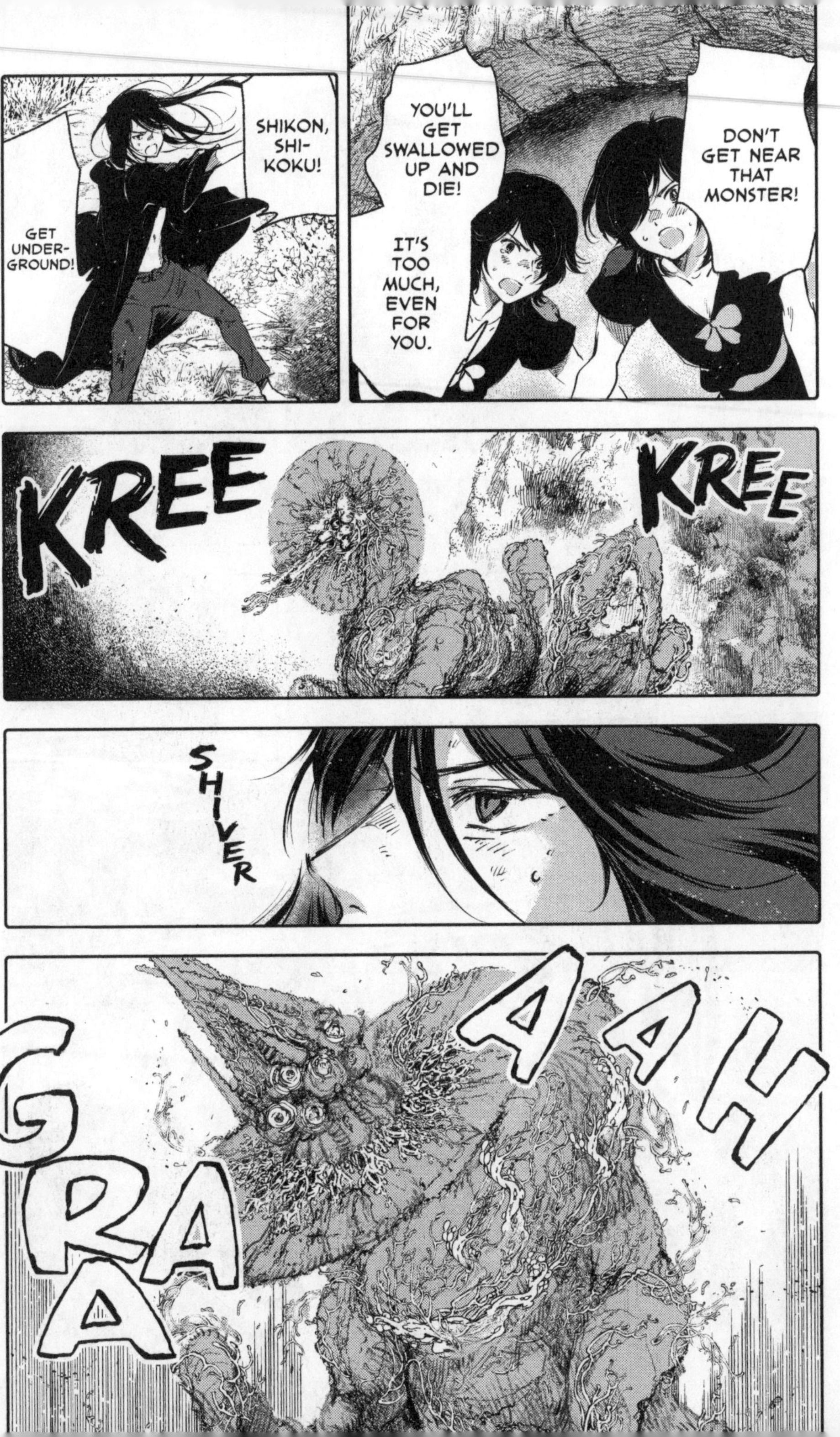
DON'T GET NEAR THAT MONSTER!
YOU'LL GET SWALLOWED UP AND DIE!
IT'S TOO MUCH, EVEN FOR YOU.
SHIKON, SHI-KOKU!
GET UNDER-GROUND!
KREE
KREE
SHIVER
GRAAAAH

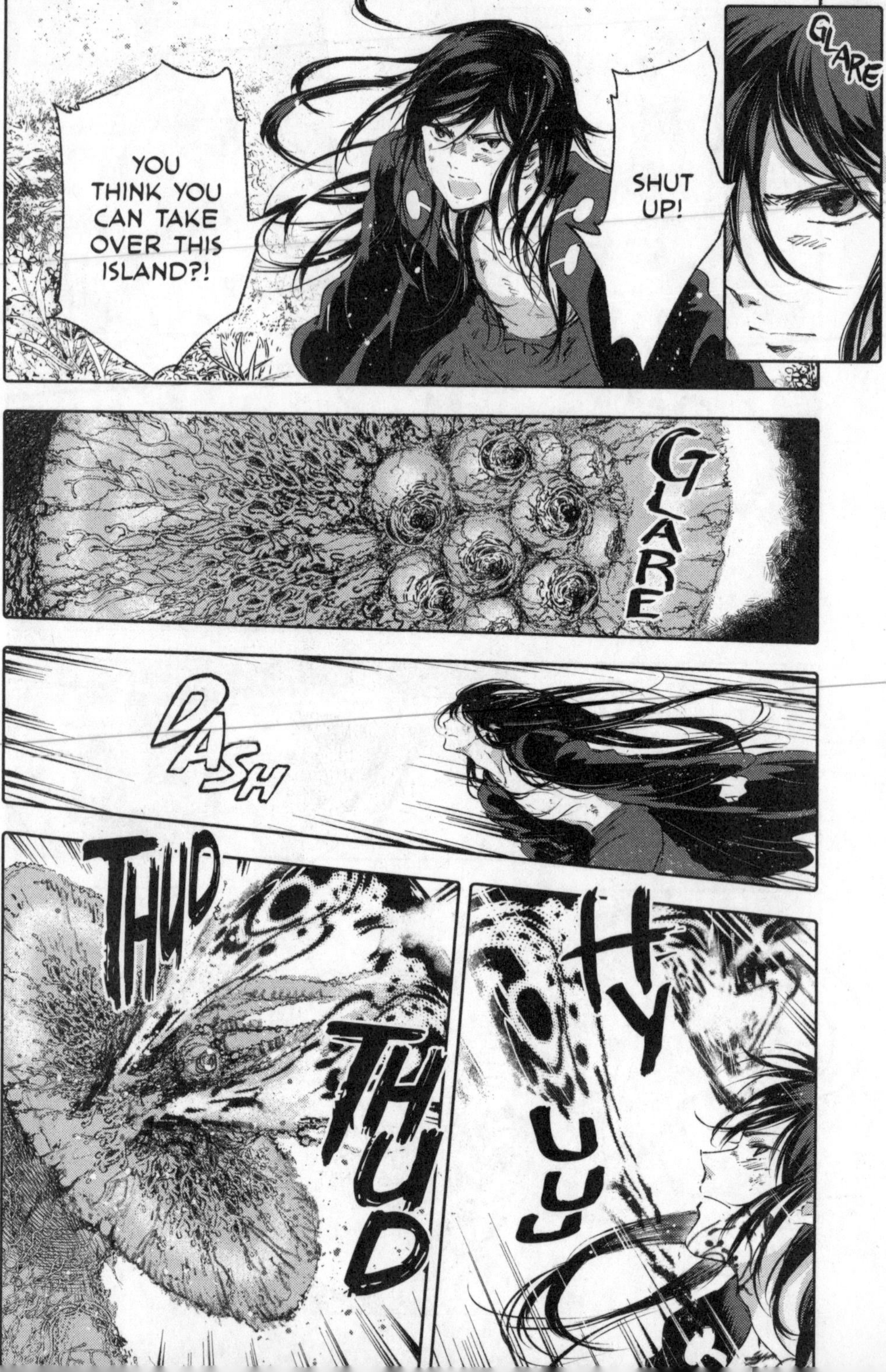
GLARE
SHUT UP!
YOU THINK YOU CAN TAKE OVER THIS ISLAND?!
GLARE
DASH
HYUUUU
THUD
THUD

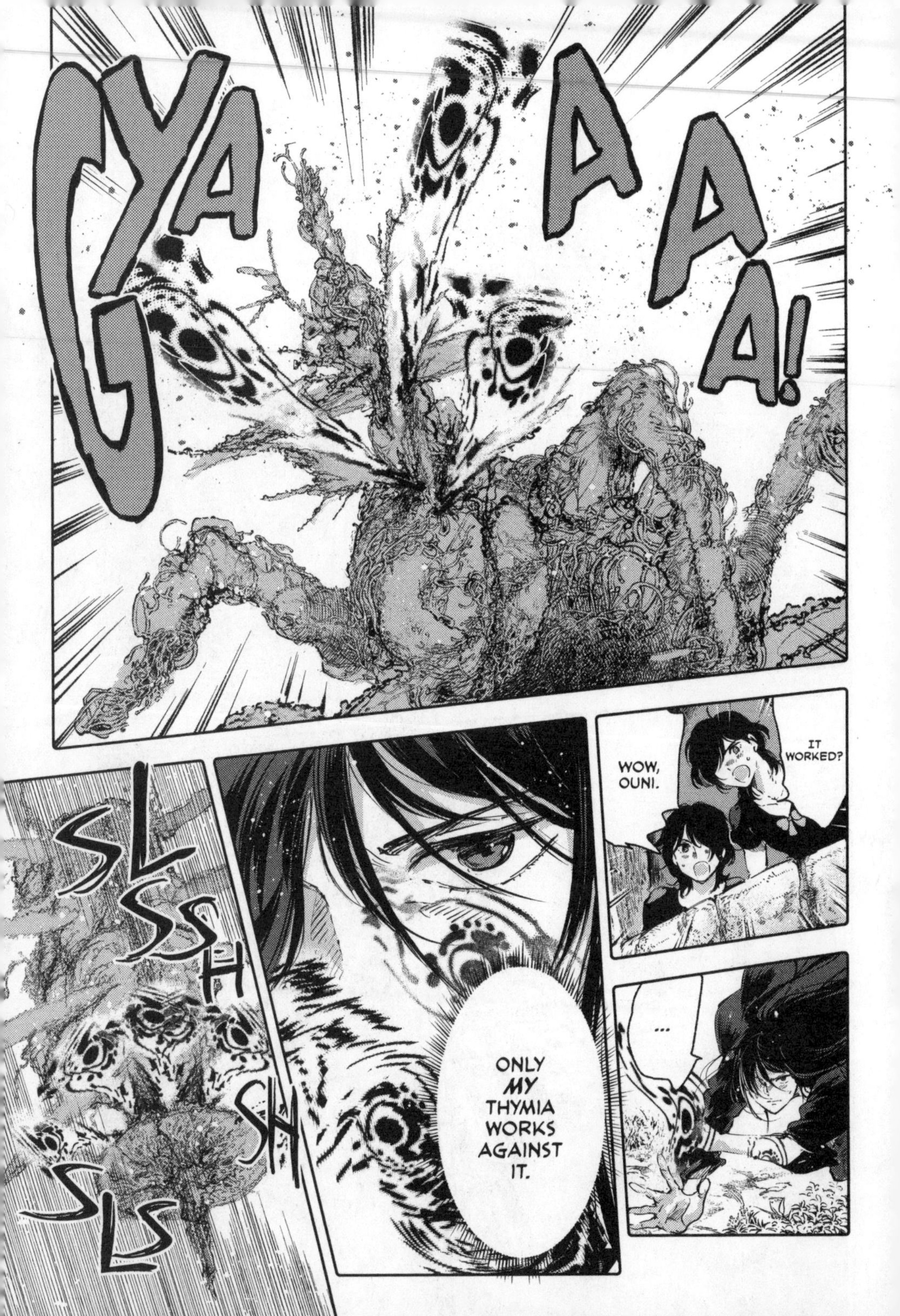
GYAAAA!
IT WORKED?
WOW, OUNI.
...
ONLY *MY* THYMIA WORKS AGAINST IT.
SLSSH
SLSSH

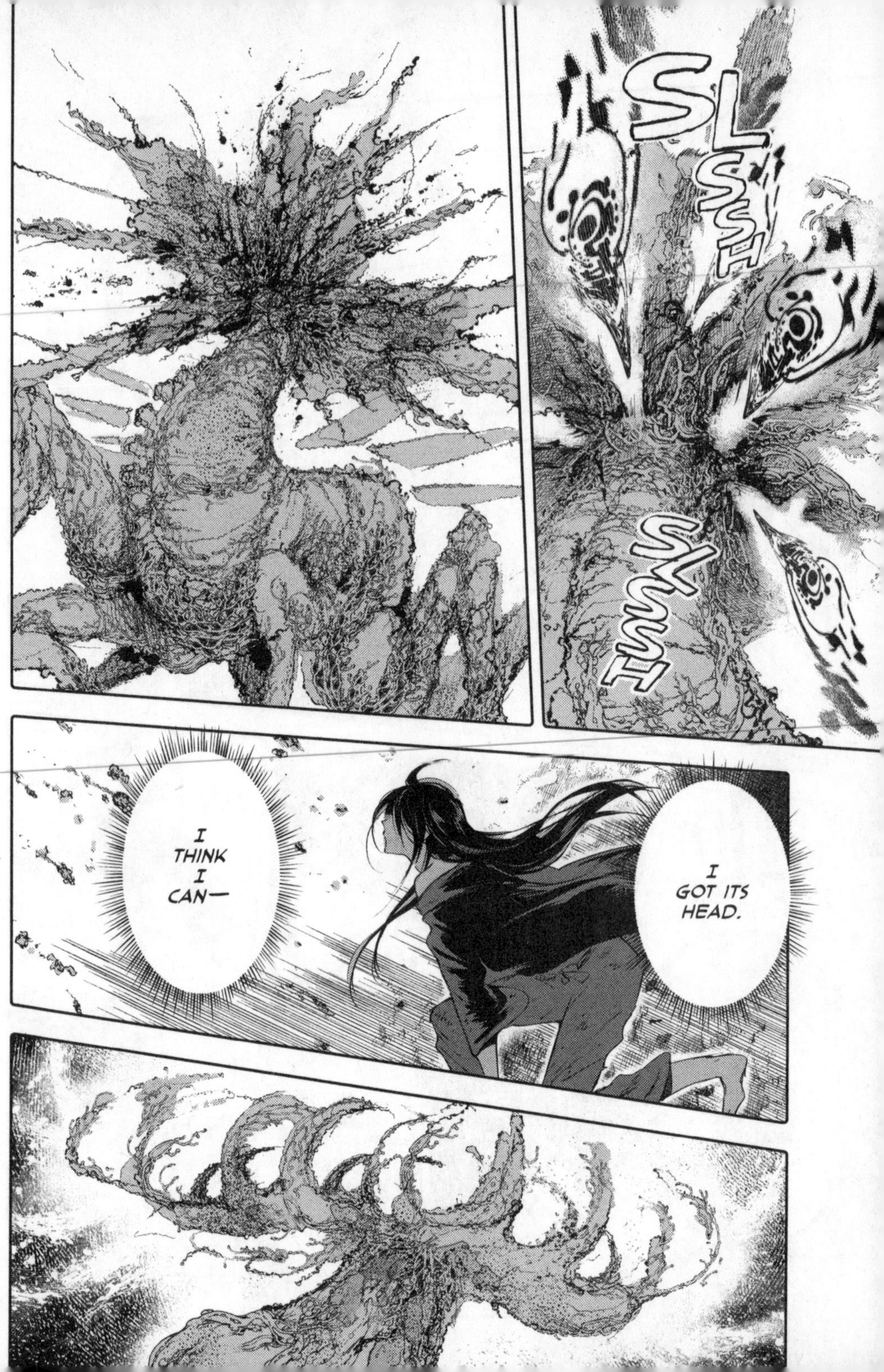
SLSSH
SLSSH
I GOT ITS HEAD.
I THINK I CAN—

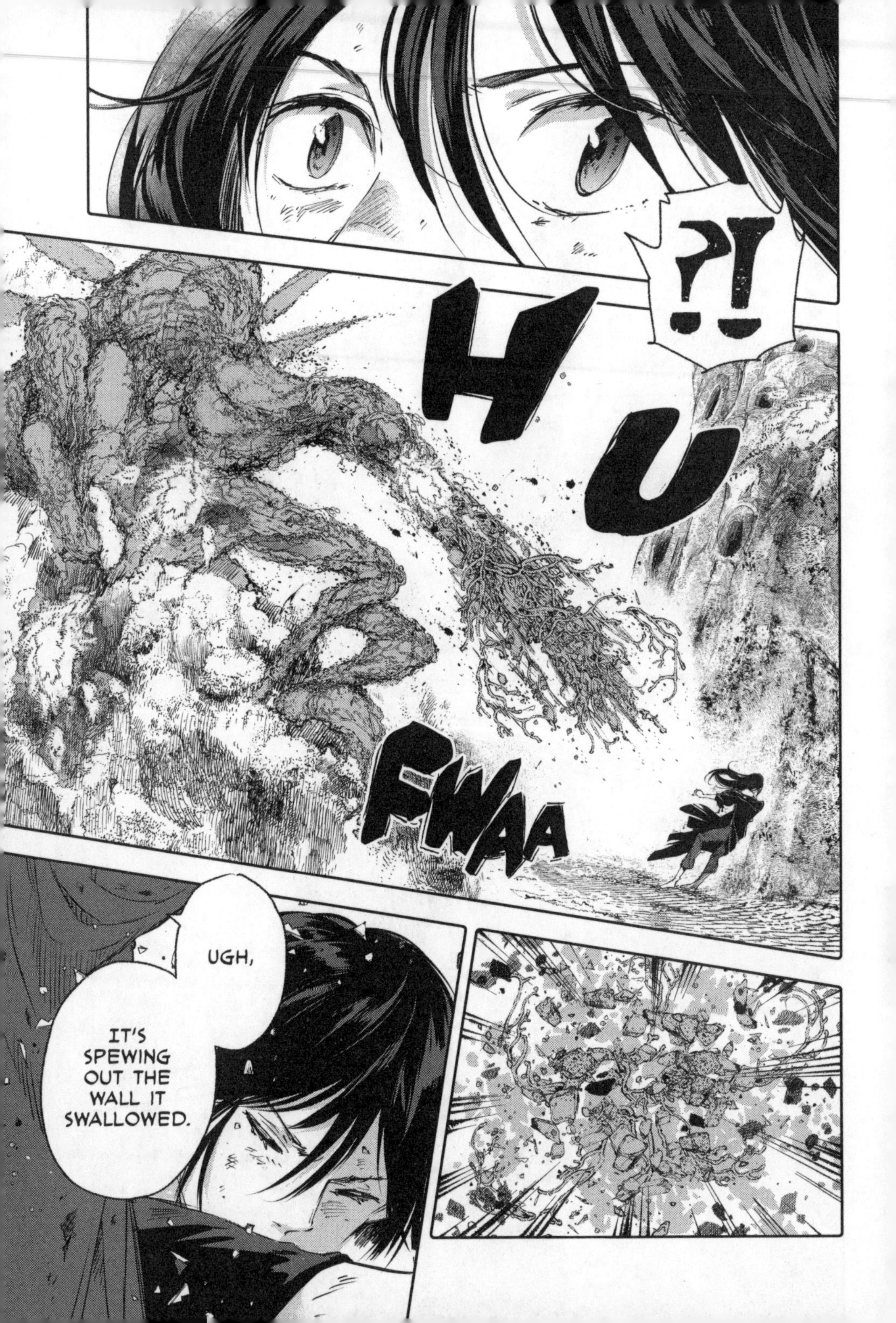
?!
HU
FWAA
UGH,
IT'S SPEWING OUT THE WALL IT SWALLOWED.

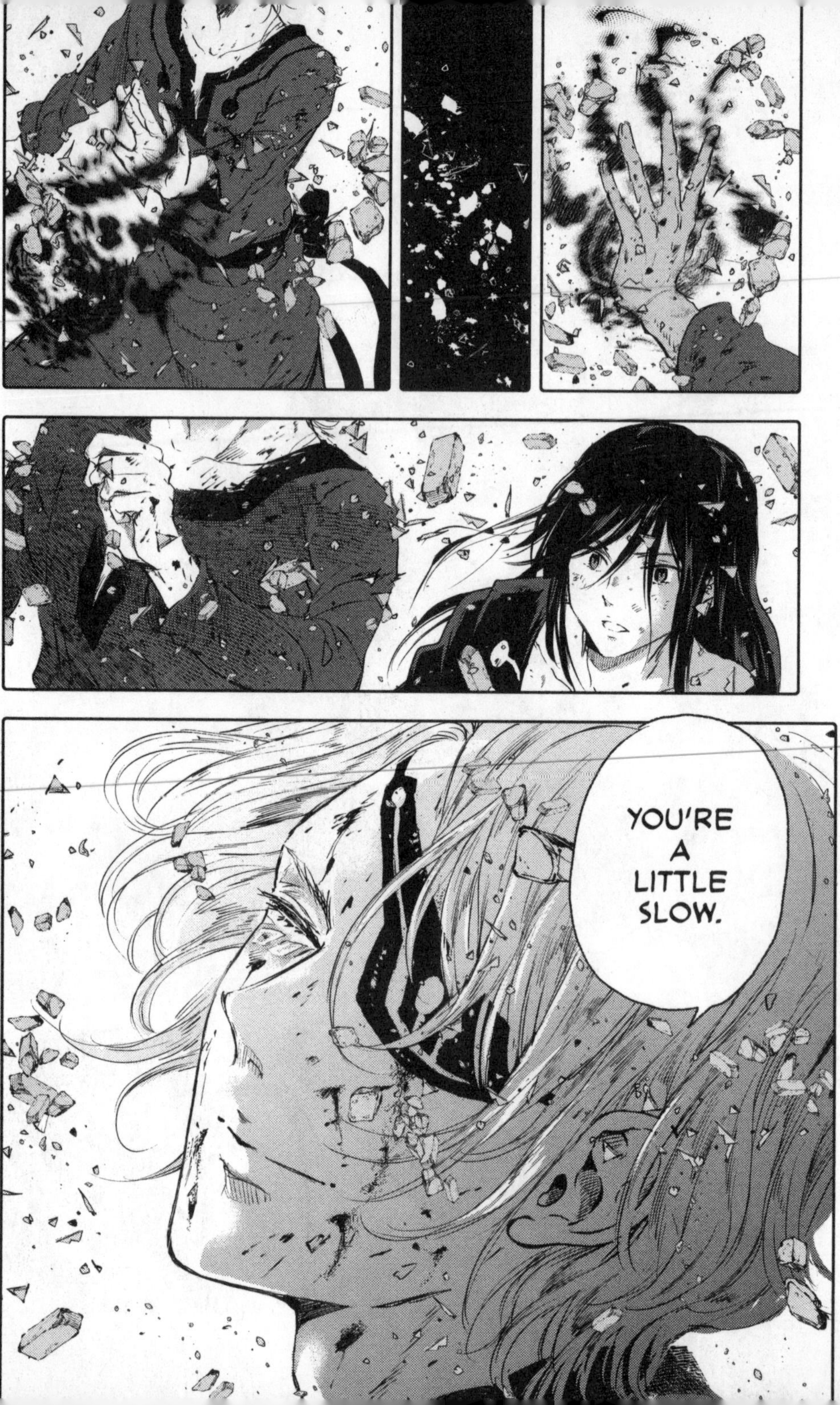
YOU'RE A LITTLE SLOW.

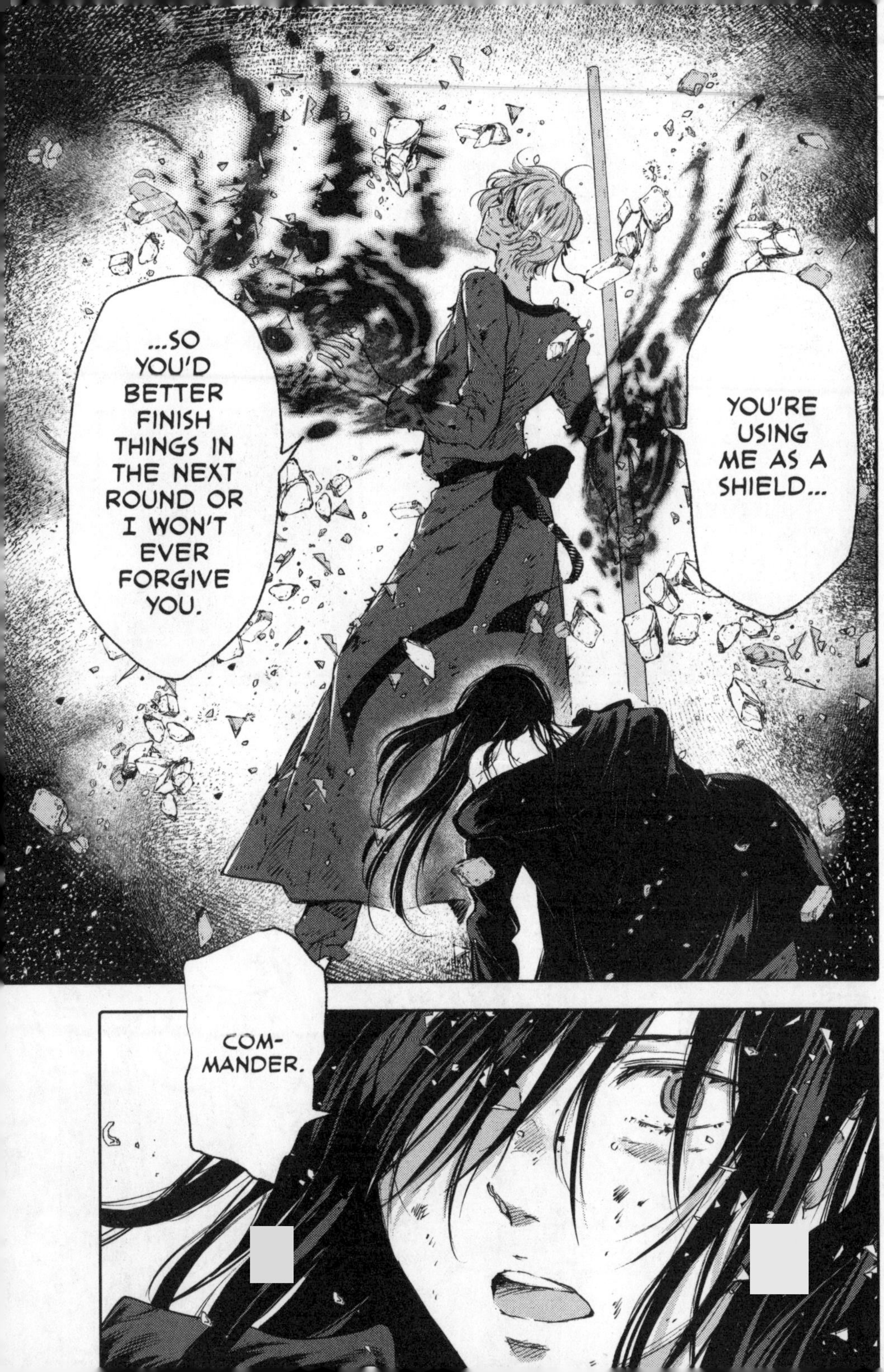
YOU'RE USING ME AS A SHIELD...
...SO YOU'D BETTER FINISH THINGS IN THE NEXT ROUND OR I WON'T EVER FORGIVE YOU.
COM-MANDER.

[redacted]

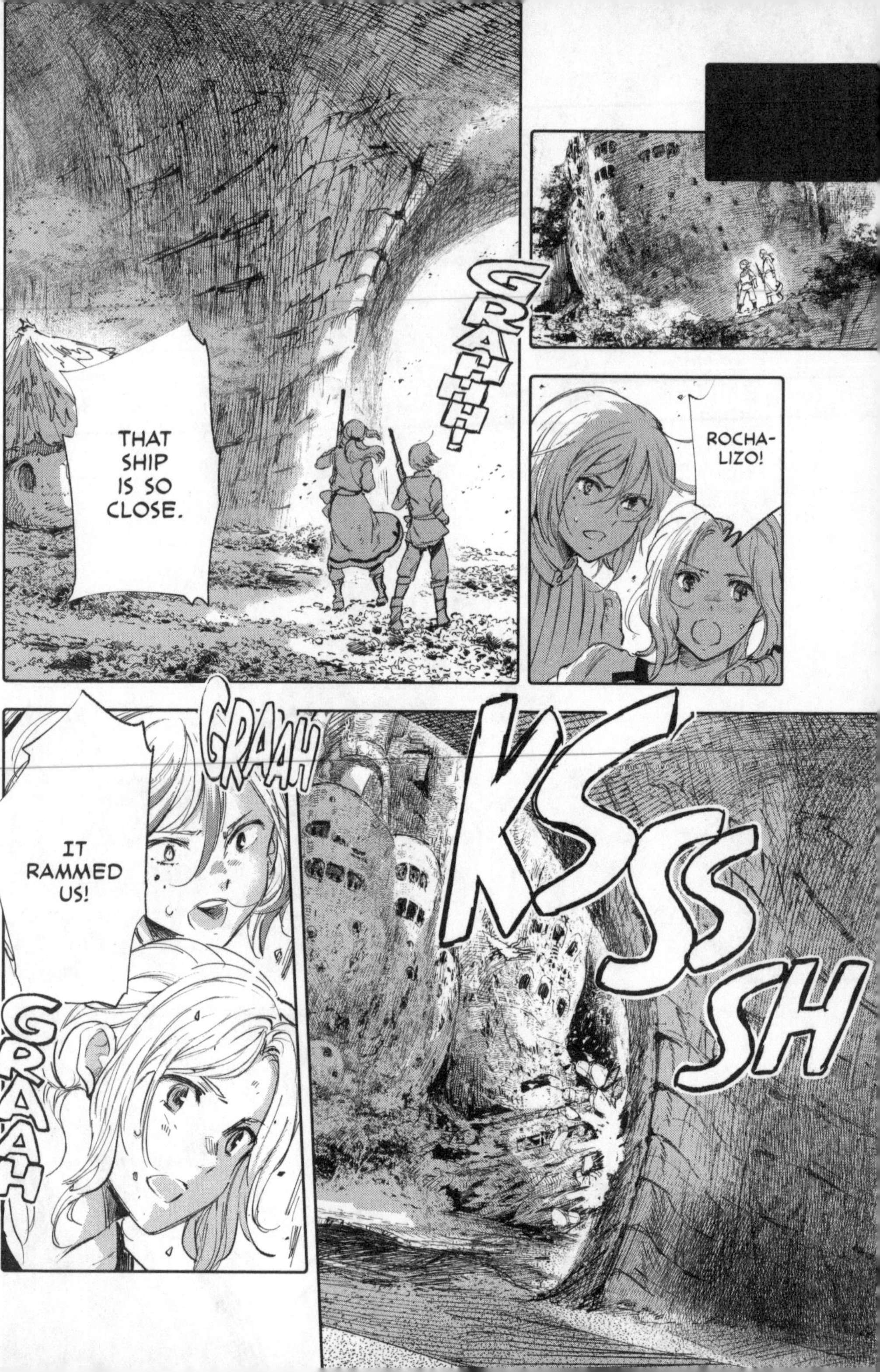

GRAHHH!
ROCHA-LIZO!
THAT SHIP IS SO CLOSE.
KSSSSH
GRAAH
IT RAMMED US!
GRAAH

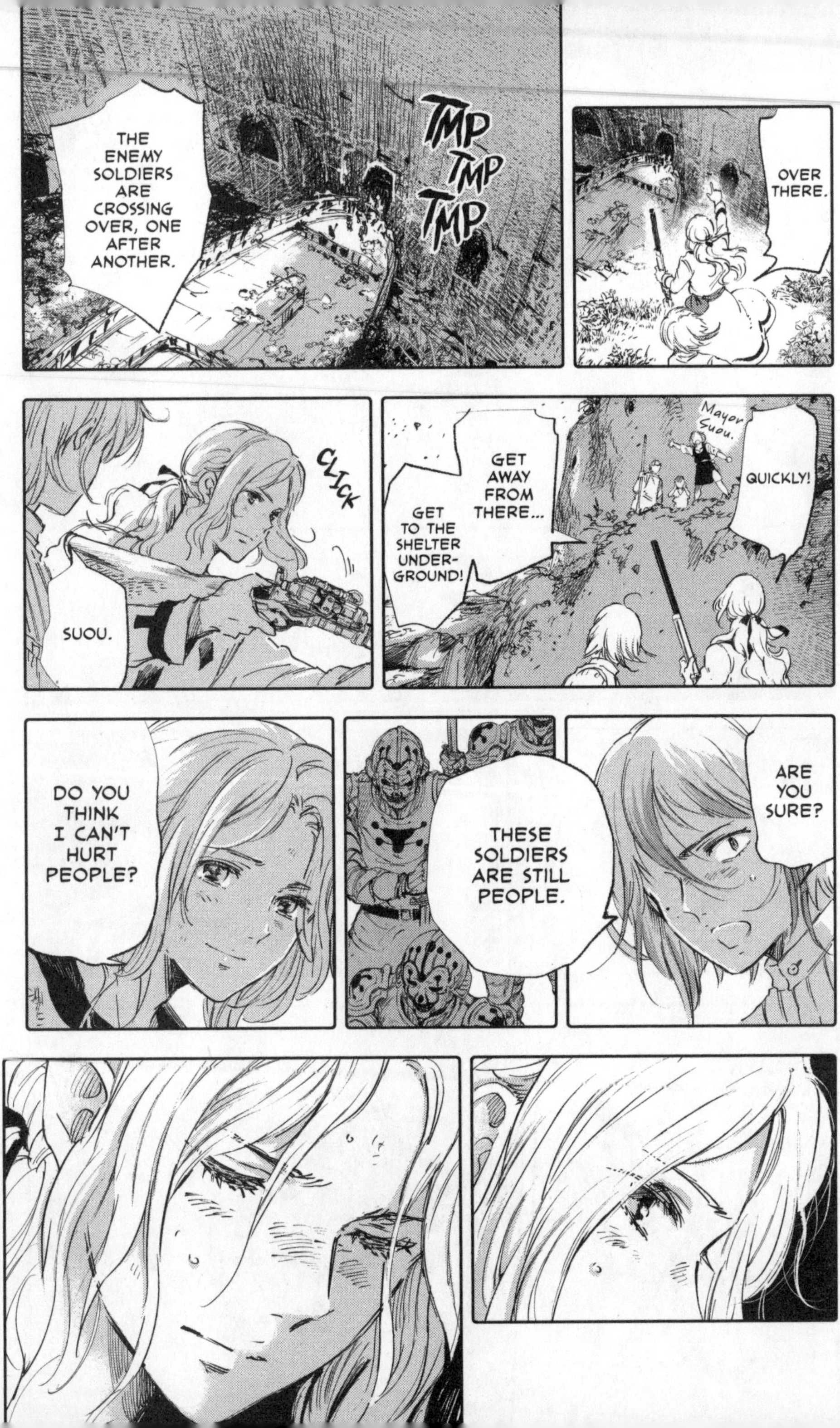
OVER THERE.
THE ENEMY SOLDIERS ARE CROSSING OVER, ONE AFTER ANOTHER.
TMP TMP TMP
Mayor Suou.
QUICKLY!
GET AWAY FROM THERE...
GET TO THE SHELTER UNDER-GROUND!
CLICK
SUOU.
ARE YOU SURE?
THESE SOLDIERS ARE STILL PEOPLE.
DO YOU THINK I CAN'T HURT PEOPLE?

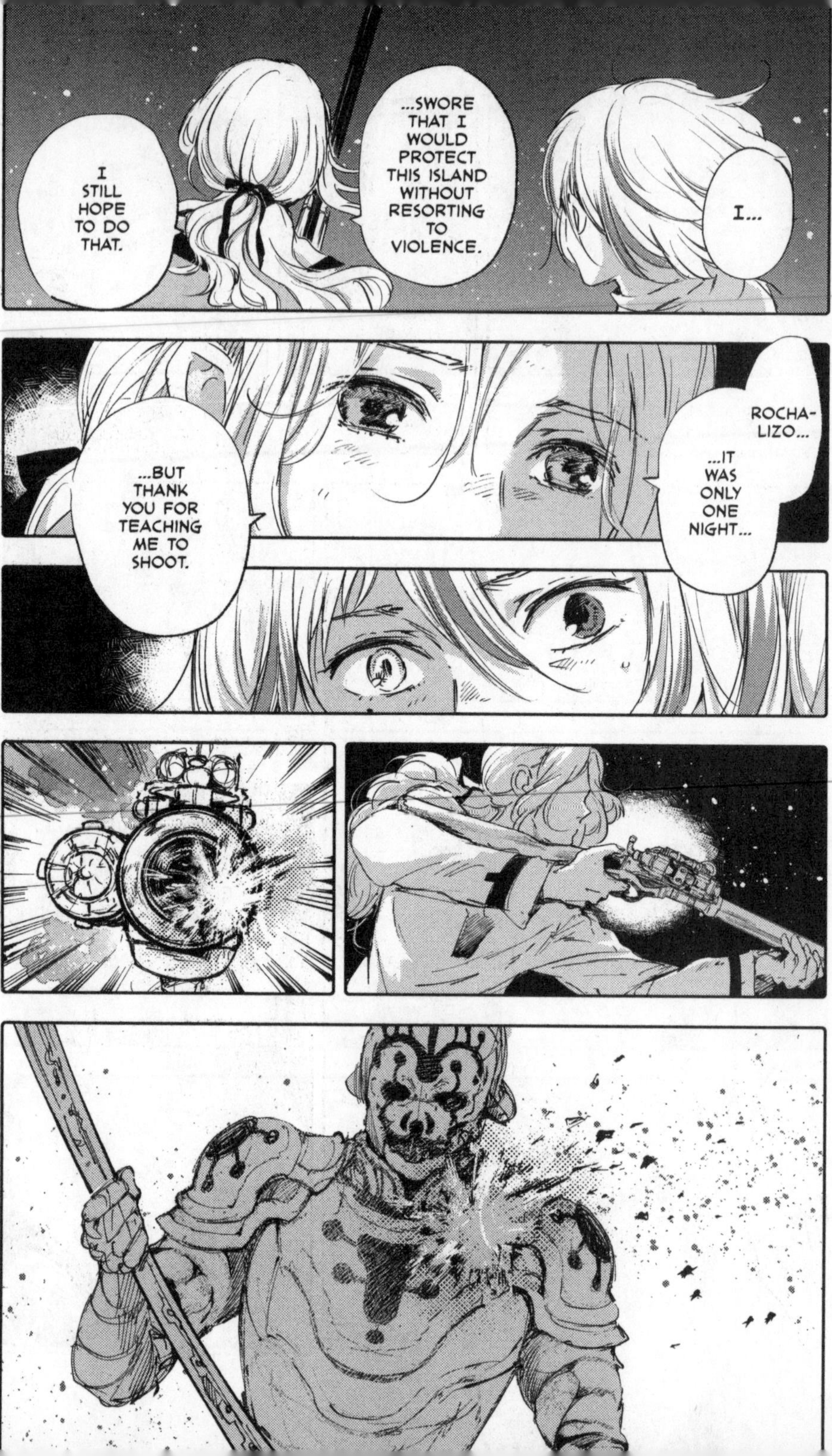
I...
...SWORE THAT I WOULD PROTECT THIS ISLAND WITHOUT RESORTING TO VIOLENCE.
I STILL HOPE TO DO THAT.
ROCHA-LIZO...
...IT WAS ONLY ONE NIGHT...
...BUT THANK YOU FOR TEACHING ME TO SHOOT.

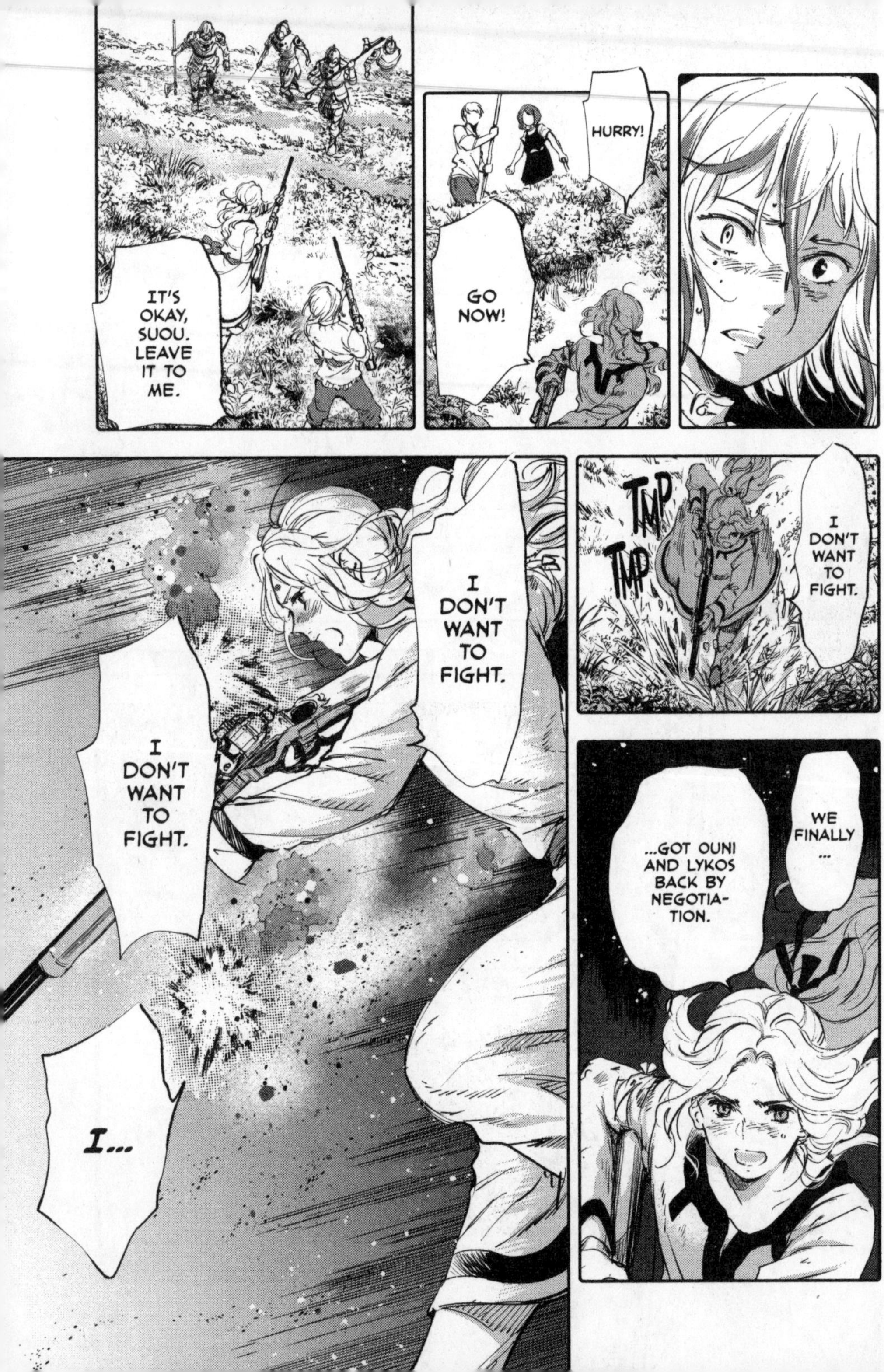
HURRY!
GO NOW!
IT'S OKAY, SUOU. LEAVE IT TO ME.
TMP TMP
I DON'T WANT TO FIGHT.
WE FINALLY ...
...GOT OUNI AND LYKOS BACK BY NEGOTIA-TION.
I DON'T WANT TO FIGHT.
I DON'T WANT TO FIGHT.
I...

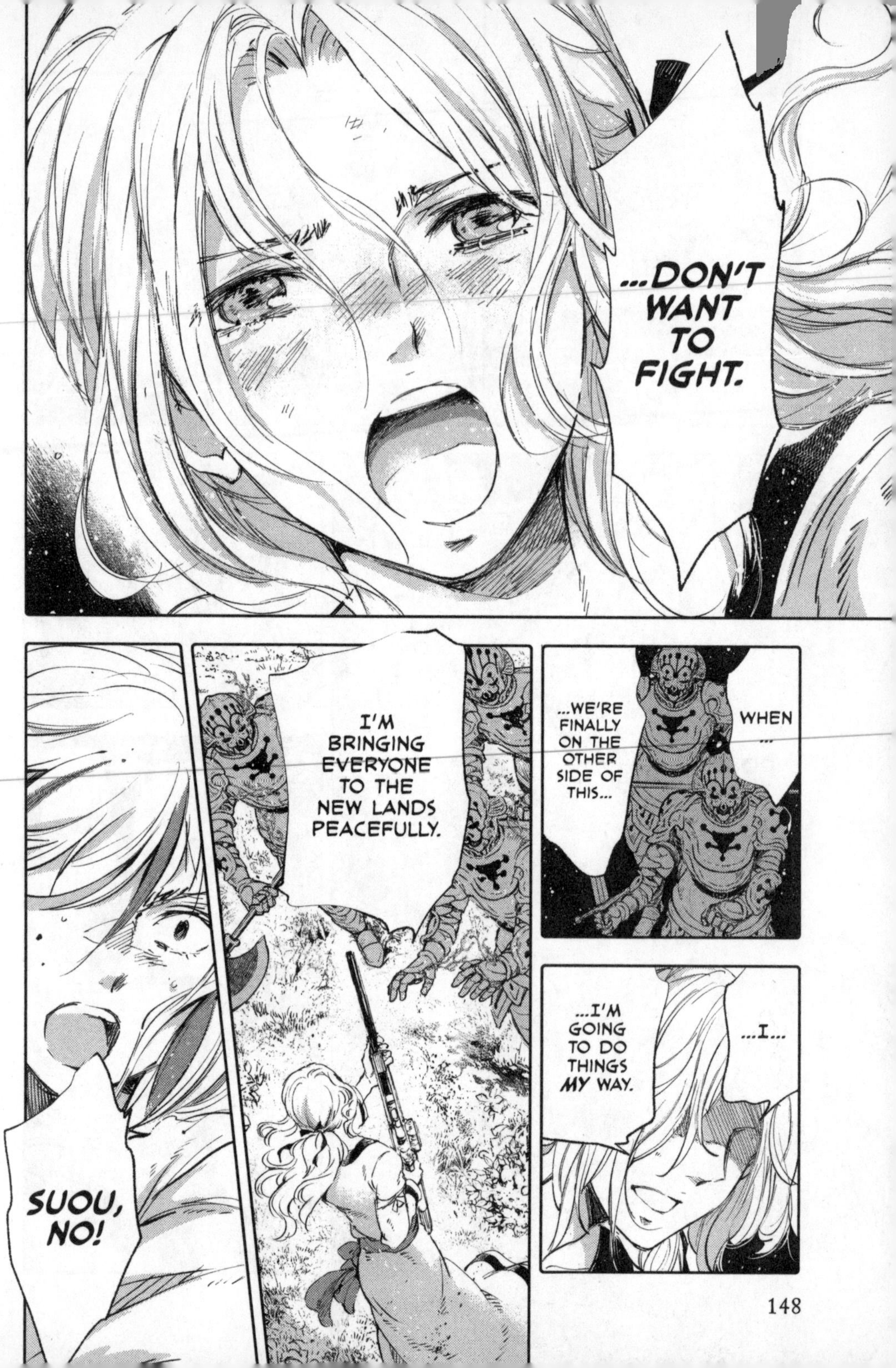
...DON'T WANT TO FIGHT.
WHEN...
...WE'RE FINALLY ON THE OTHER SIDE OF THIS...
...I...
...I'M GOING TO DO THINGS MY WAY.
I'M BRINGING EVERYONE TO THE NEW LANDS PEACEFULLY.
SUOU, NO!

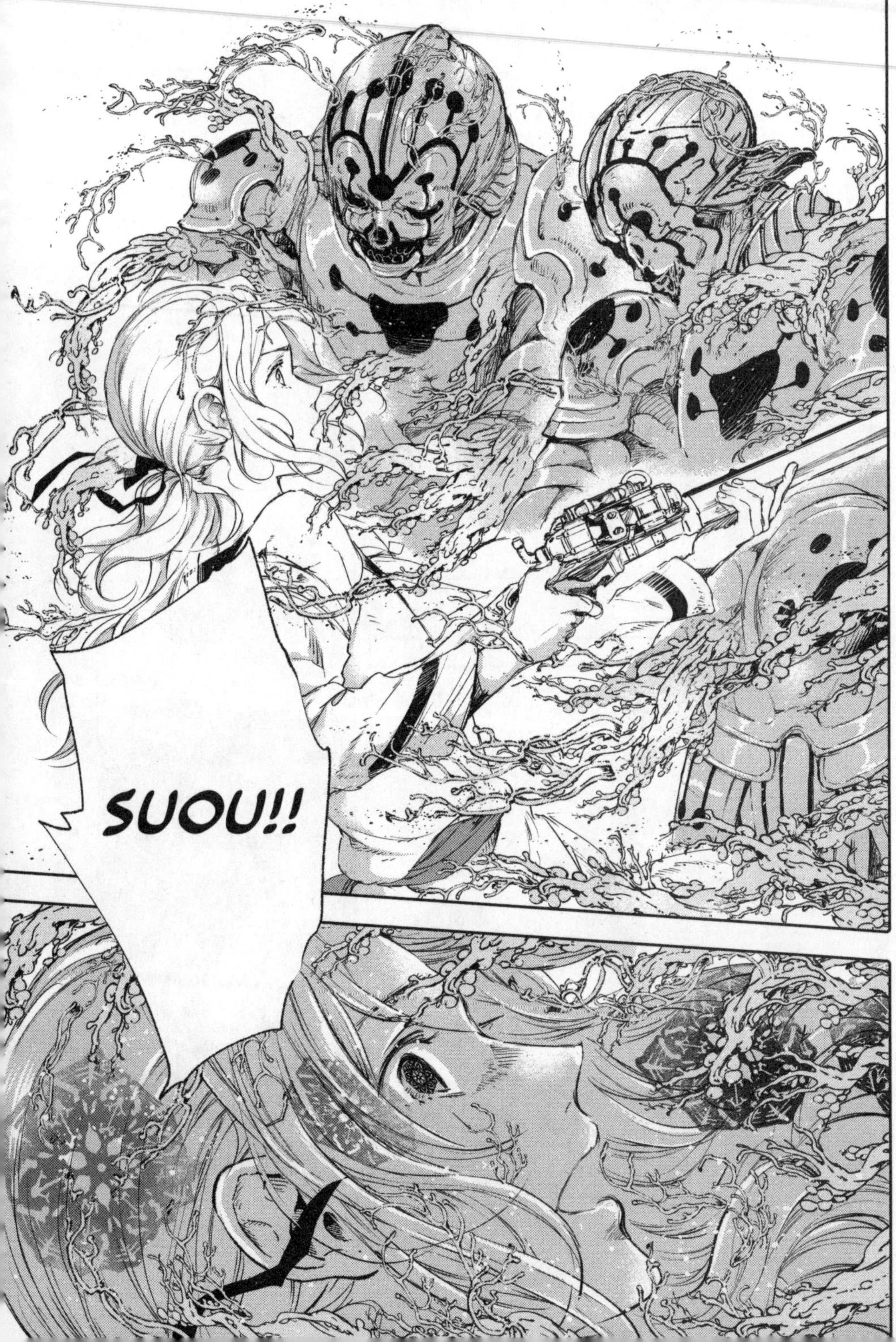
SUOU!!

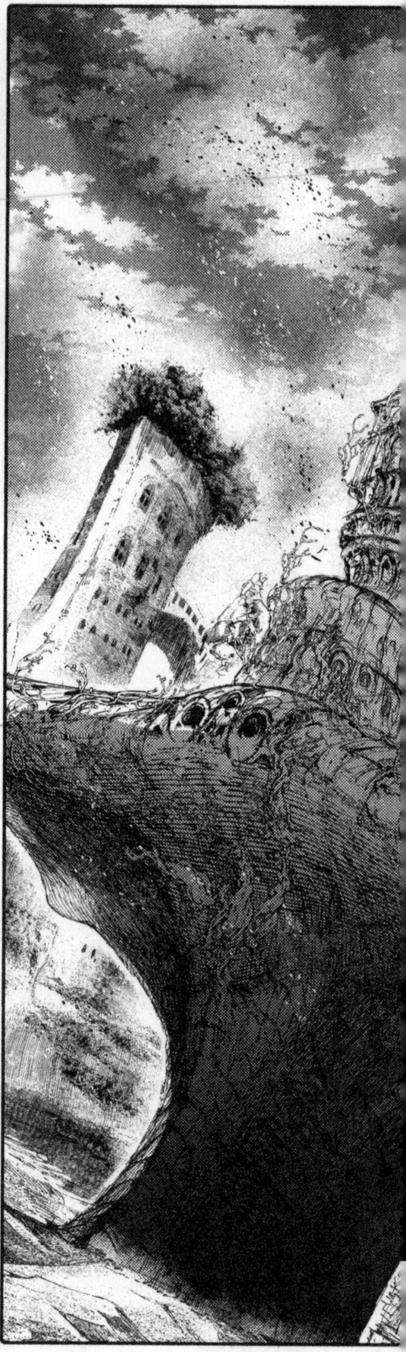

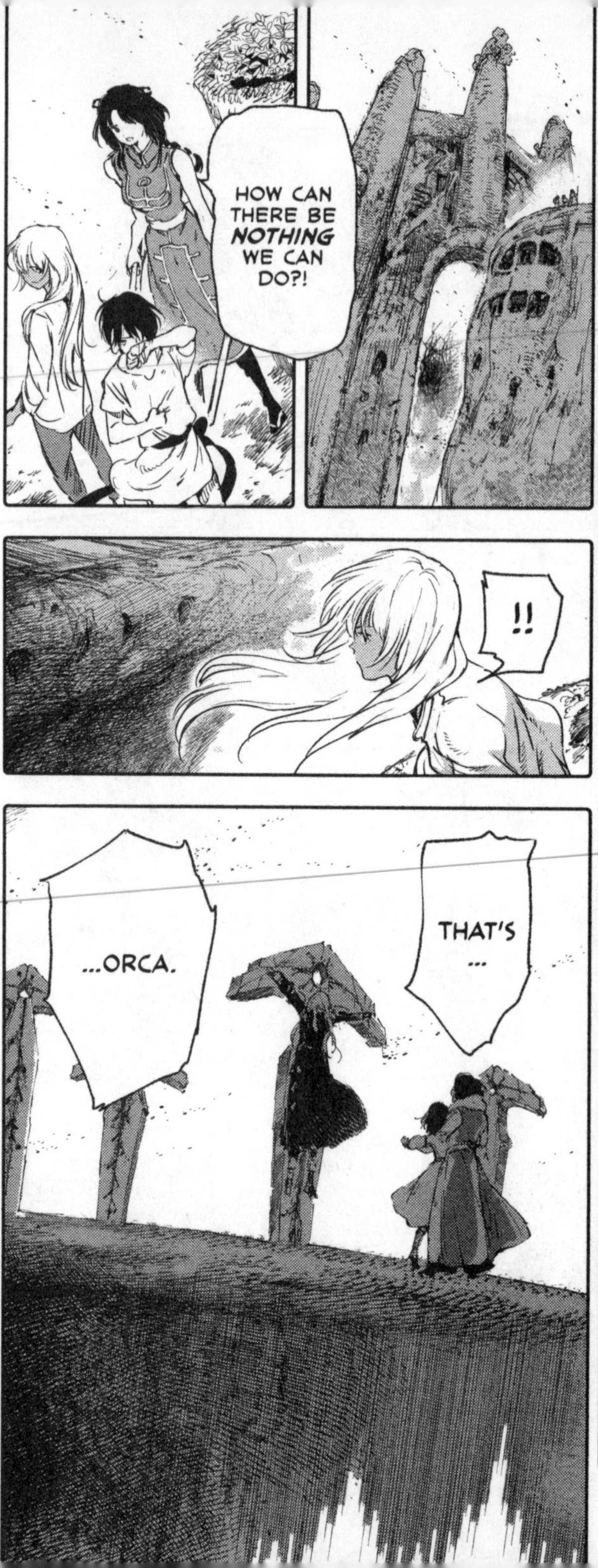
HOW CAN THERE BE ***NOTHING*** WE CAN DO?!
!!
THAT'S ...
...ORCA.

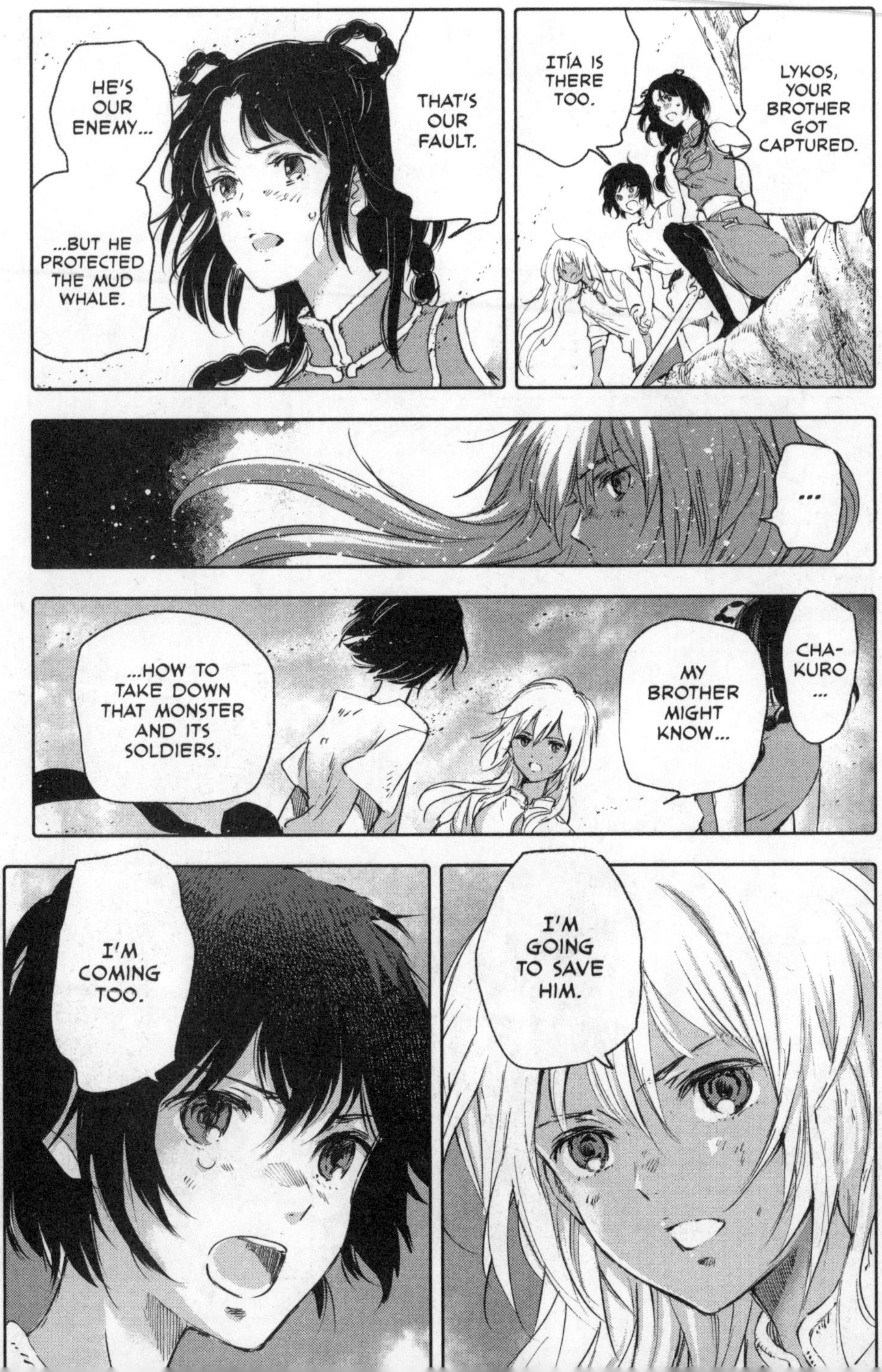
LYKOS, YOUR BROTHER GOT CAPTURED.
ITÍA IS THERE TOO.
THAT'S OUR FAULT.
HE'S OUR ENEMY...
...BUT HE PROTECTED THE MUD WHALE.
...
CHA-KURO...
MY BROTHER MIGHT KNOW...
...HOW TO TAKE DOWN THAT MONSTER AND ITS SOLDIERS.
I'M GOING TO SAVE HIM.
I'M COMING TOO.

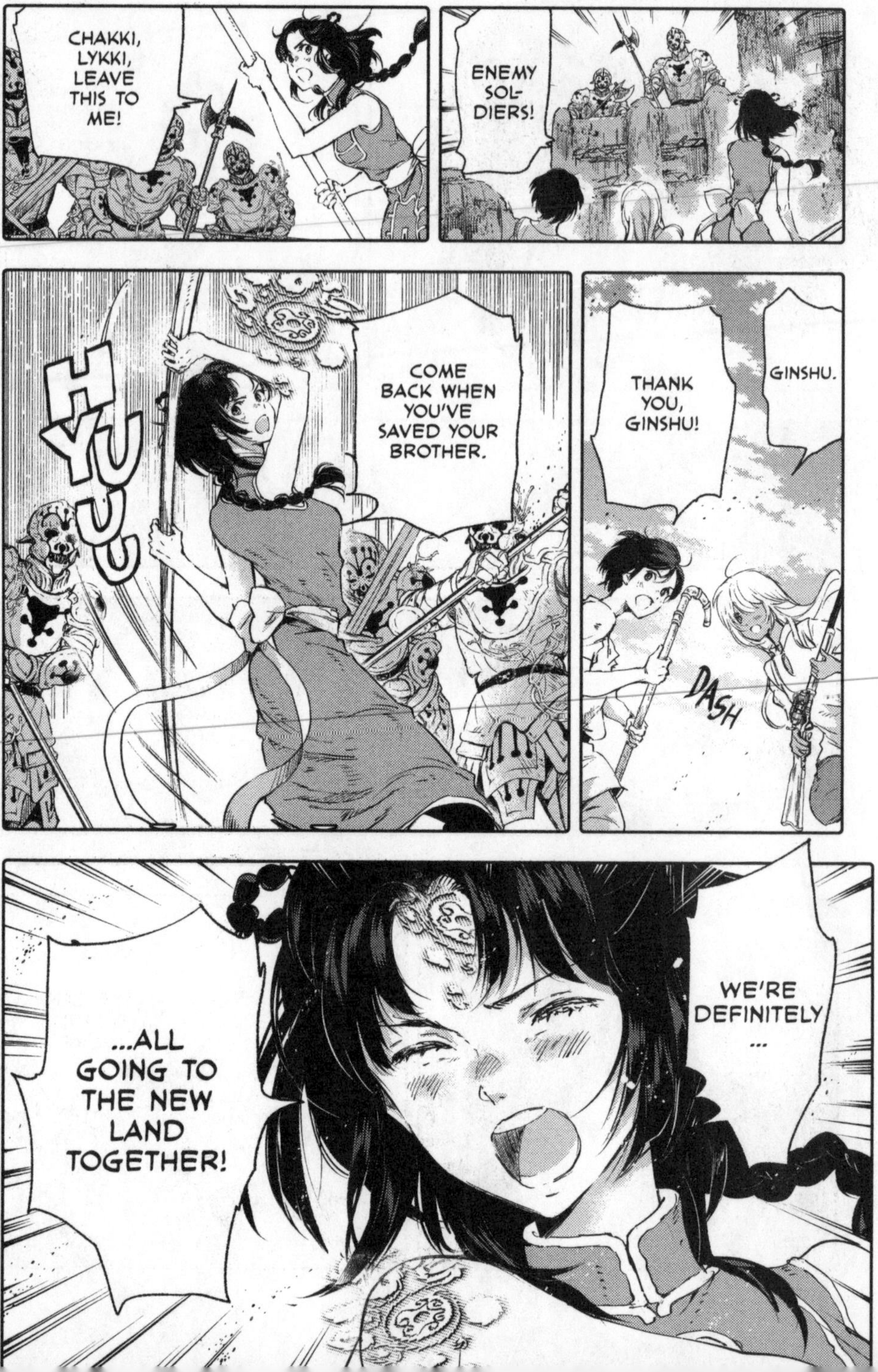
ENEMY SOL-DIERS!
CHAKKI, LYKKI, LEAVE THIS TO ME!
GINSHU.
THANK YOU, GINSHU!
DASH
COME BACK WHEN YOU'VE SAVED YOUR BROTHER.
HYUUUU
WE'RE DEFINITELY...
...ALL GOING TO THE NEW LAND TOGETHER!

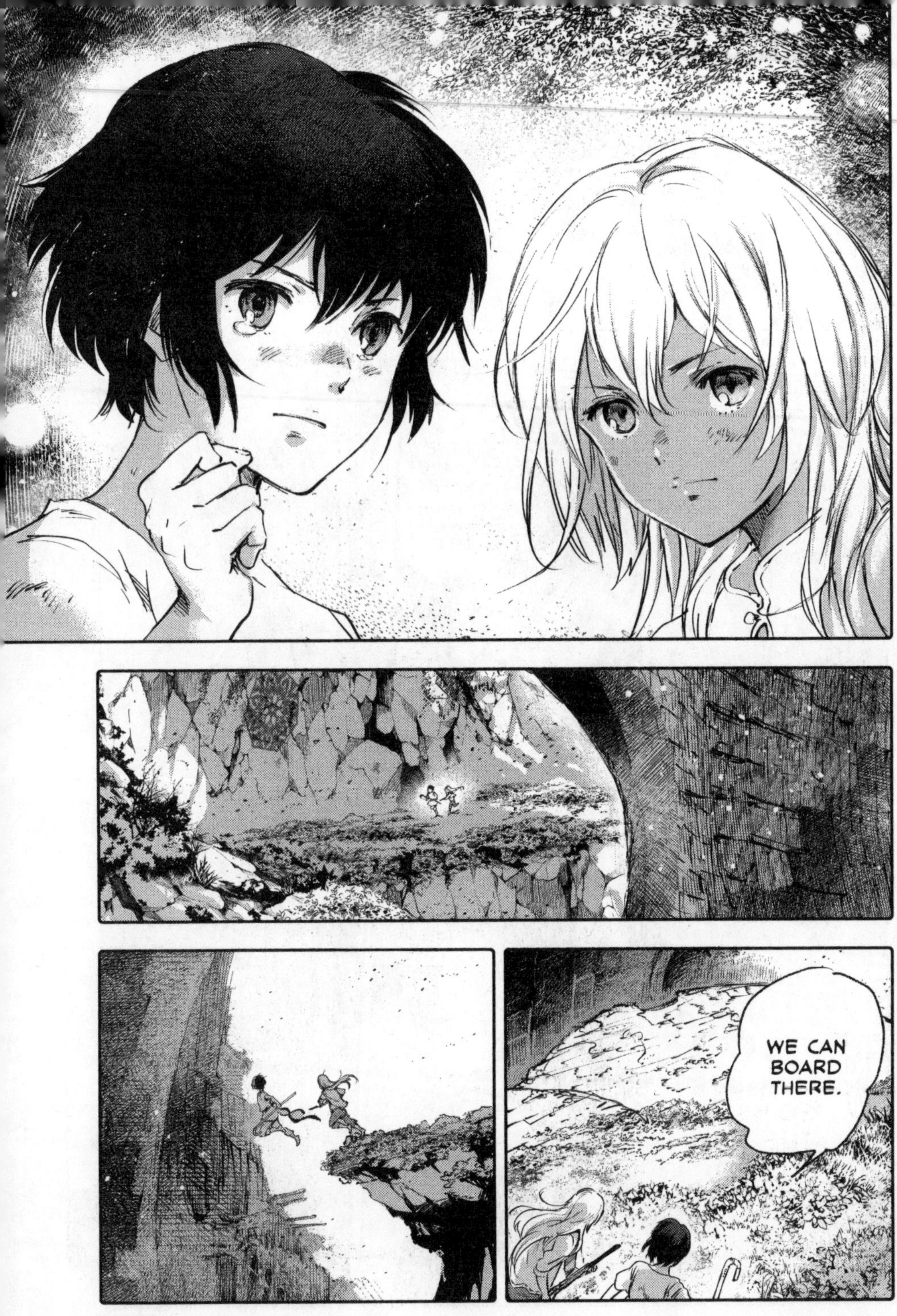
WE CAN BOARD THERE.

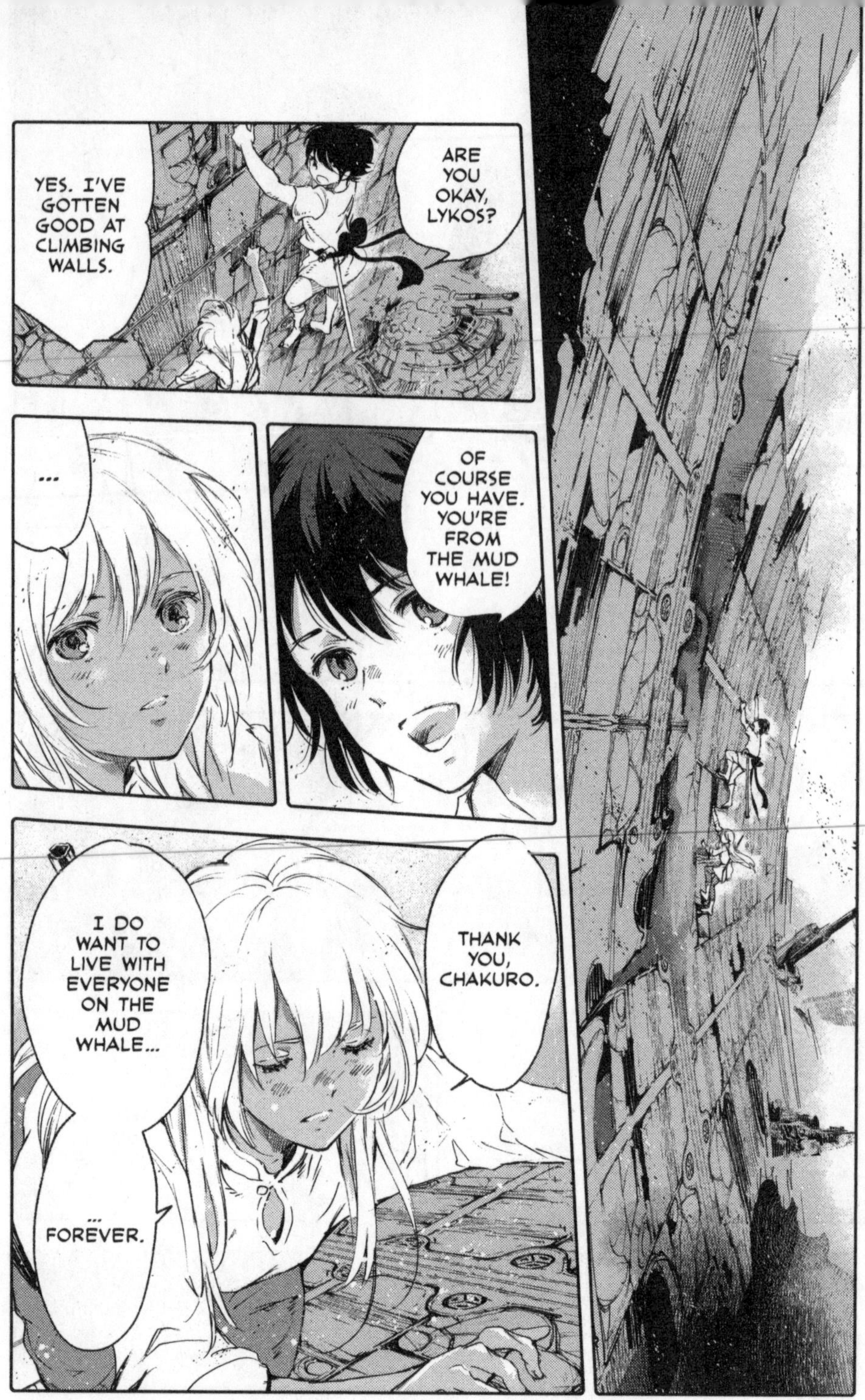
ARE YOU OKAY, LYKOS?
YES. I'VE GOTTEN GOOD AT CLIMBING WALLS.
OF COURSE YOU HAVE. YOU'RE FROM THE MUD WHALE!
...
THANK YOU, CHAKURO.
I DO WANT TO LIVE WITH EVERYONE ON THE MUD WHALE...
... FOREVER.

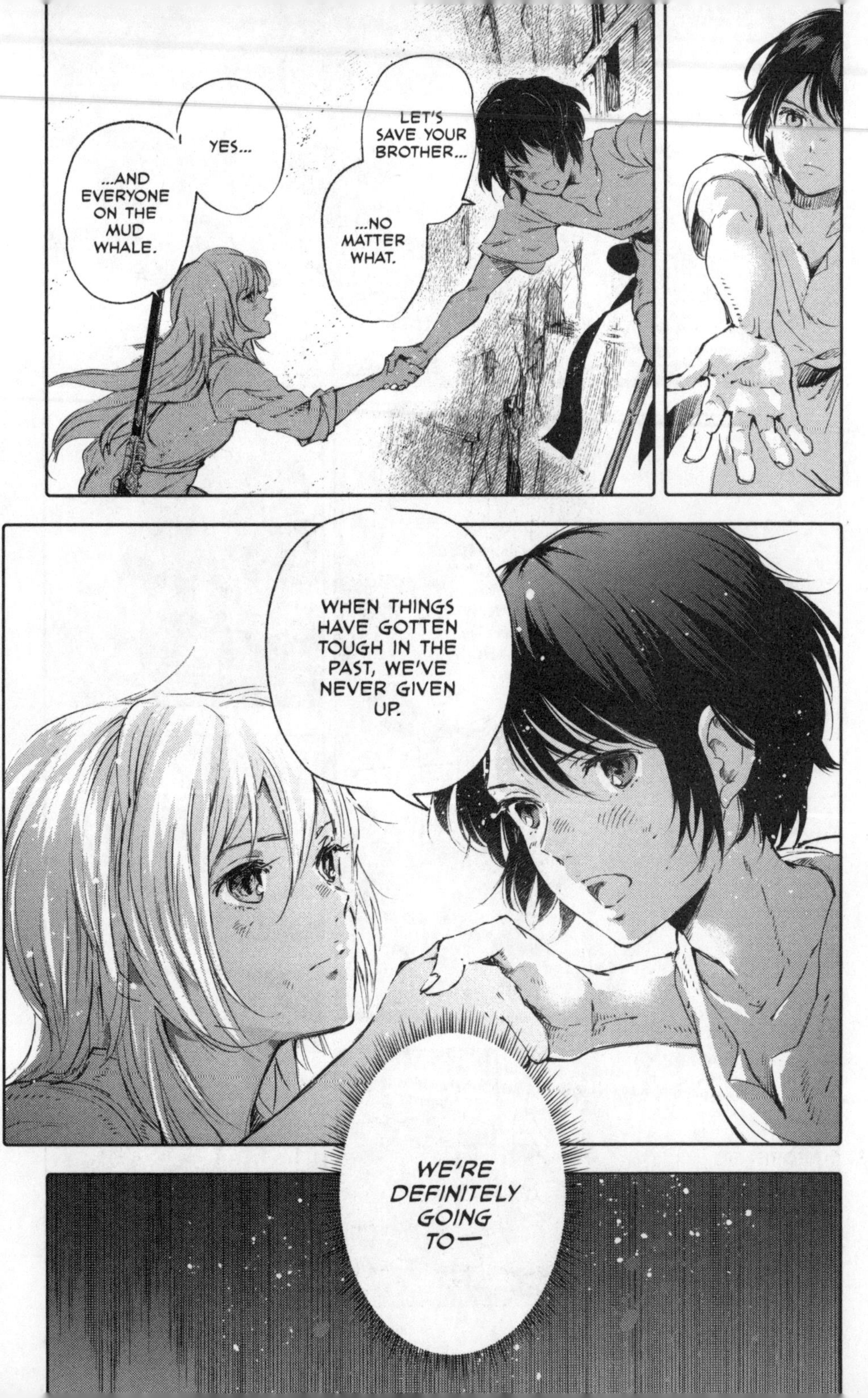
LET'S SAVE YOUR BROTHER...
...NO MATTER WHAT.
YES...
...AND EVERYONE ON THE MUD WHALE.
WHEN THINGS HAVE GOTTEN TOUGH IN THE PAST, WE'VE NEVER GIVEN UP.
WE'RE DEFINITELY GOING TO—

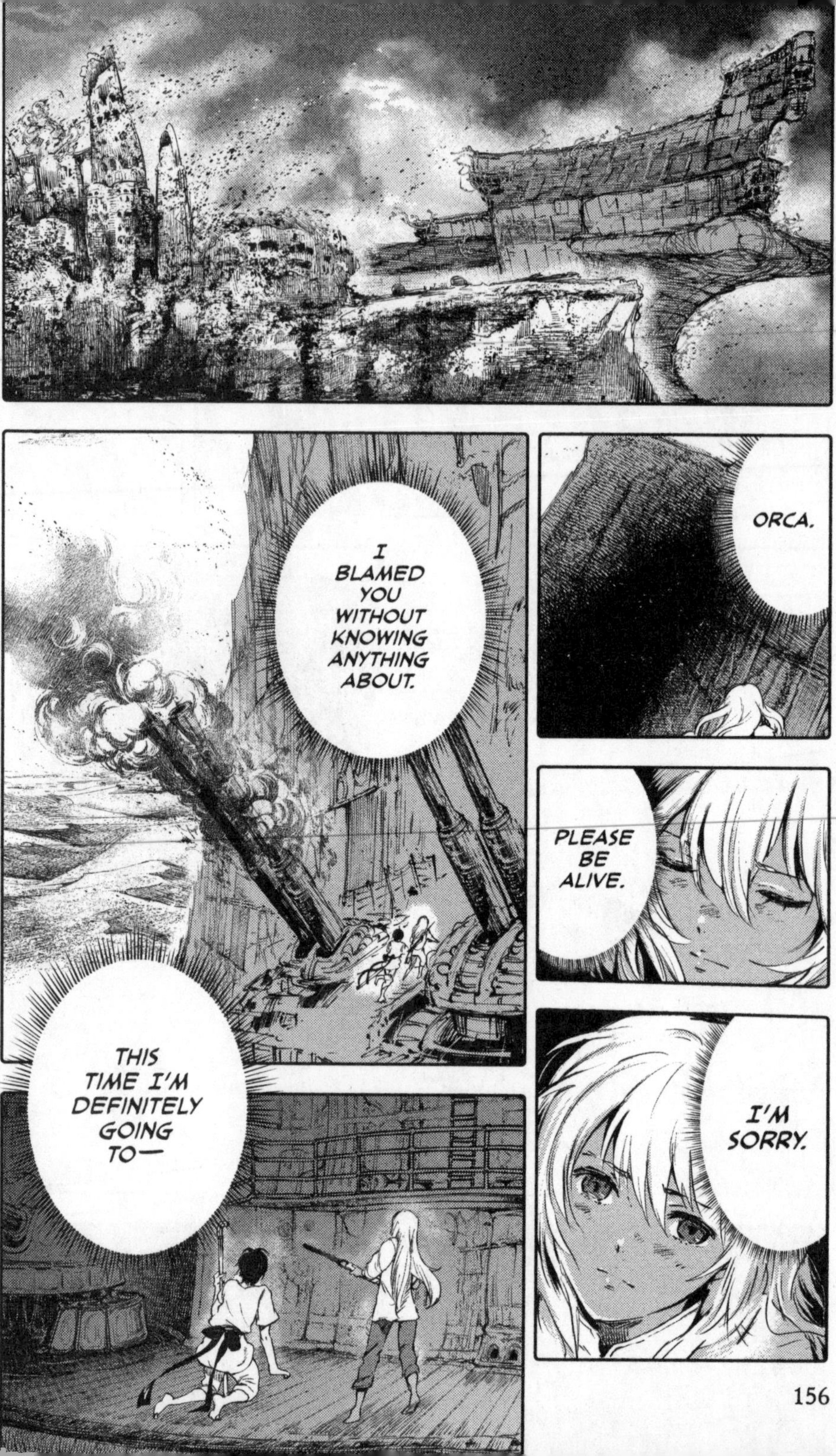
ORCA.
PLEASE BE ALIVE.
I'M SORRY.
I BLAMED YOU WITHOUT KNOWING ANYTHING ABOUT.
THIS TIME I'M DEFINITELY GOING TO—

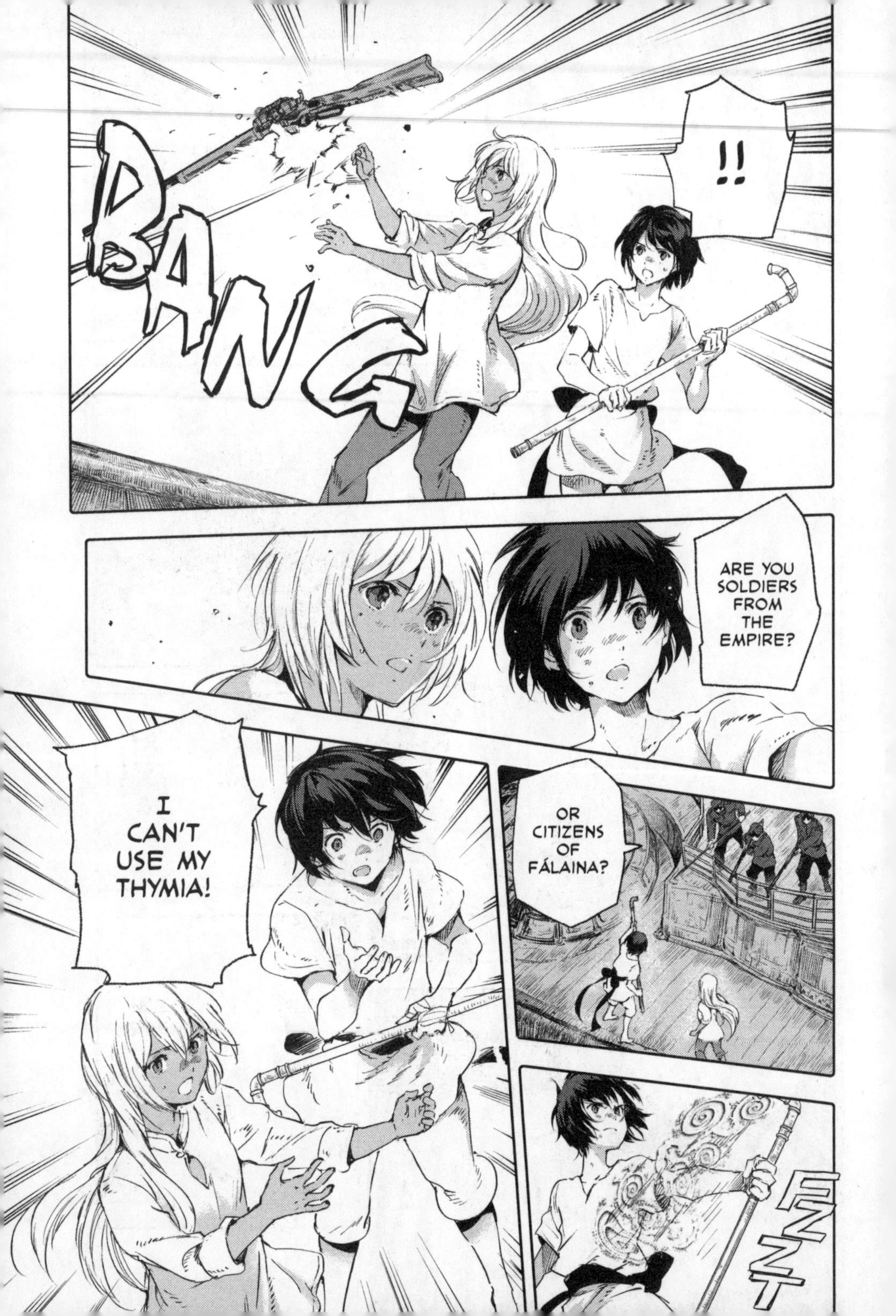
!!
BANG
ARE YOU SOLDIERS FROM THE EMPIRE?
OR CITIZENS OF FÁLAINA?
FZZT
I CAN'T USE MY THYMIA!

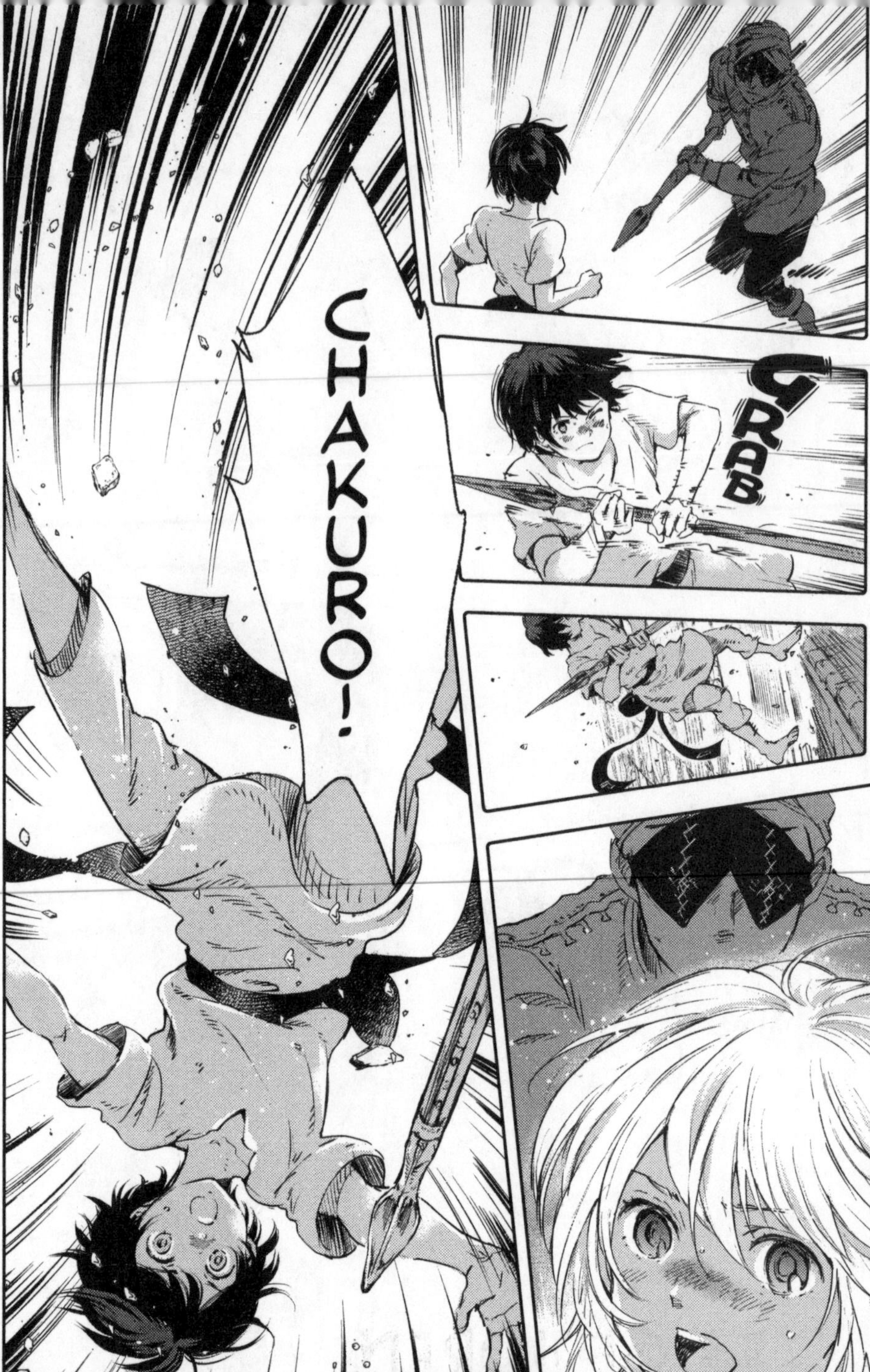
GRAB
CHAKURO!

Do Not Touch - The End-

Children of the Whales volume 16 - The End-

CHILDREN OF THE WHALES

A Note on Names

Those who live on the Mud Whale are named after colors in a language unknown. Abi Umeda uses Japanese translations of the names, which we have maintained. Here is a list of the English equivalents for the curious.

Aijiro	pale blue
Benihi	scarlet
Buki	kerria flower (*yamabuki*)
Byakuroku	malachite mineral pigments, pale green tinged with white
Chakuro	blackish brown (*cha* = brown, *kuro* = black)
Furano	from "flannel," a soft-woven fabric traditionally made of wool
Ginshu	vermillion
Hakuji	porcelain white
Jiki	golden
Kicha	yellowish brown
Kikujin	koji mold, yellowish green
Kogare	burnt muskwood, dark reddish brown
Kuchiba	decayed-leaf brown
Masoh	cinnabar
Miru	seaweed green
Nashiji	a traditional Japanese crepe weave fabric
Neri	silk white
Nezu	mouse gray
Nibi	dark gray
Ouni	safflower red
Rasha	darkest blue, nearly black
Ro	lacquer black
Sami	light green (*asa* = light, *midori* = green)

Shikoku	purple-tinged black
Shikon	purple-tinged navy
Shinono	the color of dawn (*shinonome*)
Shuan	dark bloodred
Sienna	reddish brown
Sumi	ink black
Suou	raspberry red
Taisha	red ocher
Tobi	reddish brown like a kite's feather
Tokusa	scouring rush green
Tonoko	the color of powdered grindstone, a pale brown
Urumi	muddy gray

I have a new editor. The previous one as well as the new one are both warm and fluffy. I can live with that!

—Abi Umeda

ABI UMEDA debuted as a manga creator with the one-shot "Yukokugendan" in *Weekly Shonen Champion*. *Children of the Whales* is her eighth manga work.

CHILDREN OF THE WHALES

VOLUME 16
VIZ Signature Edition

Story and Art by **Abi Umeda**

Translation / JN Productions
Touch-Up Art & Lettering / Annaliese "Ace" Christman
Design / Julian (JR) Robinson
Editor / Pancha Diaz

KUJIRANOKORAHA SAJOUNIUTAU Volume 16
© 2020 ABI UMEDA
First published in Japan in 2020 by AKITA PUBLISHING CO., LTD., Tokyo
English translation rights arranged with AKITA PUBLISHING CO., LTD. through
Tuttle-Mori Agency, Inc., Tokyo

Printed in Canada

Published by VIZ Media, LLC
P.O. Box 77010
San Francisco, CA 94107

10 9 8 7 6 5 4 3 2 1
First printing, January 2021

viz.com

vizsignature.com

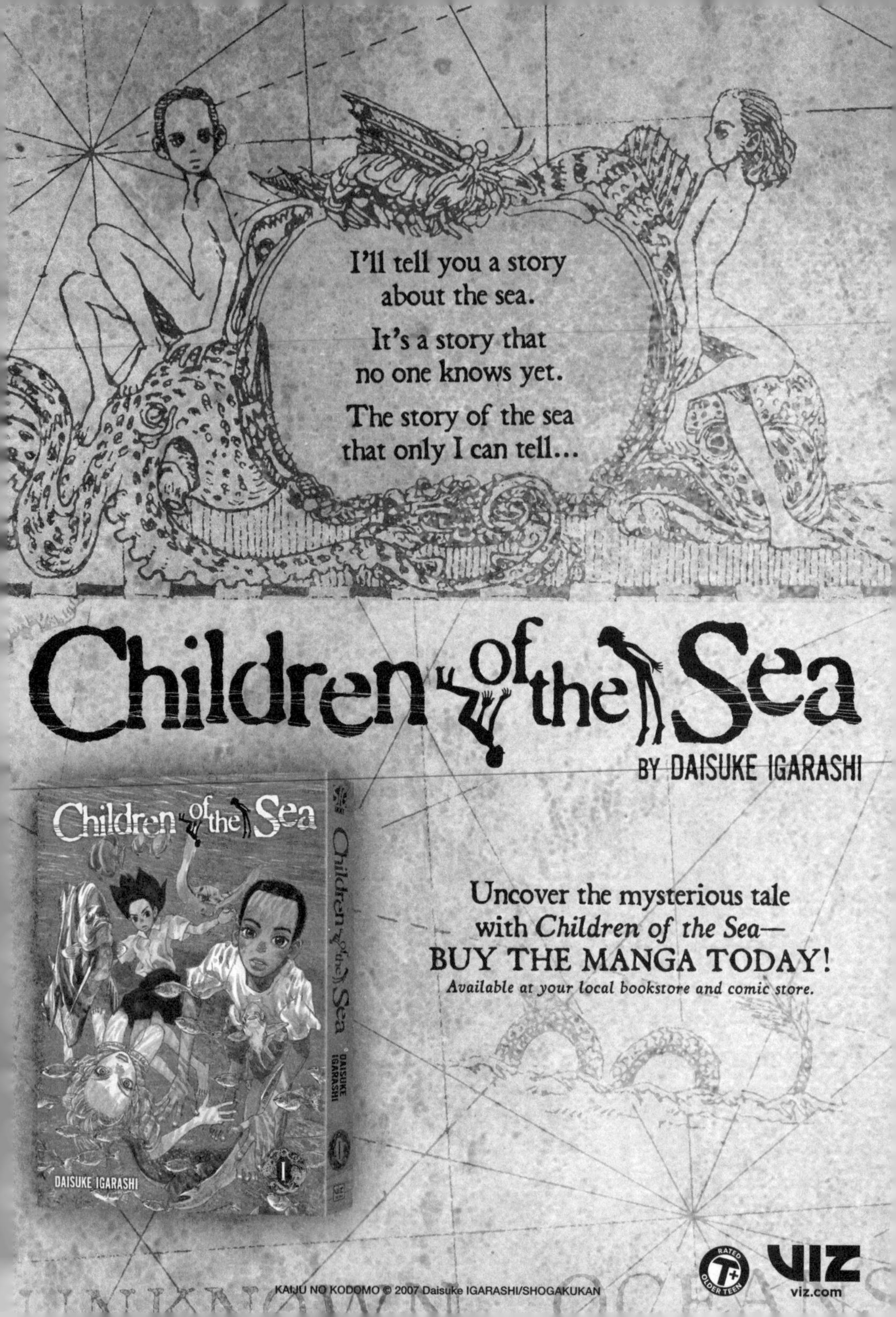
I'll tell you a story
about the sea.
It's a story that
no one knows yet.
The story of the sea
that only I can tell...
Children of the Sea
BY DAISUKE IGARASHI
Children of the Sea
DAISUKE IGARASHI
Uncover the mysterious tale
with Children of the Sea—
BUY THE MANGA TODAY!
Available at your local bookstore and comic store.
RATED T+ OLDER TEEN
VIZ
viz.com
KAIJU NO KODOMO © 2007 Daisuke IGARASHI/SHOGAKUKAN

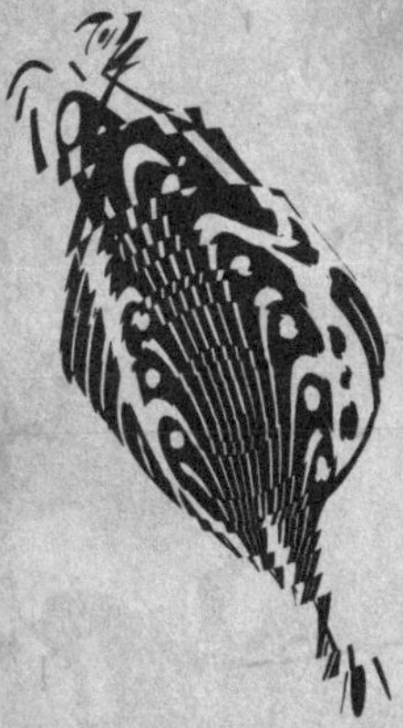

THIS IS THE LAST PAGE!

Children of the Whales has been printed in the original Japanese format to preserve the orientation of the original artwork.

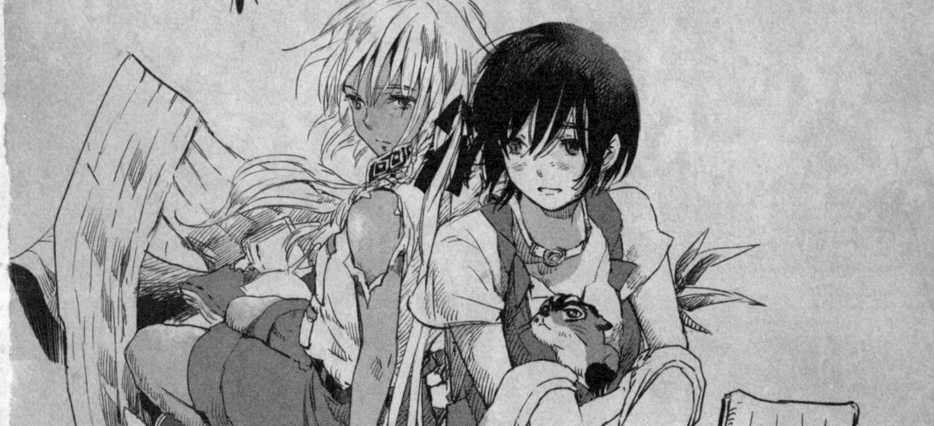

THE DRIFTING CLASSROOM

PERFECT EDITION

by KAZUO UMEZZ

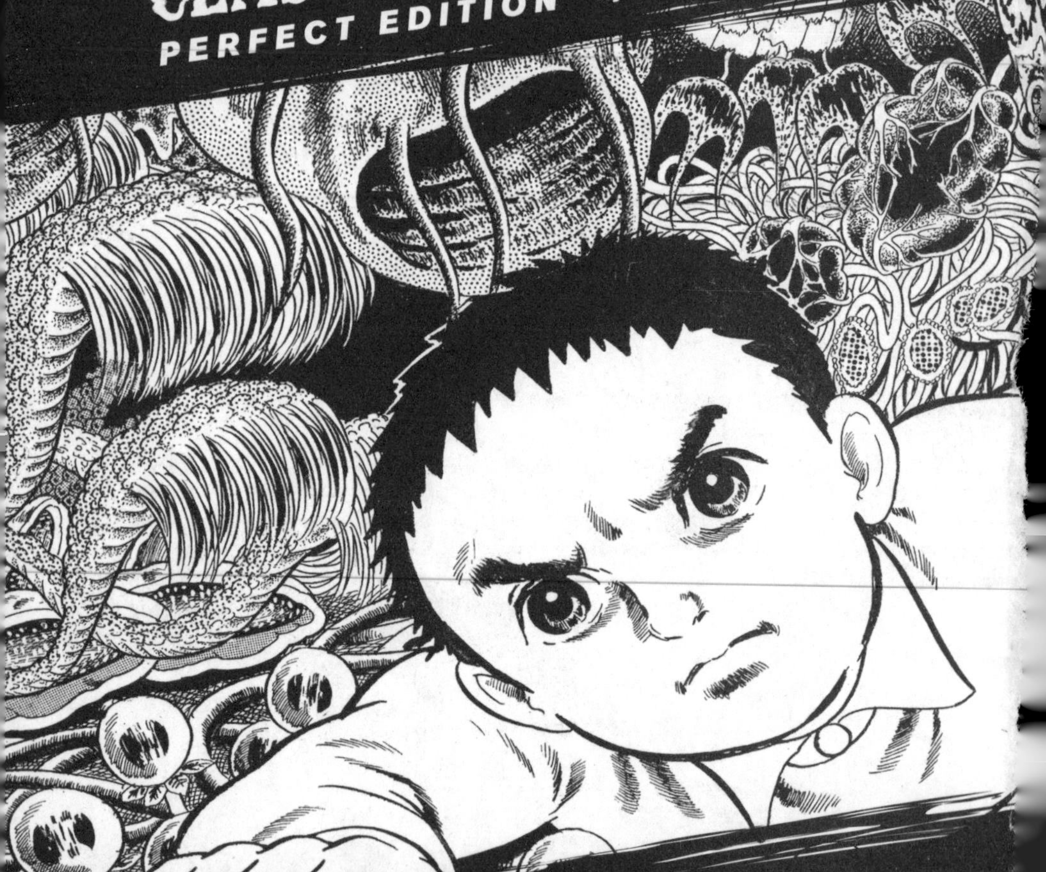

Out of nowhere, an entire school vanishes, leaving nothing but a hole in the ground. While parents mourn and authorities investigate, the students and teachers find themselves not dead but stranded in a terrifying wasteland where they must fight to survive.

COMPLETE IN 3 VOLUMES